CHILDREN'S PLAY

Mar
Tel:

CHILDREN'S PLAY

W. George Scarlett • Sophie Naudeau
Dorothy Salonius-Pasternak • Iris Ponte
Tufts University

SAGE Publications
Thousand Oaks ▪ London ▪ New Delhi

For information:

Sage Publications, Inc.
2455 Teller Road
Thousand Oaks, California 91320
E-mail: order@sagepub.com

Sage Publications Ltd.
1 Oliver's Yard
55 City Road
London EC1Y 1SP
United Kingdom

Sage Publications India Pvt. Ltd.
B-42, Panchsheel Enclave
Post Box 4109
New Delhi 110 017 India

Printed in the United States of America

Library of Congress Cataloging-in-Publication Data

Children's play / W. George Scarlett . . . [et al.].
    p. cm.
Includes bibliographical references and index.
ISBN 0-7619-2999-1 (pbk.)
  1. Play. 2. Child development. I. Scarlett, W. George.
HQ782.C438 2005
649′.5—dc22

                   2004008545

This book is printed on acid-free paper.

04   05   06   10 9 8 7 6 5 4 3 2 1

Acquisitions Editor:	James Brace-Thompson
Editorial Assistant:	Karen Ehrmann
Production Editor:	Denise Santoyo
Typesetter:	C&M Digitals (P) Ltd.
Indexer:	Pamela Van Huss
Cover Designer:	Janet Foulger
Illustrator:	David Murray
Photographer:	Kim Walls

CONTENTS

PREFACE

Why study children's play? One answer is obvious. Doing so helps those developing careers working with children. They need to understand play, because understanding is useful, even necessary, for doing their jobs. For teachers, play can be central to developing curriculum. For clinicians, it can be central to assessing and treating problems. If we consider parenting a career, for parents, play can be central to raising children. There are, therefore, practical reasons for studying children's play.

However, we don't see practical reasons as being necessary or even the most important for studying children's play, and this book was written with that thought in mind. To convey what we mean, an analogy might help. Few people justify studying music mainly as a way to foster careers. Understanding and appreciating music is in and of itself good—because music is complex and beautiful. The same is true with children's play. This book is intended to turn readers on to play's complexity and beauty.

One further preliminary note: Before knowing much about play, many see play as a small subject, a secondary aspect of children's development. Surprisingly, this view is reinforced in textbooks on child development by there being relatively little discussion about children's play. There are lengthy discussions about brain development, cognitive development, and the development of attachments and moral judgment, but not much about the development of play.

This is puzzling for two reasons in particular: First, given the opportunity, children usually choose to play. Play is, therefore, a central value for children, which should alert us to the fact that it is important. Second, some of the best minds in psychology and education have studied play and, in so doing, have shown that play is indeed complex, beautiful, and important for children's development.

However, in this book, we don't wish to explain the puzzle as to why play is not thought of or treated as being so important. In this book, we wish simply to explain children's play and foster in readers a deep appreciation for its complexity, its many forms, its many interesting uses, and perhaps most of all, its beauty. We want readers to see play for what it is at its core, namely, an expression of the human spirit.

ACKNOWLEDGMENTS

The authors would like to express their gratitude to those who contributed significantly to this book. We are particularly grateful to Kim Walls, who provided most of the book's photographs, to David Murray, who drew the sketches, and to Jason Kuhn, who assisted in the writing of two of the chapters. Audra Plewak, Rosa Maria Ares, and Gregory Chertok provided significant assistance in drafting the chapter on organized youth sports. Brett Levin provided assistance on Chapter 6, and Lamio Sol contributed to developing the original book proposal. Last, but not least, our editor, Jim Brace-Thompson, provided invaluable guidance and much-appreciated support throughout the writing process.

INTRODUCTION

I n a book on children's play, it seems permissible, even appropriate, to begin with an invitation to pretend. We might pretend that play has no adaptive value, no value for preparing children for anything except more play. We might also pretend that children's play is much more similar to adult recreation than is generally admitted. We might pretend that play is really best considered a mixture of good and bad, rather than an unequivocally good thing. Last, we might pretend that play is not a thing at all but rather an indefinable and hence immeasurable non-thing, and therefore nearly impossible to study scientifically.

Having engaged in this bit of playful pretending, you might feel there is something seriously real in what has just been said. You might feel that play may not have adaptive value, that play is very much like adult recreation, that there is indeed bad as well as good play, and that it may be impossible to pin down play scientifically.

What we have shown by this game of pretending is that when we talk about play, it often becomes something it is not, an unequivocally good *thing* that mostly children do. That is, when we talk about play as a thing, we often *idealize* play and make it be what we wish it to be, not what it is in reality.

However, when we actually play, even when we play at explaining play, we notice that something freeing and refreshing happens. The grains of truth in our playing are interesting and important, but by playing with them and not taking them too seriously, we open ourselves to the process of knowing. We focus less on wrapping everything up in a neat conclusion and more on enjoying the process itself.

Play, then, is more aptly defined as *playing*. It is a verb more than it is a noun. As a verb, playing is something one experiences and makes happen. It need not be looked for in any particular place, at any particular time, or in any particular group. At any place, at any time, or in any group, playing may break out, even when it is least expected. And in those places, times, and groups designated for play, something quite different from play may occur.

Even when children are clearly playing, they often seem to go in and out of play. A nice example of this ephemeral nature of play occurs when children build or construct with blocks, Legos, or some other construction material. As George Forman (1998) has pointed out, as long as the experience of building has a "What if . . . ?" attitude, it is constructive play, but as soon as it shifts to a "Why won't it do that?" attitude, then it is more like work. In Forman's words, "the playful child is content to change what he or she does, just to see what it yields. The task-oriented child is determined to achieve a particular goal" (p. 394).

There is, then, a great deal of difficulty in defining play and determining when play happens. What should we do in the face of this ambiguity? The ambiguousness of the concept does not mean we cannot study and understand play. Many important concepts are equally if not more ambiguous, such as the concepts of love, feeling, and religion. Each of these ideas has resisted exact definition, and yet each remains indispensable for understanding the human condition.

One response to ambiguity is to develop criteria for deciding what is and is not play, with no one criterion being sufficient (Smith, 1985). But which criteria? Some suggested criteria have turned out to be useless, such as that play is *intrinsically motivated* (Smith, 1985). Others, such as that play produces *positive affect* or that it is *flexible, voluntary, egalitarian,* and (typically) *nonliteral* (i.e., based on pretense), have been found to work much of the time but not all of the time (Sutton-Smith, 1984). We need, then, to consider multiple criteria for defining play rather than settling on one definition.

Sometimes researchers define play as what children see as play. Using this definition, we learn that, for children, play is about having fun, being outdoors, being with friends, choosing freely, not working, pretending, enacting fantasy and drama, and playing games. Furthermore, we learn that it is not about preparing for the future (Sutton-Smith, 1997).

Defining play according to what children see as play will be a main criterion used throughout this book. For this reason, we have included in our discussion phenomena that major scholars have sometimes treated as nonplay, such as humor, organized sports, and academic games. Our argument is that if play is the experience of playing, then we should not rule out these borderline activities that children see as play. We will therefore strike a balance between offering a precise but false definition of play and accepting almost anything enjoyable as play. In doing so, we will err on the side of being inclusive. We will let description and a flexible collection of criteria carry the burden of defining play.

But even with the best collection of criteria, it will always be difficult, perhaps impossible, to pin down play, which means that any theory of play cannot be a theory of some thing, some clearly bounded unit of behavior that is easily defined. With play and playing there is always ambiguity, which is why the great play theorist, Brian Sutton-Smith, has preferred that we speak of *play rhetorics* rather than of play theories (Sutton-Smith, 1997).

● EXPLAINING PLAY'S FUNCTIONS AND ITS DEVELOPMENT

Rhetorics are patterns of talk designed to persuade. They exist because, in the absence of sufficient data and clear definitions, we still need to understand, evaluate, and decide whether to support children's play. There is, then, nothing irrational about engaging in rhetoric. However, there are pitfalls when we take our rhetorics too seriously, when we forget that they are rhetorics, not well-grounded theories.

Functions of Play

Sutton-Smith suggests that there are several rhetorics of children's play, each emphasizing some presumed general function. One in particular stands out: what Sutton-Smith calls the *rhetoric of progress* (Sutton-Smith, 1997). This is talk about play as being good for children's physical, emotional, cognitive, and social development. It is talk about play preparing children for the future.

In recent decades, the rhetoric of progress has been the dominant rhetoric among scholars as well as among parents, teachers, and ordinary people in industrialized cultures such as our own. As one reviewer recently put it, children's . . . play has been hypothesized to contribute to the cognitive, motor, and social development of children, including the development of perception, attention, memory, problem-solving skill, language, communication, creativity, logical operations, emotion regulation, self-regulation, social skills, gender roles, social relationships, conflict resolution, coping with stress, and so on. (Power, 2000)

The rhetoric of progress makes good intuitive sense, which is why we adopt it throughout this book, and why it shows up not simply in older research but in the most up-to-date discussions on children's play (Harris, 2003; McCune, 1993). However, researchers disagree over whether there is solid evidence to support this rhetoric of progress. For example, after reviewing the literature on play's functions, Martin and Caro (1985) concluded, "At present, there is no direct evidence that play has any important benefits, with the possible exception of some immediate effects on children's behavior" (p. 97). In seeming contrast, Fein and Kinney (1994) concluded that

children who spontaneously engage in [make-believe play], when compared to their less playful peers, tend to be more friendly, popular, expressive, cooperative, verbal, and creative, less impulsive and aggressive, and more likely to take the perspective of others. . . . More impressive, kindergarteners' participation in sociodramatic play predicts their social and social-cognitive maturity in first and second grades. (p. 189)

Fein and Kinney's argument has to do with relatively short-term correlates of play, which is why their differences with Martin and Caro may be only apparent, not real. In sum, though the rhetoric of progress makes sense, both intuitively and perhaps for predicting short-term effects, it has yet to make the kind of tough-minded sense that comes with sufficient data and evidence about long-term effects.

Insufficient evidence for saying anything definite about play's positive functions isn't the only shortcoming of the rhetoric of progress. The rhetoric of progress can lead to serious problems. First, it can lead to the idealization of play, to overlooking its darker, harmful side—as we shall discuss shortly—so that we don't prepare ourselves for times when we need to stop or prevent bad play. Second, this idealization can justify adults taking control of children's play when they shouldn't. Some people seem to feel that if play is essential for children's future, it can't be left to children to choose how to play.

Sutton-Smith is concerned with the way adults have more and more come to control children's play. It should concern us as well, for, as Sutton-Smith (Smith, 1985) explains, "children need their play to make the present tolerable to themselves. We should defend that need and not intrude upon it for the protection of our own past values under the guise of preparing their future" (p. 146).

In the end, play need not be justified on the grounds that it prepares children for the future. It can be justified simply on the basis that it helps children thrive or at least survive in the present. But even this last statement is itself based on a rhetoric.

Development of Play

This is first and foremost a book about play's development. Therefore, we need to be clear about what we mean by *development*. We do *not* mean simply changes with age, though we will describe how play changes as children grow older. What we mean has more to do with *maturing*, with becoming more complex and organized, with functioning or achieving on higher levels and with being more sophisticated and subtle, more flexible and aware. A developmental perspective on children's play means, then, a perspective that attends to the signs of maturing, whether of children maturing or of the maturing of play.

In observing children's play, you may sense that there is development without having the words and concepts to explain it. For example, you may notice a child going from "feeding" her doll to having her doll "feed" another doll, and in noticing this shift you may sense that something has developed. However, without having the concepts and distinctions to explain this change, you may not know what exactly has developed. One of the major purposes of this book is to supply you with concepts and distinctions to explain play's development.

One further point regarding the meaning of development, again using this last example of doll play: In both instances of doll play, the theme or content remains the same (feeding a baby); however, the form or *structure* differs. This notion of *structure* and the distinction between *structure* and *content* will be crucial to understanding what is meant by development. Like many crucial distinctions, it is difficult to explain with a single definition, but it will become clear with repeated examples and explanations. You can bear this in mind whenever we use the term *development*.

Support for Play's Development

This book's approach to what supports play's development is broad and not determined by any one theoretical perspective. As Piaget (1952) and others have taught us, children support their own development through their active puzzling and problem solving. Parents, teachers, and caregivers support development not just in broad ways, such as by helping children feel secure and confident but also in narrow ways, such as by helping children fit Lego bricks together. Physical settings support development by offering materials to play with: a lake and beach to play at skipping rocks, a jungle gym to play at climbing and swinging, a shelf of blocks to play at building a fort. Children support each other's play and development, especially by suggesting new lines of play. There are, then, many forms of support for development. We need to consider them all.

Now that we have clarified this book's overall approach to defining play, its functions, its development, and the supports for its development, we can turn to discussing play theories.

KINDS OF PLAY THEORIES ●

One of the sad realities of student life is that students are often rewarded more for memorizing boiled-down conclusions of great thinkers than they are for emulating great thinkers' ability to *inquire.* That happens especially in textbooks, where restrictions on space permit only a cursory view of a thinker's perspective. Although we need to touch on key theories and theorists, we don't want to reinforce memorizing conclusions. This brief overview, then, is to be taken for what it is, an outline used only to give examples of *kinds* of play theories. For anything substantial, the reader needs to consult the original discussions.

This discussion is organized around *interests,* because different kinds of theories are generated and used by scholars with different interests. We begin with the interests associated with the psychoanalytic tradition.

Psychoanalytic Theory and Play

Those from within the psychoanalytic tradition (Erikson, 1950; Esman, 1983; Winnicott, 1977) have been interested in helping children whose problems stem from difficulty in managing feelings. They have shown how helpful it is to focus on when children are unable to express and cope with feelings, not just because feelings such as anger and love are powerful but also because feelings produce powerful *intrapsychic conflicts.* For example, "If I get angry, will she (he) still love me?" is a question pointing to an intrapsychic conflict, one that any reader can identify with. These intrapsychic conflicts get us into trouble if we don't know how to manage them.

The analytically minded also focus on feelings of helplessness. Children can become overwhelmed by their smallness and their feelings of helplessness. They need help to gain a healthy sense of being in control.

This focus on problems associated with feelings has a great deal to do with children's play. Theorists working within the psychoanalytic tradition have shown how play can reveal children's struggles with conflicting feelings and with their sense of helplessness. They show also how children can use play to master their feelings and sense of helplessness. One famous example will illustrate this last point.

Around the same time that Sigmund Freud was developing his concept of the *repetition compulsion* to explain why so many of his patients repeated the same mistakes and talked about their difficult pasts over and over again, he happened to be staying in a household with a toddler (Erikson, 1950). Freud noticed the toddler throwing objects so that they disappeared behind other objects, such as sofas and chairs, and then retrieving them, over and over again. Freud explained that the child was mastering the feelings he felt each time his mother left him. Like most toddlers, this toddler had no control over the comings and goings of his mother. He did, however, have control over the comings and goings of the objects he was throwing. In play, then, he could master feelings of frustration and helplessness that were difficult to master outside of play.

Feelings take center stage in the psychoanalytic perspective on play. In the next major theoretical perspective, thought and thinking become the principal actors.

Cognitive-Developmental Theory and Play

Consider Freud's example once again. From a different perspective, what is interesting is how the toddler's making objects disappear and then reappear rests on his ability to imagine or think about objects even when they are out of sight. The great Swiss psychologist, Jean Piaget, called this the ability to think about the permanence of objects or, to use his shorthand, *object permanence* (Piaget, 1952). Object permanence is a thinking tool that develops over time; it isn't there from the beginning. For the very young infant, out of sight can mean out of mind. Object permanence indicates the ability to *symbolize,* and the ability to symbolize is crucial to understanding the world. Therefore, to a Piagetian, the toddler's play in Freud's example seems to *consolidate* acquisition of object permanence as a tool for thinking symbolically—no trivial function indeed (Piaget, 1951).

A Piagetian explanation does not negate Freud's explanation. The toddler in Freud's example could have been using his play both to manage his feelings and to consolidate a newly acquired ability to think symbolically. Theoretical perspectives often complement rather than compete with one another.

The Piagetian explanation represents another common feature of cognitive-developmental approaches, namely, a focus on explaining development in terms of structural changes that define different *stages*. Piaget gave us three broad stages for explaining play's development: a stage dominated by nonsymbolic *practice games*, followed by a stage dominated by make-believe and *symbolic games*, followed by a stage dominated by *games with rules*. These stages are about the form or structure of play and not about its themes or content.

Piaget's Stages of Play

The great Swiss psychologist and stage theorist, Jean Piaget, developed three major stages for play's development, which are still used today. They are based on changes in play's *structure* rather than in play's *content*, and they reflect Piaget's major interest in the way play's development reflects children's developing capacity to think *symbolically*. The shift from the first to the second stage is a shift from presymbolic to symbolic play. The shift from the second to the third stage is a shift from symbolizing from one point of view only to symbolizing from multiple points of view, as children come to realize that the rules of games are constructed so that games can be played uniformly and fairly. Here are the stages with their approximate ages.

Age (Approximate)	Characteristics
Early to late infancy	Nonsymbolic practice games
Early childhood (before age 6)	Make-believe and symbolic games
Late childhood (before age 12)	Games with rules

Lev Vygotsky, a Russian psychologist and educator, is another well-known cognitive-developmental play theorist (Vygotsky, 1976b). Being an educator as well as a psychologist, Vygotsky was interested in how children learn and how learning contributes to development. Perhaps his most valuable contribution was his demonstrating how children's development rests on their actively participating in their culture. After all, no child develops in a vacuum. We will have more to say about this later on when discussing play and culture.

Vygotsky also emphasized the way parents and teachers help children learn by working within their *zone of proximal development,* that psychological "space" just beyond children's comfort zones, where they are used to functioning, but not so far beyond that they cannot stretch and grow.

Finally, Vygotsky saw in young children's make-believe play their use of play as a bootstrapping operation to help them *free thought from perception.* Vygotsky, then, saw play as a leading source of children's cognitive development. In later chapters, we will have more to say about exactly what this means.

Jerome Bruner is yet another central figure in the cognitive-developmental tradition. One of his many contributions to our understanding of play's development is his concept of *scaffolding* (Bruner, 1982). For example, in playing with their infants, parents often provide scaffolding so that their infants can participate in the play, such as by holding their infants' attention, giving a clear "play" face, and using a high-pitched voice—all to help their infants see their play as play. Play's development (and children's development too) can happen, then, because more skilled play partners support the development of play skills.

Piaget, Vygotsky, and Bruner attended to how play reflects and fosters children's cognitive development. Today's cognitive-developmental theorists do the same. However, in the past 30 years or so, there have been two major shifts in how cognitive development is conceived. The first shift was away from seeing thinking as developing toward being logical (Harris, 2000, 2003). Piaget's view was that children outgrow make-believe by becoming more logical, when, for example, they give up make-believe play for games with rules. However, today's cognitive-developmental psychologists argue that imagination continues to develop well into adulthood, as evidenced by how imagination operates in older children's and adolescents' play (Singer & Singer, 1990). We will have more to say about imagination in Chapters 3 and 4.

The other great shift has been toward appreciating how culture, play, and cognitive development work together (Rogoff, 2003). Today's cognitive-developmentalists have been listening to anthropologists, and the result has been to picture play as but one of several supports for cognitive development. In many cultures, work, not play, is the principal domain in which children are supported to think and develop, and these children turn out just fine (Gaskins, 2003). There are, it seems, many roads to maturity.

Today, then, cognitive-developmentalists are more likely to emphasize that development never occurs in a vacuum or in a single, unchanging environment. Rather, children develop through *participating* in their culture, which may or may not emphasize play. This thought is further developed by cultural-ecological theoretical perspectives on play.

Cultural-Ecological Theory and Play

As we have just indicated, development never occurs in a vacuum. That is as true for the development of play as it is for any other development. Play occurs within multiple and nested contexts (home, neighborhood, etc.) that deeply affect whether and how children play. Those theories that explain play in terms of contexts are often referred to collectively as *cultural-ecological theories.* In this book, there will be plenty of examples of cultural-ecological theories, as when we discuss Anthony Pellegrini's research on school recess and Gary Moore's research on the design of early-childhood classrooms.

Throughout this book, we will look at several contexts important for understanding children's play. In particular, we will look at the home, neighborhood, and school settings and at how they influence the way children play, so there is no need right now to say much about settings. However, because *culture* is such a misunderstood concept, we need to say a few words about it.

Culture is often treated as a single variable tied to particular geographical regions. However, culture is far more pervasive and subtle than this treatment implies (Rogoff, 2003; Roopnarine, Johnson, & Hooper, 1994). With respect to play, culture can be found in the smallest details—in an offhand reference to a TV show during doll play, in the particular materials chosen for building a playhouse, in the preference for one type of play over another, in whether or not parents encourage children to play, or in whether certain kinds of play are considered good or bad. The list is long.

Much of the list refers to surface matters, details that can be observed and measured. However, much also refers to what is hidden, to underlying assumptions, values, and worldviews. For example, some cultures are *interdependent:* They define development in terms of a child's needing to "fit in." In these cultures, harmony among group members is valued. Therefore, play in interdependent cultures is less likely to feature competition. In contrast, *individualistic* cultures define development in terms of a child's needing to "stand out." Individual achievement is what matters, so play in individualistic cultures is likely to feature competition (Rogoff, 2003).

To illustrate how culture works to influence play, consider the game of Monopoly. Monopoly was first developed in 1904, but it was not until 1935, during America's great economic depression, that a modified version became popular (Freitag, 1998). That version emphasized winning by accumulating

Photo 1.1   Young people's social and cultural contexts shape the materials they use and how they play. Here, a girl enjoys playing with a hula hoop at an outdoor basketball court.

wealth that put competitors out of business. The game reflected not only the individualistic nature of American culture but also the hard times of the Depression era. However, though the rules of Monopoly reflect a Western, individualistic culture, the way it is played need not, as illustrated in the accompanying box.

Playing to Emphasize Interdependence

Two East Asian girls had been playing Monopoly for quite a while when it was clear that one girl was about to go bankrupt. Rather than let that happen, the other girl gave her a sizable chunk of her own play money. From a cultural perspective, this seeming act of charity was not simply charity. It was an expression of an East Asian culture's emphasis on *interdependence* between individuals and maintaining harmonious relations.

But perhaps the most relevant points to make right now about culture and play have to do with basic assumptions about children's play. In the dominant North American culture, most assume that play is good, even essential, for children. Most assume that adults should be actively involved in supporting and at times coaching children's play. And most assume that children's age-mates are children's natural play partners. These assumptions turn out to be cultural assumptions, not universals. That is, other cultures make very different assumptions about children's play, as we will see in later chapters.

Evolutionary and Comparative Theories and Play

In this book, we won't say much about evolutionary and comparative theories of play, but readers should know that these theories have played important roles in the history of play theories (Sutton-Smith, 1984). Evolutionary theory has been particularly important in developing the rhetoric of progress. For example, Jerome Bruner (1972) argued that play is a major precursor to the emergence of language and symbolic behavior in higher primates and man. He made much of the fact that old-world monkeys play less than later-evolving new-world monkeys, and of the fact that new-world monkeys seem to use play to imitate and practice important skills.

The study of play among nonhuman animals has also contributed enormously to the development of play theory. Comparative studies have dispelled misconceptions about play in general, including misconceptions about play's being practice for the future. For example, the "galumphing" movement characterizing play fighting among juvenile baboons exists side by side with remarkably agile movements carried out when fighting is for real; the one does not lead to the other (Bruner, 1972).

Perhaps what is most important about the research having to do with evolution and nonhuman animals is that it has bolstered the argument for studying children's play. Play, it turns out, is ubiquitous. It connects not only different groups within the human species but different animal species as well. When we play with a family pet or observe a colt cavorting, we feel this connection. Paradoxically, then, by studying the diverse ways that different species play, evolutionary and comparative theorists have fostered a sense of unity among all animal species. In observing play, we better understand that we humans share a great deal with our nonhuman cousins.

So much for the major kinds of play theories. We need now to say something about play and the influence of major group characteristics: gender, socioeconomic status, and disability.

● MAJOR GROUPINGS AND PLAY: GENDER, SOCIOECONOMIC STATUS, AND DISABILITY

Gender

Gender has a profound influence on play. Very early on there are expectations with regard to how girls, as compared with boys, should play, expectations placed not only by adults but also by children themselves. Around age 3½, girls and boys separate themselves into same-sex play groups (Maccoby, 1998; Pitcher & Hickey-Schultz, 1983). This *gender segregation* continues throughout childhood, and it deeply affects how children play. Crafts, make-believe with domestic themes, and noncompetitive jumping and rhyming games often characterize girls' play. Trucks, war play, and physically vigorous competitive games and rough-and-tumble play characterize boys' play (Meany & Beatty, 1985; Rubin, Fein, & Vandenberg, 1983). But the main overall differences have to do with physical aggression, activity level, play fighting, and interactional style; boys are higher on the first three items on this list. As for interactional style, boys are more likely to draw attention to themselves, and girls are more likely to facilitate conversation (Maccoby, 1998). With respect to children's play, then, the world is fairly gender stereotypical.

There is, however, no evidence that girls and boys differ significantly in their overall development as players. Boys and girls are equally playful and imaginative, and the overall structural development of their play is roughly the same. This is why we have chosen to focus on the similarities in the way boys' and girls' play develops.

Boys' and Girls' Play: Differences in Content but Not in Structure

Boys and girls generally play at different play content, boys more with aggressive themes and girls more with domestic themes. In addition, boys' play is more physically active. These and other features have distinguished boys' and girls' play. However, there is no difference in terms of overall structural development. Girls and boys develop their play in the same stagelike progression described by Piaget. And both genders follow the same transformation from playing in parallel to eventually playing cooperatively with others.

Socioeconomic Status

Socioeconomic status (SES) became a focal point of discussions about children's play when, in 1968, Sara Smilansky published her book comparing the play of immigrant children from poor families with the play of children from middle-class families. She found immigrant children's play to be deficient (Smilansky, 1968). However, since then, there have been numerous criticisms of the way that Smilansky drew her conclusions, and today the trend is away from evaluating SES differences as indicating deficiencies. Poverty never stands by itself; it is usually confounded with other variables such as culture and race (Ramsey, 1998), making it difficult to make evaluative statements about the play of children from different socioeconomic groups.

We will have more to say about Smilansky, socioeconomic status, and play in Chapter 3 when the focus is on play in early childhood. For now and with respect to socioeconomic status and play, the best we can say is that it is premature and unfair to make assumptions about poor children being deficient in how they play.

Disability

The term *disability* covers a wide range of conditions, making it unfair to lump all disabilities together. Furthermore, doing so can lead to wrong generalizations. Certain disabilities have profound effects on the way children play. Autism, for example, renders children seriously impaired in their ability to generate make-believe (Cicchetti, Beeghly, & Weiss-Perry, 1994). Other disabilities, such as mental retardation, simply slow down the stagelike progression we expect in the play of all children. And still others render children without access and opportunity to play, as when children in wheelchairs don't have access or the opportunity to engage in sports. The main issues, then, have to do with the special supports and opportunities needed for children with disabilities to play.

With regard to special supports, aside from special equipment and techniques employed by occupational therapists and special educators, many of the supports needed for children with disabilities are the same supports needed for typical children, though they may be for children at younger ages. Therefore, it is important to remember that the discussions in this book about supports for children's play are applicable to children with and without disabilities.

The issue of opportunities may be more subtle and complicated to resolve. The history of rehabilitation psychology and special education tells us that excluding children with disabilities from the mainstream has created painful problems having to do with denying basic opportunities (Biklen, 1989). Later on, we will have more to say about this issue of disabilities and opportunities.

BAD PLAY ●

Most of this book is about positive instances of play. Therefore, to avoid idealizing play, we need to say something about bad play and play that is ambiguous with respect to whether it is good or bad.

Some readers may object to the term *bad play.* It can suggest that we are judging children as bad and that what is good and bad is something objective. However, in using the term *bad play,* we are not implying anything about the goodness or badness of children, and we certainly aren't saying that judging what is bad is a simple and objective process. What we are saying is that thoughtful, responsible caregivers stop or try to prevent certain forms of play because those forms are harmful or potentially harmful to children. In fact, we thought of calling this kind of play *stop-it play,* but we decided in the end that *bad play* would suffice. Furthermore, there is scholarly literature acknowledging that certain forms of play are indeed "bad" (Sutton-Smith, 1984).

Types of Bad Play

Risky Play

By "bad play," we mean first of all *risky play,* or play that puts children at risk for serious harm: lying down on railroad tracks to wait as long as possible for oncoming trains is a dramatic example. But there are less dramatic and much more common examples. Throwing sand at one another and stones at cars are among them, as are the many examples having to do with jumping off and into something. Visit certain country bridges crossing shallow, rock-strewn rivers on a hot summer day, and you are likely to see what we mean. This is bad play because it is risky play.

Mean-Spirited Play

Bad play also includes the many forms of *mean-spirited play,* play at making someone else unhappy or terrified. Teasing falls under this category, unless it is affectionate teasing among friends. So too do bullying and beating someone up "for the fun of it." We also include here the numerous kinds of inappropriate sexy play often carried out by preadolescent boys both to excite the perpetrator and to embarrass the victim. Bra snapping is one example; there are many others. This too is bad play.

Misbehaving Play

A third category of bad play consists of certain forms of *misbehaving play* that are both chronic and compulsive. We say "certain forms" because not all misbehavior is bad. The child who never misbehaves is not healthier for being so good. That said, chronic misbehaving play that reveals psychological problems because it is chronic and compulsive is indeed bad. The preschooler who constantly gains attention by showing off at circle time and the 11-year-old who constantly adopts the role of class clown are examples. Therefore, when misbehaving play is chronic and compulsive, it is bad play.

Ambiguous Play

The same cannot be said for a whole host of examples in which the presumed badness of the play rests on differences in taste and perspective. Children have different tastes than adults. They take delight in what is disgusting or offensive, such as jokes about nose picking and farting. These are ambiguous examples in terms of whether the play is good or bad. The amateur will rush to make a judgment. The professional will pause to ask questions. This book will provide many examples of these ambiguous types of play and show how questions can lead to an appreciation of their hidden value. In the meantime, we give two examples of *ambiguous play* to further clarify what this type means.

The first is of three preschoolers, age 4, playing at being "robbers"— what they called themselves when pretending to dismember baby dolls. What are we to make of this play? Is it unequivocally bad play? Or is it ambiguous? Here, we treat it as ambiguous for three reasons. First, the boys were clearly pretending. They weren't actually destroying the dolls, and they weren't being themselves; they were "robbers." Second, they were carrying out pretense collaboratively, always an achievement for children this young. Third, they engaged in this play sporadically, not all the time. Given these additional observations, we are still left with some concern because of the brutal and odd nature of the play's content, which is why we call this play ambiguous.

Take another example, this time of much older children playing a rougher game. These were children living in the city, children often stereotyped as being "tough" and "inner city," as if the basic differences between them and other children are great, when they are not. Their game was as follows: Each member was expected to contribute to the group's fun by occasionally telling a joke. However, if any member told a joke that the others did not find funny, the others had to pummel him hard. No member enjoyed being pummeled, and no member bullied.

On the surface, this might be considered "bad" play. Someone is getting hurt. But the fact that all the members accepted the play should give us pause. Was this play helping members feel closer to one another? Was it making members become more thoughtful humorists? Was it helping them develop a degree of toughness needed in this neighborhood? The answers to all three questions might well be "yes," which is why we treat this as an example of ambiguous play.

In sum, bad play and ambiguous play exist alongside good play. We need to distinguish between them if we are to understand children's play.

SUMMARY ●

We have seen, then, that although play is difficult to define and its functions are difficult to observe directly, play still has been a focus for scholarly discussion. Furthermore, we have seen how most scholars view play positively, as promoting children's overall development. We have seen how play's development never occurs in a vacuum, how it derives from children's participating in their cultures and in particular settings. Finally, we have seen that not all play is good, that there are several forms of bad play. We move, now, to more focused discussions on these and other issues, beginning with discussions of age changes and play's development.

KEY WORDS, NAMES, AND IDEAS ●

Ambiguous play

Bootstrapping play

Bruner, J.

Cognitive-developmental theory

Cultural-ecological theory

Development

Freud, S.

Gender segregation

Individualistic society

Interdependent society

Intrapsychic conflicts

Mean-spirited play

Misbehaving play

Object permanence

Piaget, J.

Psychoanalytic theory

Repetition compulsion

Rhetoric of play

Rhetoric of progress

Risky play

Scaffolding

Structure vs. content

Sutton-Smith, B.

Symbolic games

Vygotsky, L.

Zone of proximal development

PART I

The Development of Play From Infancy Through Late Childhood

Part I discusses age changes in how children play. It is divided into four chapters, one on infancy and the toddler years (0–2), one on early childhood or the preschool years (3–5), and one on late childhood or the elementary school years (6–12). We end Part I with a chapter on children's humor, because children's humor deserves its own chapter and also because charting its development throughout childhood provides a way to summarize the main points about age changes in how children play.

In this section on age changes, three main points become apparent. First, play's development is tied to children's overall physical, cognitive, and social-emotional development. So, for example, infants play mostly in non-symbolic ways, because their ability to symbolize is as yet undeveloped. Similarly, preschoolers like action jokes more than they like jokes about logic, because their ability to think logically is rudimentary. These and other examples of what is present and what is missing in children's play at different ages indicates what we mean by play's development being tied to children's development.

The second main point is that play develops as separate lines of development within separate play media. Each play medium has its own special opportunities and limitations. So, for example, dolls or replicas lend themselves to developing stories, whereas blocks lend themselves to developing three-dimensional constructions.

The third main point is that play's development is more about structural change than it is about content. Going from presymbolic to symbolic play is a prime example. There are many other examples as well.

Part I, therefore, gives a broad overview of play's development in childhood. In doing so, it shows that despite individual differences and differences in context, there is much that children everywhere have in common with respect to how their play develops.

CHAPTER 2

THE EMERGENCE OF PLAY IN INFANCY AND THE TODDLER YEARS

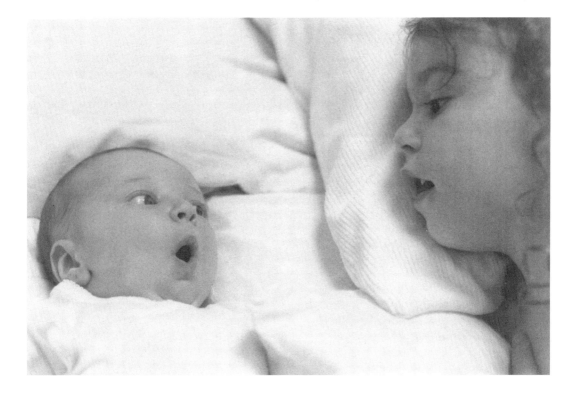

I n the introduction to this book, we explained how challenging it could be to define play. Indeed, there seems to be no single and clear attribute of play. Yet most theorists, practitioners, and informed observers agree that although play cannot be easily defined, it can be recognized, at least most of the time. What makes for play, then, seems to be a rather complex combination of behaviors that can only be perceived and understood as a whole and within a particular context.

In infancy (i.e., the first year of life) and the toddler years (i.e., roughly the year and a half following), defining play is especially difficult. Some link play to pretense, thus ruling out play in infancy since pretense does not emerge until the second year of life. However, infants definitely play. A smile, a giggle, or an engaging pattern of interaction all point to the existence of infant play. As an example, take Piaget's observation of his 6-month-old daughter Jacqueline:

> At 6 months and 25 days, J. invented a new sound by putting her tongue between her teeth. It was something like *pfs.* Her mother then made the same sound. J. was delighted and laughed as she repeated it in her turn. Then came a long period of mutual imitation. J. said *pfs;* her mother imitated her, and J. watched her without moving her lips. Then, when her mother stopped, J. began again, and so it went. Later on, after remaining silent for some time, I myself said *pfs.* J. laughed and at once imitated me. There was the same reaction the next day, beginning in the morning (before she had herself spontaneously made the sound in question) and lasting throughout the day. (Piaget, 1951, p. 19)

Jacqueline's inventing a new sound, "pfs," was not itself play. Most likely, it was a by-product of her exploration into making sounds with her tongue.

We need to say more about exploration because, as this example illustrates, exploration in infancy closely resembles and often leads to play. Play versus exploration, then, is the first section of this chapter. Through several vivid examples of what young children can or cannot do at different ages, we see and feel the ambiguity in calling much of their behavior play, but we also see the unquestionable instances of play. In doing so, we become more aware of the difficulties involved in defining play and the boundaries around play.

In the second section of this chapter, we look at the different types of play in which infants and toddlers engage. We see how children progressively learn about play by repeating known actions, by imitating others, by taking turns, and by eventually initiating play activities themselves, including pretense activities.

Finally, in our last section, we revisit what happens when infants and toddlers play with their parents or with other children. There, we show that from the very first months of life onward, children's cognitive, emotional, and social development converge in play. We also explain that the value of play varies across cultures and settings, and that children play differently and with different partners accordingly. We learn that what can be adaptive in one culture is not necessarily adaptive in others.

PLAY VERSUS EXPLORATION ●

In Theory

Some emphasize the similarities between play and exploration because both are intrinsically motivated or carried out for their own sake (Weisler & McCall, 1976). However, most scholars agree that there are significant differences between the two, for at least two reasons. First, exploration is "stimulus- dominated" and play is "organism-dominated" (Hutt, Tyler, Hutt, & Christopherson,

1989)—meaning that in exploration it is the object's characteristics that matter most, whereas in play it is the player's interests that are most important. To clarify this distinction between exploration and play, Hutt (1970) refers to two implicit questions that the child might be asking herself: What does this object do? in the case of exploration, and What can I do with this object? in the case of play (p. 169). For example, exploring a rattle is a means to find out about its properties and its methods of use, whereas playing with a rattle entails using it in any way that is interesting, including using it as if it were not a rattle.

Second, exploration is about reducing uncertainty and forming goals, whereas play is about displaying known actions and having a clear goal (Piaget, 1951). Referring again to the rattle example, when an infant explores a rattle, the infant's only goal is to become familiar with it. In contrast, when an infant plays with a rattle, the infant already knows something about how the rattle can be used, and it is the desire to use the rattle in a particular and pleasurable way that motivates the infant.

Although these distinctions may be clear conceptually, they often are unclear when we try to apply them. Therefore, we need to know the specific behavioral cues to distinguish between exploration and play.

In Practice: Cues for Distinguishing Exploration From Play

Affect and Words

Consider the following children, both engaged in what some would consider to be play. Three-month-old Jeremy sticks his fingers in his mouth, sucks them for a while, and makes gurgling sounds. Twenty-two-month-old Nicholas puts his fingers in his mouth, looks at his mother, giggles, and says, "hum . . . yummy chocolate pudding." Clearly, Nicholas uses his mouth and fingers to pretend and play. We know this not only by his giggles but also by the words he uses to indicate he is pretending. Jeremy, on the other hand, neither giggles nor uses words. Without these cues, conservative interpretation tells us that he is exploring—exploring what he can do with his fingers to make interesting sounds. Giggles and positive affect provide cues for distinguishing between exploration and play. So too do words that mark behavior as pretending.

Context

Consider another example of a common cue, context. Two 6-month-olds, Lucie and Kevin, both shake rattles. Lucie's grandparents visited the day before and gave her a brand new pink and blue rattle. Kevin has two older siblings, and he often inherits their toys. His rattle has been around for quite some time, and Kevin has had many opportunities to shake it.

Given this background information, information distinguishing the *context* of Lucie's play from Kevin's, we can conclude that Lucie is more likely to be exploring. That is, Lucie is more likely to be shaking the rattle to see what it feels like to hold it in different positions, to hear what sounds it makes at different shaking speeds, and so forth. On the other hand, because Kevin already knows what can be done with the rattle, he is more likely to be playing by making "a happy display of known actions" (Piaget, 1951, p. 93). Context, therefore, is an additional cue to use when distinguishing between exploration and play, even for infants of the same age.

How Is This Distinction Useful?

Making the distinction between exploration and play helps us to realize how complex it is to define play and how hazardous it can be to try to capture its essence in a single definition. Moreover, making such a distinction on the basis of affective, linguistic, and contextual variables helps us to change our focus when seeking to discover when play first appears in children—from focusing on the age or time of appearance (e.g., 4 months versus 6 months) to focusing on the cues that indicate whether or not infants are playing (e.g., positive affect versus serious face). We are now ready to distinguish among the various types of play in infancy and the toddler years.

TYPES OF PLAY IN INFANCY AND THE TODDLER YEARS ●

Clearly, play in infancy and the toddler years appears in many forms, and children of different ages clearly play differently. Consider the following examples:

● At 4 months, Tom throws his head backward and looks at his surrounding environment. He repeats the action over and over again with what seems to be increasing pleasure.

● At 9 months, Clara mistakenly touches her nose with her finger while trying to scratch her irritated cheek. Her father looks at her, puts his finger on his own nose, and says "pouet-pouet" in a clown-like voice. Clara looks at him, laughs, imitates the gesture, and even makes an attempt to reproduce the noise. Her father repeats the whole sequence again. Clara laughs, repeats the gesture again, and waits for her father to take his turn. For the next few days, Clara responds with great excitement when her father touches his nose, and the exchange sometimes continues for several minutes at a time.

● At 16 months, Isaac lies down in his crib, closes his eyes, and smiles broadly. He then opens his eyes, looks at his mother, and smiles again. In the following few minutes, he repeats the same pattern—opening and closing his eyes while smiling. A few weeks later, Isaac repeats the same sequence, this time using a stuffed animal as a pillow. Again, he smiles broadly, and then moves on to using other random objects in place of the pillow.

We know, both intuitively and from the cues already mentioned, that these children are playing, but obviously Tom, Clara, and Isaac are playing in different ways. How should we describe the differences?

There are two major distinctions to make when categorizing types of infant play. The first is between *sensorimotor* (nonsymbolic) and *make-believe* (pretend) play. The second distinction is between *nonsocial* (solitary) and *social* play. The first distinction reveals a central development in infancy; namely, the development of a capacity to symbolize or represent, and so we will use it to organize this discussion of play types. However, while discussing sensorimotor and make-believe play separately, we will also make use of the social/nonsocial distinction. We will then revisit this social/nonsocial distinction in the third section of this chapter, where we describe how infants and toddlers play next to, and sometimes with, each other.

Sensorimotor Play

Tom's and Clara's play are examples of sensorimotor play because, on the surface, nothing is represented. However, Tom's repetitions are of a different type than Clara's. Tom repeats an action in response to one of his own actions. These repetitions and playful actions are called *circular reactions.* They are usually nonsocial, or solitary, insofar as no playmate is involved.

Developmental Milestones: Circular Reactions

Following Piaget (1952), most authors distinguish among four types of increasingly complex circular reactions:

● *Primary circular reactions* first emerge between 1 and 4 months of age, when infants discover pleasurable actions with their own bodies (e.g., their thumbs). These actions, first discovered by chance, are then purposely repeated to generate pleasure.

- *Secondary circular reactions* are similar to primary circular reactions to the extent they are first discovered by chance and then repeated over and over again. However, secondary circular reactions involve an external object (e.g., a rattle). They usually appear between 4 and 8 months of age.
- *Coordination of secondary circular reactions* tends to appear between 8 and 12 months of age. At this stage, children may use two different objects at once to create a new result (e.g., knocking a spoon on a cup to make a new noise).
- *Tertiary circular reactions* signal the emergence of new trial-and-error exploratory schemes. Between the ages of 12 and 18 months, children experiment with several objects at a time, usually toys, to see if they can reproduce interesting results or create new ones (e.g., reaching out to a faraway toy with a stick).

Clara, on the other hand, repeats an action in response to her parent's imitations. Most significantly, she goes on to engage in *turn-taking*.

Turn-Taking as a Precursor to Social Play

Comparing these two types of play, we can say that in Clara's case, but not in Tom's, there are indications that she is representing something, not in the play itself but in her thinking. Indeed, she waits for her father to take a turn and anticipates (that is, represents internally) how her father will touch his nose and make the funny sound.

The significance of turn-taking play, however, is not simply its ability to indicate the capacity to imagine or represent internally. It is also a milestone in relating to another person. Imagine what our lives would be like without taking turns. For one thing, without turn-taking, we could not converse, and without conversing, we could not communicate and develop ideas together (Kaye & Fogel, 1980). Indeed, as Collis (1979) pointed out, human beings are limited in their capacity to speak and listen at the same time, hence the necessity for alternating between speaking and listening to others. The advent of turn-taking, then, is no small accomplishment for children, and the fact that we often see turn-taking first in play—before children can communicate through language—provides one of the many reasons to value play as a support for children's development (Papousek & Papousek, 1982). In this respect, Clara's father is playing an instrumental role by providing scaffolding.

Scaffolding, Zone of Proximal Development, and Social Play

As we explained in Chapter 1, the term *scaffolding* was first crafted by Bruner (Bruner & Sherwood, 1976; Ratner & Bruner, 1978). It is often used to describe the caregiver's role in promoting a child's development. Vygotsky (1978) further hypothesized that children first develop their skills with their caregivers before they apply these skills with less advanced social partners (e.g., siblings or other children). He used the term *zone of proximal development* to describe the developmental space between what a child can do by herself and what she can do with the support of a mature social partner (e.g., her caregiver).

Several other scholars have explored how scaffolding operates in play. Hodapp, Goldfield, and Boyatzis (1984) reported that mother-infant games such a roll-the-ball or peekaboo had positive benefits on infants' social development. In their study of 26 infants at ages 6 and 9 months, Vandell and Wilson (1987) also showed that the quality of infants' playful exchanges with their mothers positively influenced their subsequent play activities with siblings and peers, especially with regard to turn-taking.

In the third section of this chapter, we will revisit how caregivers—and siblings, to a lesser extent—can help young children develop their social abilities through play.

Patterns and Rules

There is another important observation to make about Tom's and Clara's sensorimotor play; namely, through infants' behavior repetition, they come to understand behavior sequences by their *patterns*. The raw experience of life does not sort itself neatly into recognizable patterns; we do the sorting, and we do it first by either actively repeating experiences (as in the previous two examples) or by noticing that repetitions happen on their own. In either case, repetition helps to sort and organize experiences into patterns. We see this in many ways, including the ways that infants play, which gives us another reason to link play to knowledge about infant development.

After observing infants' repetitive play, Piaget (1951) assigned to play the important function of *consolidating* knowledge. Infants' repetitive play, he says, is not the first way that infants learn about reality, but it is the way they consolidate what they have already learned, namely that the world is patterned.

However, the most important aspect of this sorting into patterns is that infants come to know reality as *rule governed*. After all, a pattern is defined by the rules that allow for its repetition. In Tom's case, the rule is to throw one's head back and look upward. In Clara's case, the rule is to touch one's nose and make a sound. Although these rules may not seem significant and are implicit in infants' actions rather than explicit in their language, defining them constitutes an important step forward in a child's development.

The presence of rules in infants' play also justifies referring to these early instances of infant play as *games*. Doing so allows us to move on to another important distinction for understanding infants' and toddlers' play, namely, the distinction between *reading* games and *inventing* games that can be read by others.

Reading and Inventing Games

Peekaboo!

At 5 months, Erica seems to have quite a bit of fun when her father throws a blanket at her face while changing her diaper and then says "Peekaboo" when partially removing the blanket. For the past month, Erica and her father have developed a routine of engaging in such inter-actions several times a day. Each time, Erica smiles, sometimes laughs, and always kicks her feet up and down with great excitement, com-municating that she is having a good time. Sometimes, the changing of Erica's diaper is just the excuse that leads into the game, as the game usually extends far beyond the time necessary to actually change the diaper. It is clear, then, that certain signals are being sent and received by both Erica and her father—otherwise, how would Erica know that the throwing of the blanket is a game and not an aggressive act on the part of her father?

Reading games comes first, followed by inventing games. Peekaboo pro-vides the earliest and almost universal example. Peekaboo has many varia-tions, but its essential game-defining rule states that something disappears and then reappears. That something may be a parent, an object, or the infant herself. However, whatever or whoever disappears is not what matters. What matters is that the infant learns to "read" the disappearance and reappear-ance as a game.

Peekaboo becomes a first game for many infants because it is such a simple game initiated and repeated by supportive caregivers. Caregivers provide many cues and supports to help infants discriminate peekaboo as play—using a high-pitched voice, maintaining focused attention, showing a playful facial expression (Lillard, 2003), and other cues say, in effect, "This is play."

What develops in the process? Most likely, Erica is becoming more and more proficient at reading others' cues—in this case, her father's cues. She is, therefore, developing into a proficient playmate and a social being, thanks to her father's scaffolding. Is Erica also developing cognitively? Remember that she is only 5 months old. At this young age, it is most likely that she has not yet mastered a major developmental milestone in cognition: *object permanence.* Yet, when hidden, Erica seems to know that her father is still there, somewhere behind the blanket that covers her face. She also knows that her father is not being aggressive. In fact, she apparently understands that he is being playful, and she responds with great excitement herself.

Developmental Milestones: Object Permanence

As we already explained in Chapter 1, object permanence, or the notion that objects and people continue to exist even when out of sight, is considered to be one of infants' most important cognitive achievements. According to Piaget (1952), children usually start mastering this capacity around 8 months of age. According to others (Bjorklund, 2000), even very young infants know that objects continue to exist; they just forget about these objects when the objects remain hidden for more than 1 or 2 seconds. Whatever the interpretation, children younger than 8 months of age usually do not seek to retrieve hidden objects or people. But infants' capacity may vary depending on the object or person and context. In fact, some argue that children are able to understand the permanency of their primary caregiver's face before they can do so with inanimate objects.

As children grow up, caregivers naturally adapt, and their sensorimotor games tend to become more challenging to read. The following example illustrates one such sensorimotor game:

At 14 months old, Roger approaches his father, who is eating his supper. Roger whines, and his father hands him his napkin. They briefly engage in a game of tug-of-war. But then Roger retreats back around the corner of the dining area and into the hall. Roger's father takes the napkin, and, without looking around the corner, he throws it at Roger. Roger laughs and reappears holding the napkin—gesturing that he wants his father to repeat this game. They do so by waiting for Roger to retreat into the hall, followed by his father tossing the napkin around the corner again, followed by Roger reappearing with the napkin in hand. The game goes on for several minutes and occurs several times throughout the following weeks.

As in the case of peekaboo, this type of play entails having an adult invent the game. However, as opposed to peekaboo, reading the rules is much more complicated. There are far fewer cues for Roger to use to discern that his father's behavior is indeed play. Roger is becoming more skilled in discerning others' play. As we shall see in the last section of this chapter, he will need these skills when playing with peers who are not as adept as his parents at providing cues for him to "read" their play.

By the second year of life, we start to see children regularly inventing sensorimotor games on their own—games that can be "read" by others and hence responded to by others, either caregivers or other children. Just watch a toddler jumping in a silly way and another doing the same to see what we mean.

Now that we have seen different ways that infants and toddlers engage in sensorimotor play—in solitary or social ways—we can begin discussing the origins and development of make-believe play. In doing so, it will become clear that many of the same points made about sensorimotor play's development can be made about make-believe play's development as well.

Make-Believe Play

The emergence of make-believe play in the second year of life marks another extraordinary mental achievement. Consider what even a "simple" act of make-believe entails. For a 16-month-old to play at, say, falling asleep (see the previous example of Isaac), he has to (a) image falling asleep in his head, (b) animate that image by bringing it out into the open, that is, by making it visible in his gestures, and (c) deny that what he is doing is serious (Ariel, 2002). There is, then, a lot to think about, even in very simple make-believe.

The example of pretending to fall asleep also raises another point about beginning make-believe; namely, that it is highly imitative. So, how do we

Photo 2.1   During the toddler years, make-believe play often involves imitating realistic scenes—such as calling someone on a telephone.

distinguish early instances of make-believe play from the many instances of imitation that infants show us that are not play?

Make-Believe Play and Imitation

The question of how to distinguish between make-believe play and imitation is similar to the question of how to distinguish between exploration and play. And the answer is similar too—through the affective, linguistic, and contextual *cues*. But why this reliance on cues? Surely what is being pretended should be enough to define the child's play as play. The content of play, however, is often not enough to say whether it is play. A child's pretending to fall asleep or drink from a cup may look identical to the real action. We have no way of knowing from its content whether it is play, imitation, or a mistake on the child's part (e.g., trying to drink from a cup and finding it already empty).

This means that whether or not a child's action is make-believe play, imitation, a mistake, or something in between the three depends on inferring something about the child's mental state. It also depends on whether what is depicted is understood by the child to be "just pretend." Affect (e.g., laughter) and context (e.g., going through the motions of sleeping when the child is clearly rested) give us a peek into a child's mind.

However, just as exploratory and play behaviors are not always clearly distinguishable from one another, imitative behaviors and make-believe play often go together during the second year of life, when children make their first attempts at pretending while still engaging in many imitative behaviors. In Piaget's view (1951), whereas imitation is viewed as a continuation of accommodation (i.e., the process by which children incorporate or adapt to new experiences) and play as a continuation of assimilation (i.e., the process by which children incorporate new experiences into their existing schemes), both converge in fostering development and "intelligence, [the] harmonious combination of the two" (p. 104). As make-believe play emerges and develops in the second year of infancy, the distinction becomes more obvious. But how does this occur?

Language leads to an important development in an infant's capacity to initiate make-believe play. As the example of Isaac's pretending to sleep indicates, language is not necessary to pretend. However, language adds extraordinary power and flexibility for turning ordinary imitation into make-believe. As indicated in the example of Nicholas saying "Hum, yummy chocolate," simply labeling or mislabeling an action or object can be all it takes to make clear that an action is pretend. Thus, in the toddler years, make-believe develops by becoming more verbal.

Solitary Pretense and Social Pretense

The other major development in make-believe play in the toddler years is that it becomes increasingly social. At first, make-believe events are largely solo performances or performances in front of another but not *with* another. Several researchers (e.g., Belsky & Most, 1981; Tamis-LeMonda & Bornstein, 1991) have documented that pretense themes tend to be first directed toward the self (e.g., pretending to eat from a plate, pretending to fall asleep) before they can be applied to other inanimate objects (e.g., pretending to soothe a doll), and finally toward other playmates. The box on the next page summarizes how.

Toddler's Play Levels		
Play Level	Definition	Examples
1. Unitary functional activity	Production of an effect that is unique to a single object	Squeeze ball, dial telephone
2. Inappropriate combinatorial activity	Inappropriate juxtaposition of two or more objects	Put ball in vehicle
3. Appropriate combinatorial activity	Appropriate juxtaposition of two or more objects	Put lid on teapot, nest blocks
4. Transitional play	Approximation of pretense but without confirmatory evidence	Put telephone receiver to ear without vocalization
5. Self-directed pretense	Clear pretense activity directed toward self	Pretend to eat from spoon or empty cup
6. Other-directed pretense	Clear pretense activity directed toward others	Hug doll, pretend car makes sound
7. Sequential pretense	Link two or more pretense actions	Dial telephone and speak into receiver
8. Substitution pretense	Pretend activity involving one or more object substitution	Talk into block as if it were telephone

Source: Adapted from Tamis-LeMonda & Bornstein (1991).

Gradually, children engage in pretense with others, and pretense activities become events whereby the toddler "plays off" the make-believe of another. Consider the following example:

At 22 months old, Seth sits in his bath holding his toy rubber lizard. He pretends the lizard bites him. His father gives a mock cry and pretends to comfort Seth by giving him medicine. His father also pretends to spank the lizard. This game is repeated several times, and the next day, Seth starts the game again. Father and son repeat and develop the story line together.

But "playing off" the make-believe of another involves two preliminary steps: the capacity to read others' make-believe and the ability to initiate make-believe oneself.

Reading Make-Believe Play

Just as in sensorimotor play, children often learn how to refine their own pretense by becoming more proficient at reading others'. This is demonstrated in the following example:

Mom Pretends, I Smile . . .

At 18 months old, Pedro is still a relatively difficult child when it comes to feeding. The whole family has a different schedule, and Pedro is usually in bed long before his parents and older siblings sit together at the dinner table. Eating is no fun for Pedro!

Yet, for the past few weeks, his mother seems to have found a new trick: she sits at the dinner table with Pedro and pretends to have a meal herself while he actually has real food and real milk. "Hum . . . ," she says, "These vegetables are really really good. I think I'll have some more. What do you think, Pedro? May I have more vegetables?" While his mother pretends to eat, smiling and looking at her son in the process, Pedro starts smiling and looking at his mother in return. After a while, he picks up his spoon and starts eating. Clearly, Pedro seems to 'get' the trick, and he begins to enjoy the interaction with his mother. In fact, he enjoys it so much that eating becomes tolerable, even fun.

In the example above, Pedro knows, somehow, that his mother is not really eating vegetables. But how does he know? After all, he is only 18 months old, and he is probably not yet capable of fully engaging in such elaborate pretense himself. In fact, Pedro's mother is probably quite happy that he is not capable of such developed pretense, for if he were, the game could go on and on with Pedro pretending and never eating his vegetables.

To discover how infants read their caregivers' playful pretense, Lillard (2003) researched the types of social cues that can help infants distinguish between real and pretend. In a study with American dyads of 18-month-old children and their mothers, she showed that most mothers usually engaged in pretense activities with their children (e.g., pretending to eat cereal and drink juice) and that most children—especially those who had had repeated experience with such interactions—reacted positively to them.

Along with Kaye (1982) and other scholars (Smolucha & Smolucha, 1998), Lillard takes a Vygotskyan perspective by assuming that early pretense is as much a social activity as it is an output of children's cognitive development. In particular, she explains, infants between the ages of 12 and 18 months have three important skills that help them to precociously understand pretense in social contexts: (a) They can make sense of incomplete acts and read the intentions behind these acts (Meltzoff, 1995); (b) they can attend to others' actions with great interest and focus, thus displaying what Bruner (1995) calls *joint attention;* and (c) they often engage in *social referencing* when confused by the ambiguity of a given situation (Feinman, 1992). All three skills, then, might contribute to the child's early understanding of pretense.

Developmental Milestones: Social Referencing

Social referencing refers to the use of others'—often the caregiver's—facial expressions to infer the meaning of ambiguous situations (e.g. a strange noise, a pet coming toward the child, etc.). This behavior starts becoming obvious in infants between 8 and 10 months of age and becomes increasingly common with age, especially during the toddler years.

Inventing Make-Believe Play

Finally, by the end of toddlerhood, make-believe becomes less imitative and more *inventive.* Consider the following invented make-believe by a 2½-year-old playing with his father:

Cory sits in the sink where he is getting cleaned off. He hands his father a small doll figure, makes a sad face, and tells his father, "He's sad, Daddy." The father tickles the doll and makes the doll laugh uncontrollably. Cory laughs and then repeats the game by giving his father more dolls and an animal figure to tickle and make happy. But then he goes a step further. He hands his father a toothbrush, saying, "It's sad, Daddy," then a drinking cup, hand lotion, and dental floss—each time saying, "It's sad." His smile indicates he understands clearly that he has made a joke by introducing these objects and calling them "sad."

In this last example, we see how far young children can come in their play. They begin with nonsymbolic play that is largely carried out by a caregiver. They continue by inventing make-believe play that can be read and "played off" by another. Several scholars have documented this development. In their study with 13- and 20-month-old toddlers, for instance, Tamis-LeMonda and Bornstein (1991) noted that older children increasingly engaged in "spontaneous" pretense—pretense in which the child exhibited a behavior that was neither elicited nor demonstrated by the caregiver—whereas younger children engaged in "prompted" pretense most of the time. Nicolich (1977) also pointed out that children increasingly plan their pretense activities as they become more mature players. Twenty-four-month-old children, for instance, will sometimes verbally announce their intentions beforehand and/or look for the objects needed for their planned pretense scenario to begin.

By the end of the toddler years, we find children often passionate about their make-believe. We find their make-believe increasingly identified and supported by their language, and we find their make-believe becoming more social through joint make-believe, be it caregiver-prompted or child-initiated. However, these are just first attempts at developed make-believe. There is much more yet to be developed. These first tries merely set the stage for the golden age of make-believe, which is the subject of the next chapter.

SUPPORTING INFANTS' AND TODDLERS' PLAY ●

Before moving on to the next chapter on play in early childhood, we need to say a bit more about how adults, and sometimes other children, can support the development of children's play in infancy and the toddler years.

When Caregivers Play With Their Children

We already have seen many examples of caregivers playing with their infants, so here our purpose is mostly to label the different kinds of supports that have already been described. There are four types: *initiating play, imitating the imitator, extending children's play,* and *collaborative co-playing.* We will discuss each in turn.

Initiating Play

The first and most obvious support that caregivers give is initiating play, even with newborns who have no capacity to play. From caregivers taking hold of newborns' hands and clapping them together to play patty-cake to caregivers initiating all kinds of hard-to-read make-believe with older infants and toddlers, children acquire considerable experience "reading" the games of others.

Five Steps for Initiating Play

In their study with 2- to 20-week-old infants and their mothers, Brazelton, Koslowski, and Main (1974, p. 64) list five steps to describe how mothers initiate play activities with their newborn infants:

1. Reduction of interfering activity.

2. Setting the stage for a period of interaction by bringing the infant to a more alert, receptive state.

3. Creating an atmosphere of expectancy for further interaction by her behavior.

4. Acceleration of the infant's attention to receive and send messages.

5. Allowing for reciprocity with sensitivity to the infant's signals, giving him/her time to respond with his/her own behavior, as well as time to digest and recover from the activation the mother's cues establish.

Not surprisingly, the games infants first initiate on their own are often modeled after the games that their caregivers have initiated. For example, after months of watching and laughing at their parents' peekaboo games, many infants who can crawl will crawl behind an object such as a living-room sofa and emerge laughing on the other side.

Imitating the Imitator

We saw this phenomenon in the very first example, when Piaget's wife imitated her daughter Jacqueline's making the sound "pfs," which prompted Jacqueline to reciprocate the imitation. Parents imitate their infants all the time, without coaching and often without realizing what a clever tactic it is for eliciting and supporting play. In the process, infants and toddlers learn how to take turns. In his study on the origins of reciprocity in preverbal parent-infant interactions, Papousek and Papousek (1982) showed that a clear progression takes place through these interactions. Indeed, whereas young infants (i.e., those up to 3 or 4 months of age) and their caregivers tend to vocalize at the same time in the context of pleasant interactions, a new type of interaction emerges later on as the child engages in more vocal activities when the caregiver pauses. By 12 months of age, the rate of simultaneous vocalizations (or "vocal clashes") diminishes significantly, and between 18 and 24 months of age, children start playing an active role in regulating the turn-taking sequence (Schaffer, Collis, & Parsons, 1977).

Extending Children's Play

We saw this phenomenon when Seth pretended his toy lizard bit him, and then his father extended the make-believe by "dressing" the wound and "punishing" the lizard. This too parents do all the time, especially in the beginning stages of make-believe when infants initiate make-believe with only single acts. By extending their children's play, parents show them new possibilities.

Collaborative Co-Playing

Co-playing occurs whenever caregivers and infants play as play partners. This includes instances of imitating the imitator and extending play, but it also includes instances when caregivers collaborate and play as equals, when each partner both initiates and follows. We got one glimpse of this kind of co-play in the example of Cory and his father making sad objects happy. The toddler initiated by reporting on the sad feelings of various objects, and the parent initiated tickling to make them "happy." Together, they produced a delightful piece of make-believe.

In addition, several authors (e.g., Vandell & Wilson, 1987; Bronson, 1981) have shown that co-playing with their caregiver can also prepare infants and toddlers for play with other children.

When Children Play With Other Children

Play in infancy and the toddler years does not always happen with a parent. In many instances, infants and toddlers play with other children—with little friends at day care or in the neighborhood, or with siblings and other relatives. In a study of young children's play in Civita Fantera, a small Italian town near Rome, New (1994) showed how primary caregivers, usually mothers, are the least likely to play with their infants.

What happens, then, when children play with other children? We need to distinguish between children playing with older children or siblings, and children playing with same-age peers.

Play With Older Children and Siblings

When infants and toddlers play with older children, we can legitimately assume the older, more competent children provide *scaffolding,* perhaps not as much or as well as the scaffolding provided by parents, but scaffolding nonetheless. Just as children as young as 4 years of age engage in motherly behaviors (i.e., by using simple language) when talking to infants (Tomasello & Mannie, 1985), we often see these same children adjusting their play behaviors to coincide with their perceptions of younger playmates' capacities. For instance, they might play more gently with a toddler than they would with another 4-year-old by adjusting the level of their pretense to better fit the younger child's capacities, and so forth.

Yet, older children (preschoolers in particular) have more limited perspective-taking abilities than their parents, which may limit their capacity to scaffold their younger siblings or peers. Consequently, they might not have the same motivation and patience to engage infants in turn-taking activities (Vandell & Wilson, 1987). In fact, in a study with infants at 6 and 9 months of age, their mothers, their preschool-age siblings, and their same-age peers, Vandell and Wilson (1987) found that infants spent more time in turn-taking exchanges with their mothers than they did with their siblings. They also found that the average length of each exchange was longer in the context of infant-mother interactions and that the nature of turn-taking activities varied depending on the play partner. In particular, they showed that 3- to 6-year-old siblings were more likely to elicit behaviors in the infant (e.g., by making a funny face or by giving the infant a toy) than to extend and elaborate on the infant's behaviors as parents often do. However, despite these developmental limits in how preschoolers scaffold

Photo 2.2   Infants and very young children often find age-mates to be very satisfying play partners—and in ways different from when they play with older siblings and parents.

infants' play, Vandell and Wilson also found that infants' play experiences with an older sibling predicted more turn-taking exchanges between infants and same-age peers later on. Siblings, then, can help young children become constructive players, albeit at a different level and pace than parents do.

Play With Same-Age Peers

On the other hand, the whole play scene is quite different when infants and toddlers play with age-mates (e.g., two toddlers delighting in running up and down a hall together). Yet, this is not to say that all play within infants or toddlers is exactly the same. How does play develop in such contexts?

Mueller and Lucas (1975) listed three stages of development in peer play among toddlers: object-centered contacts, simple and complex contingency interchanges, and complementary interchanges. In Stage 1, they say, children are most interested in an object, without regard for what the other child is doing. For instance, two children might be exploring the same toy truck without really interacting with each other. Because they are in the same space at the same time, and because they are both interested in the same object, they might take turns, not so much because they want to but rather because they have to. This is the distinction made between Stages 1 and 2 in Mueller and Lucas's model. Indeed, while children are mostly interested in things, not peers, in Stage 1, they progressively start becoming proactive partners in Stage 2, when they actively seek and receive signals from one another. Between Stages 1 and 2, then, toddlers' play evolves from being primarily solitary to becoming more social. Finally, in Stage 3, toddlers play by giving complementary interchanges—that is by building on one another's actions to develop new patterns of play. For example, when one child puts a small doll replica in the toy construction truck, another reaches for the container holding different kinds of replicas, selects another doll, and puts it next to the first one in the truck.

To summarize Mueller and Lucas's model, children play by themselves, imitate, take turns, and progressively initiate new forms of play through interacting with their age-mates, just as they did with their parents. Mueller and Lucas suggest that play interactions between age-mates are at least complementary to adult-child interactions. In doing so, they extend Piaget's view (1951) that even at a very young age, peers play an active role in fostering children's development.

In addition, peers also have different interests than adults—interests that most often match the infant's or toddler's own interests (Howes, 1988). Two things are implied here. First, peers are less likely than caregivers to play off those children's behaviors that do not interest them, which means that children benefit from less scaffolding—if any scaffolding at all—when playing with same-age peers. Second, some social abilities (e.g., jumping in a silly way 10 times in a row) are more likely to be acquired from peers than from adults (Howes, 1988). Play with same-age peers, then, is complementary to play with adults, older children, and siblings.

There is one more distinction we need to make, the distinction between play with familiar peers and play with nonfamiliar peers. Eckerman, Davis, and Didow (1989) conducted a longitudinal study with pairs of same-age unfamiliar peers at ages 16, 20, 24, 28, and 32 months. Following and expanding Mueller and Lucas's model (1975), they found a marked increase in social play throughout this age period; in particular, they discovered actions coordinated to the actions of a peer (mainly imitative acts) and extended social interactions (see table below).

Major Types of Play Between Same-Age Toddlers	
Categories	*Definitions*
Unrelated (solitary)	Acts on different play material than peer or on the same play material (e.g., beanbag) but at a distance from peer and without any coordinated or interfering features
Tangential (solitary)	Acts neither coordinated nor interfering with peer's that involve the same play material as peer's or occur near peer; also, gestures or words directed to peer that are somehow related to peer's actions, words, or gestures but fail to meet the criteria for coordinated or interfering
Interfering (presocial)	Acts that interrupt or interfere with peer continuing his or her ongoing actions, or requests for an interruption or stopping of peer's actions
Coordinated (social)	Acts thematically related to the specifics of peer's acts that allow peer to continue his or her activity while expanding that activity to include both children
1. Imitative	Performing the same action as peer, one or more of the distinctive elements of peer's actions, a thematic variant of peer's actions (e.g., hiding but at a different location), or an elaboration of peer's actions (e.g., marching around the box before jumping off it)
2. Complementary	Performing the same action as peer, one or more of the distinctive elements of peer's actions, a thematic variant of peer's actions (e.g., hiding but at a different location), or an elaboration of peer's actions (e.g., marching around the box before jumping off it)
• Complementary role	• Performing an act that together with peer's act forms a common play theme (e.g., "finding" a "hiding" peer); performing a role in an established game that differs in content from peer's role (e.g., "leading" in follow-the-leader games)
• Complementary directive	• Use of conventional gestures or words to direct a peer in the continuation or elaboration of his activity (e.g.,"go jump") or the joint activity of the two children
• Complementary response	• Responding appropriately to the complementary, interfering, or tangential directives of peer (e.g., going where peer directs)

Source: Adapted from Eckerman, Davis, & Didow (1989).

Eckerman et al. (1989) further note that, at least with nonfamiliar peers, imitative behaviors seem to be predominant in the toddler years, even when they coexist with more advanced behaviors such as complementary role relations. As they explain, the experience of imitating and being imitated can foster each child's perception of his or her connectedness with the other, especially in the absence of fully developed language.

When peers know each other well, a whole different dynamic often appears, and children might engage in play behaviors at a level of proficiency that they cannot reach so easily with unfamiliar peers (Vandell & Wilson, 1987). In fact, the complexity of infants' and toddlers' interactions with peers tends to be more strongly correlated with previous peer experience than with age (Howes, 1988). All experiences with peers help children develop their social competence, but the familiar routines that are established in the context of play with familiar peers can lead to an increased proportion of complex behaviors (Howes, 1988). Therefore, it is important to consider children's individual differences and their levels of exposure to different types of play experiences and playmates before assessing their play behaviors in a given context. This is particularly true in cultures and socioeconomic contexts in which play is present and promoted to a lesser extent than it is in middle- and upper-class families in most industrialized cultures. In the next section, we explain why.

When Feeling Secure Is What Matters Most

There is one overarching and seemingly universal support we have yet to mention: supporting play by helping infants feel secure. Play happens only when infants feel secure; infants fail to play when they feel anxious. In infancy, feeling secure entails feeling that one's caregiver is accessible.

Developmental Milestones: Attachment, Separation, and Individuation

When speaking about how parent-child relationships form and develop, Mahler, Pine, and Bergman (1975) speak of the separation-individuation process. This process, they explain, gradually takes infants from simply being an extension of their primary caregiver, usually the mother, to developing into autonomous individuals. Bowlby (1969) and Ainsworth (1979) add that infants and their caregivers develop a strong emotional relationship in the process, usually referred to as "attachment." Thomas and Chess (1986), in their theorizing of the "goodness of fit" model, emphasize the caregiver's responsibility in such a relationship by explaining that they need to be sensitive to their children's temperaments in order to adjust their own behavior accordingly. Erikson (1963), on the other hand, tends to put the emphasis on the child by showing that the complex process of separation-attachment-individuation does not go without psychosocial crises. In fact, he says, children develop by going through two major developmental crises in their very first years of existence: "basic trust versus mistrust" and "autonomy versus shame and doubt." However, he adds, children go through these crises more successfully when they are provided with the ego support they need. In this respect, then, the infant-caregiver relationship is fully reciprocal. Indeed, both agents perceive each other's signals and try to adapt to them, therefore evolving as a system (Bowlby, 1969). When the system functions well, infants feel secure.

In many cultures, adults show little interest in supporting play. In some cases, as we already saw through New's (1994) description of Italian culture, play is valued but simply not promoted because it is assumed to take place naturally. In other cases, and in traditional societies in particular, children simply do not have many opportunities to play. Mothers or older siblings often carry infants on their backs while they work in the fields or carry out household chores (Power & Radcliffe, 2000). An infant's place, then, is on her caregiver's back, not on the ground where she can play.

Yet, this lack of opportunity for play is particularly adaptive in many environments. For example, in some environments, if infants were left exposed on the floor, they would most likely get hurt, because of snakes or other dangers on the ground. In very high altitudes, infants are similarly spared because the harsh climate does not harm them if they are kept asleep on their mothers' backs (Tronick, 1982). Feeling secure, then, takes a different meaning depending on the context, and survival, not play, sometimes comes first.

These cultures teach us that play, as we describe it in this chapter, is not always necessary for children to develop. Indeed, infants and toddlers seem to reach the same developmental milestones near the same age across cultures, particularly when the environment is secure enough to provide them with the support and means they need to do so. The same can be said of socioeconomic contexts in which parents are simply too poor to buy their children many toys. In these contexts too, children develop fine when they receive the emotional and cognitive support they need.

Much support and stimulation can be provided through play, but there are many other ways to support an infant's development. Therefore, as discussed in the book's introduction, we have to be careful not to idealize play. Indeed, indulging in such idealization would imply that other cultures or contexts, in which play is not necessarily present or promoted, are deficient when, really, they are merely different. With this in mind, we can move on to explore how play develops in early childhood.

● SUMMARY

In infancy and the toddler years, it is often difficult to disentangle play behaviors from nonplay behaviors. This difficulty partly comes from the fact that play emerges from other types of behaviors, such as exploration. Yet certain cues (e.g., affect, context) often make it clear to the observer whether an infant is playing or exploring. Later on in development, toddlers become even more proficient at play. They learn to take turns, they learn about patterns and rules, and they become increasingly able to read games, especially when these games are initiated by such familiar figures as their caregivers or siblings. In the process, they also learn to initiate games of their own, either by themselves or with others. Finally, all these skills converge to help children develop a new and extraordinary capacity for pretense.

How these skills develop in infants and toddlers is a matter of many intertwined influences. The child's intrinsic development, both cognitively and socioemotionally, promotes the development of play in many ways. But extrinsic agents, such as the child's caregivers, siblings, peers, and other community members, often support the development of play as well, albeit through different means in different cultures.

In the following chapter, we will see how play continues to develop through various means as children grow older and develop new capacities. In particular, we will explore the development of make-believe play in the preschool years, for this is the time when play is most apt to be "just pretend."

KEY WORDS, NAMES, AND IDEAS ●

Attachment

Bruner, J.

Circular reactions

Collaborative co-playing

Contextual cues

Exploration

Extending children's play

Familiar peers and nonfamiliar peers

Feeling secure

Individuation

Inventing games

Joint attention

Kaye, K.

Lillard, A.

Object permanence

Patterns and rules

Piaget, J.

Reading games

Scaffolding

Sensorimotor play

Separation

Siblings

Social play

Social referencing

Solitary play

Turn-taking

Vygotsky, L.

Zone of proximal development

CHAPTER 3

PLAY IN EARLY CHILDHOOD

The Golden Age of Make-Believe

T he early childhood years could well be renamed the golden age of make-believe, because make-believe is what young children do so well. If adults played with dolls, they would likely use them for self-therapy and talk to the dolls about their feelings and troubles. Compare that dreary scene with a 4-year-old's tea party with imaginary friends or to the thrilling war play of a young boy shouting out battle orders to plastic soldiers. There's no question who is the more imaginative, more fantastic, more playful. The child wins every time. Why, though, focus on make-believe when young children play in so many different ways, such as by roughhousing, building with blocks, or drawing? Here, we do so because in whatever way a young child is playing, there is usually make-believe.

This point was brought home in a classic case study by Sylvia Feinburg (1976) in which she described her son Douglas's combat art. As a young boy, Douglas drew hundreds of pictures of battle scenes. To the casual observer, Douglas's drawing would simply be seen as drawing, but Feinburg saw it differently. She noted how Douglas, while drawing, made battle sounds, shouted out military orders, and otherwise indicated that, for him, drawing was hardly a matter of producing pretty pictures. Rather, it was a matter of make-believe.

Make-believe and fantasizing, then, lie behind much of young children's play, even when we don't see it directly. In fact, one of the major challenges for this age-group is learning how to transfer some fantasy in the head to some play medium such as dolls, paper, blocks, or clay.

● MOTIVES FOR MAKE-BELIEVE PLAY

The capacity and motivation for rich and imaginative make-believe play seem to come, in part, from the preschooler's basic predicament, which Lev Vygotsky (1976b) explained so well. On the one hand, for the first time, children between ages 2 and 3 can symbolize not only what is directly in front of them but also the wishes and fantasies that are in their heads. On the other hand, they have many wishes that cannot be satisfied: to drive a car, to control their parents—the list can be quite long. Think of what life would be like if you had so many powerful wishes that could not be adequately expressed in words and that could never be satisfied, or at least not satisfied for a very long time. How frustrated you would feel, perhaps to the point of despairing or of being constantly frustrated and angry.

To escape this predicament and to realize unrealizable wishes, preschoolers play. In play, they drive cars, become superheroes, spank babies, and give shots to protesting children. In play, then, they satisfy wishes. However, satisfying wishes is only part of the story. Interests are another.

Young children have decided interests, not just in the world at the end of their noses but in worlds in the past, in distant lands, and in their fantasies. For example, dinosaurs fascinate young children, for their size, to be sure, but also for their diversity, and no doubt for their being monsters that have been tamed by extinction. And because they fascinate, young children bring dinosaurs into their play. This is what Piaget (1951) meant when he said that children, in their play, assimilate reality to their interests.

Wishes and interests are what drive most young children's make-believe play, but there is more. That young children become anxious and fearful is clear. What is not so clear is how they manage their anxieties. At certain moments, they don't manage well. Children's phobic reactions and night terrors are prime examples. However, at other moments, make-believe play helps them manage well enough. For example, one young child had been frightened when he went with his mother through a car wash. The swishing in confined and darkened spaces had disturbed him greatly. For several days, he did nothing to recover from his trauma, but then he built a long funnel out of blocks and drove his matchbox cars down the funnel while making swishing sounds. Clearly, he was reconstructing the car wash, and his furrowed brow indicated equally clearly that he was managing his car wash anxieties.

Wish fulfillment, interests, and anxiety management might seem enough to explain why preschoolers are so enamored of make-believe play, but there is one more item to add to the list. When young children play alongside each other, it isn't only their own play that interests them; it is also the play of others. Furthermore, this shared interest in each other's play begins a process that often ends in friendship. Once this happens, friendship becomes another motive for why young children play.

These, then, seem to be the main motives explaining why make-believe play preoccupies young children. However, scholars have raised at least four additional questions.

Photo 3.1　　Make-believe play seems to function as an important way for young children to *understand reality*. Here a young girl pretends to be a grown woman.

● QUESTIONS ABOUT MAKE-BELIEVE PLAY

The first and most important question has been *"What are the functions of make-believe play?"* Here, scholars have struggled to determine the precise role that make-believe play serves in children's cognitive, emotional, and social development. Does it cause or support children's development, or is it like cartoons and pacifiers, something young children enjoy or find comforting but don't really need?

A second central question has been *"How should we classify young children's play?"* This is a question leading in two complementary directions. The first, what we might call a vertical direction, leads one to think in terms of different levels of maturity or development. For example, a stack of blocks intuitively feels lower down or less developed than a fully constructed fort with enclosed spaces, doors, and windows. The stack deserves to be classified as one type, the fort as another.

The second, what we might call a horizontal direction, leads one to think in terms of play occurring in different *media* or through using different kinds of actions. For example, playing with plastic soldiers leads to a very different type of play than playing with markers and paper. However, one is not more developed than the other; rather, they are on the same level, or horizontal. Similarly, gross motor and small motor play refer to different kinds of play actions. One is not more mature than the other.

A third central question has been *"How should we describe, evaluate, and explain group differences?"* At first glance, answering this question might seem straightforward and easy, as one can easily document differences. However, close observation reveals not only that this question is difficult to answer but also that it is risky to try. As discussed in the introduction, falsely claiming there are differences or misinterpreting actual differences can lead to harmful stereotypes and prejudices. Too often, differences have incorrectly been taken to mean deficiencies.

The fourth central question has to do with the concerns that caregivers (parents, teachers, and therapists) sometimes have that certain kinds of play may cause or indicate problems. We put this question as follows: *"How valid are the common concerns about young children's play?"* We will look at concerns about two common kinds of play, play with imaginary companions and war play, to show what scholarship and theory have to offer. In doing so, we see that scholarly observation and interpretation have applied, practical value. We begin with the first question.

What Are the Functions of Make-Believe Play?

This is a hard question to answer when one cannot rely on experimental design to separate out causes from effects, and so scholars have relied mostly on careful observation and interpretation. The discussion that follows illustrates a few of the main insights gathered.

Cognitive Development and Make-Believe Play

With respect to cognitive development, careful observation and interpretation have revealed much. First, make-believe play seems to help young children to *understand reality*. Scholars note that it begins as reconstructing familiar events, such as driving a car, going to sleep, and eating, as if the repetition of these events is a way to better understand them (McCune-Nicolich, 1981).

Furthermore, even when make-believe turns fanciful, the physical and psychological rules governing fantastic worlds usually mirror the physical and psychological rules governing the real world, again pointing out that make-believe is about re-presenting and reflecting on reality (Harris, 2000). Dragons and superheroes may fly, but they do so because the conditions (wings) and motives (to fight bad guys) are not altogether different from those in the real world.

As a tool for understanding reality, make-believe play also serves to digest information. Once again, take dinosaur play as an example. Many pre-schoolers become dinosaur experts by gathering information on dinosaurs from books, museums, and films. However, this information needs digesting. For that to happen, preschoolers play by having plastic brontosauruses eat leaves, not meat, by drawing stegosauruses with those wonderful bony plates marching down their backs, and by having everyone flee before them when they pretend to be *Tyrannosaurus rex*. This idea about play functioning to digest information has been most closely associated with the work of Jean Piaget (1951), who emphasized that children often play with that which they have recently acquired.

The observations so far have to do with processing information and consolidating knowledge. Other observations have to do with acquiring *new tools for thinking*. The main thinking tool developed by make-believe play is that of symbolizing. Where would we be without the ability to symbolize and re-present reality? Without this ability, life would be like a waking dream in which events simply happen and pass on without a moment's reflection.

As ability to symbolize develops, thought is freed from perception and objects take on meanings that are not determined by their physical properties. We see this especially in children's make-believe. As Vygotsky (1976b) pointed out, when a child uses a stick to stand for a horse, it isn't the stick itself that matters, but the meaning the child gives to it, the meaning that defines the stick as a horse.

To illustrate the significance of this playing with meaning, Vygotsky (1976b) cited the example of two sisters playing at being sisters. They did so by holding hands and dressing alike, actions they almost never performed in reality. However, by acting as they did, these sisters played with the meaning of being sisters, namely, that sisters are closer to and more alike to one another than are nonsisters.

A similar point has been made recently by Paul Harris (2003). Harris distinguishes between the reality we know through direct observation and the equally important unobserved reality we know through the testimony of others. This unobservable reality becomes central when children are later asked to think about distant objects and events, such as historical figures and historical events, and also about microscopic objects and events, such as the actions of germs and viruses on our immune system. To understand unobserved reality, one has to imagine, which is why Harris argues we should value the imagining going on in children's make-believe.

Recent observations have also stressed the contributions of make-believe play for developing narrative as a *framework for thinking* (Singer & Singer, 1990). The distinction is made between *paradigmatic* and *narrative frameworks* for thinking (Bruner, 1986).

Paradigmatic frameworks organize thinking around propositions, distinctions, and logic. They are used in conversations in which explanation and argument are most important. Narrative frameworks organize thinking around events and characters, and they are used when it is important to describe real and imagined dramas. Each framework has its place in the ongoing need to understand and know reality.

Finally, with respect to make-believe play's cognitive functions and value, some scholars speculate that in children's make-believe, one can find the beginnings of *multiple intelligences* (Gardner, 1983). They observe that the various media used in make-believe (words, dolls, blocks, etc.) provide the means to develop verbal, spatial, and other types of intelligences. It is not that one can draw a straight line from block building to, say, architecture, or from doll play to writing novels. Rather, one can see in the early forms of make-believe play prototypes of later, more adult activities. The great architect Frank Lloyd Wright claimed that his architectural career began with his playing with blocks as a child (Wellhousen & Kieff, 2001).

Emotional Development and Make-Believe Play

We take for granted the distinction between feeling and thinking. We tip our hat to the fact that it is hard to separate the two, but we rarely question the value of making the distinction. Indeed, there seems to be value in recognizing that one can think and communicate with or without passion. However, what often gets overlooked in our focus on feelings is that they are never separated from thinking. In fact, the two (thinking and feeling) always influence one another. The lifelong struggle to mature means, in part, a struggle to connect thoughts and feelings. Posing the problem or challenge of development this way suggests that a major function of make-believe play is to connect thought and feeling.

For most of its history, clinical child psychology has focused on the *content* of children's make-believe when assessing children's problems with feelings. For example, if a child plays at spanking babies, the content of spanking might suggest feelings about newborn siblings or perhaps about violence in the home.

However, more recently clinicians have focused on the *structure* of children's make-believe play, or how well developed that play is, regardless of its content (Scarlett, 1994; Slade & Wolf, 1994). They see make-believe play as a tool for expressing and managing emotion and think that, for many children, the problem is not so much with having emotions as it is with not having a developed tool for expressing and managing emotions (Scarlett, 1994).

Take an example of two boys engaged in war play. The first simply repeats the act of pointing his finger and saying, "Bang, I shot you." The second, before shooting, announces he is G.I. Joe and then enacts scenes featuring army maneuvers. Neither play is well developed, but the second is more developed structurally because the child is assuming a fictitious role and constructing a scene removed from present reality. It turns out that these structural differences matter. Observation shows that the first boy is more apt to have problems that involve actually being aggressive (Gould, 1972; Lynch, 1997). We will have more to say later about using structural criteria to evaluate war play.

Make-believe play seems, then, to support young children's emotional development by helping them *put symbols between their impulses and actions.* Rather than acting out their impulses, they can, in make-believe play, express them symbolically. This is an enormous step forward. The important point is not that make-believe allows children to express emotions; they can express emotions in their actions. What matters most is that make-believe play allows children to express emotions symbolically.

This same thought might be better communicated with a different word than *express,* which conjures up the image of letting off steam, and indeed the cathartic function of make-believe has often been explained using this image. However, a better term might be *embedding,* or putting emotions into something rather than leaving them to float freely. Consider the example in the text box.

Battle Scenes and Embedding Feelings

Two boys of the same age drew pictures, both about dramatic battle scenes. However, the first boy's picture was simply a piece of paper covered with green finger paint. It was only by interviewing the boy that an observer could understand the boy's make-believe. He explained that the picture was of good guys sneaking up on bad guys and engaging them in a fierce battle. He pointed to different sections of the picture to indicate where the soldiers were positioned and how the battle was being fought. Despite this clear explanation, the fact that the picture was unreadable indicated that the feelings and war drama were solely in the child's head rather than embedded in the picture.

In contrast, the second boy drew his battle scene with everything easily readable. There was an airplane dropping bombs, a building on the ground about to be destroyed, and combatants on both sides. The feelings and drama of this boy's make-believe were embedded in his picture and not just in his head. Not surprisingly, with respect to how he expressed and managed his feelings outside of play, the second boy showed much more maturity.

This is the primary way that clinicians and scholars have seen make-believe play and emotional development: Make-believe play allows children to express and embed feelings symbolically. In so doing, children link feelings to thinking and not simply to action. But clinicians and scholars have observed even more about make-believe's functions with respect to emotions. We will mention two specific functions, using Piaget's terminology.

Piaget (1951) pointed out that make-believe play is often more than simply a way for children to express their interests. It also serves the emotional function of *liquidating* conflicts to get rid of bad feelings or, at least, to lessen their intensity. An example is the boy liquidating his car wash anxieties.

Interestingly, this kind of play occurs only when anxious or bad feelings are at medium intensity, not at high levels of intensity (Watson, 1994). After all, the boy with the car wash anxieties did not play out his feelings immediately. Rather, he went through a cooling-down period before he was ready.

Besides liquidating bad feelings, make-believe play can also compensate for frustrations suffered in reality. We have already encountered this compensatory function when discussing Vygotsky's observation that make-believe play helps young children realize unrealizable wishes. However, what has not been discussed is how this constitutes a step forward in the long process of maturing emotionally. Toddlers, much more than preschoolers, rely on adult caregivers to soothe and manage their emotions. For example, toddlers in a doctor's office are more apt to fuss and cling to their mothers, whereas older preschoolers are more apt to use medical toys to pretend to give shots and so on, and in so doing to manage their anxieties and frustrations on their own. The liquidating and compensating functions of preschoolers' make-believe, then, are a step toward learning how to manage their own emotions.

Social Development and Make-Believe Play

Scholars have made two primary observations on this subject. The first is that young children do not ordinarily relate to one another except when they are playing. Play in general and make-believe play in particular are primary contexts in which young children can connect and develop friendships. If a young child does not play or does not play well, he or she is apt to be socially isolated.

This point is illustrated by the example of young children who are sometimes referred to as "watchers and wanderers" (Kohn, 1966), children who have the intellectual and emotional wherewithal to make friends but who rarely do so in settings such as early childhood education classrooms. Close observation reveals that these children remain isolated not because they are rejected by other children but because they spend a good deal of time watching other children and wandering *rather than playing.* By not playing, they do not give other children the usual entrée for connecting (Scarlett, 1980).

The second observation is that make-believe play becomes increasingly joint make-believe. Even between parents and young children, there is usually a playing off of one another's make-believe, as when a parent responds to a child's "Have a (pretend) cookie, mommy" with pretend eating.

In early childhood, this joint construction of make-believe provides two conditions that develop friendships. The first condition is sharing feelings and experiences (Selman & Hickey-Schultz, 1990). That is, constructing make-believe together connects children by giving them shared feelings and shared experiences. The second condition is negotiating conflicts. Joint make-believe often proceeds through a series of negotiations marked by the ubiquitous "Let's pretend . . ." and "No, let's pretend . . ." These low-key negotiated conflicts help young children practice the needed skills of selling their wishes and ideas even as they remain responsive to the wishes and ideas of others. To be sustained over time, even young friendships demand equality between partners, so it is important for children to learn how to both lead and follow (Selman & Hickey-Schultz, 1990). Here is where social skills and cognitive skills combine. When young children engage in joint make-believe, they foster the most important of all social skills: thinking about others' thinking. Joint make-believe gives them practice in taking perspectives, or so scholars have assumed. Furthermore, when young children construct a full-blown story in make-believe, a story with different characters and scenes, they create characters with different points of view. In sum, make-believe provides an important context for developing social skills.

This, then, is how scholars have spoken about the main functions of make-believe play. As should be evident, these scholars have been among the most ardent proponents of the rhetoric of progress.

How Should We Classify Young Children's Play?

The purpose of classifying young children's play is to describe, evaluate, and explain play, but not all classifications attempt to do all three. Classification that maximizes *description* in order to capture the variety of ways young children play may focus simply on play materials and actions. It gives lists of play types based on different play materials—sand play, Lego play, play with clay, and so forth—and lists based on different actions, such as jumping and swinging actions or small motor and gross motor actions.

Generally, classifications of types of play according to types of materials and actions imply no developmental sequence, although play with certain types of materials, such as dolls, usually appears earlier than play with other types of materials, such as markers and paper. Once again, classification in terms of types of play materials and types of actions is along a horizontal dimension.

Classification that emphasizes *evaluation* and *explanation* often does so by characterizing the *structural* features of play, such as whether it is symbolic or not. This kind of classification is used to explain the development of play in terms of underlying structural changes in the way a child thinks. For example, as discussed in the introduction, Piaget's division of play into *practice games, symbolic games,* and *games with rules* explains the underlying development in children's capacity to think symbolically. In a similar vein, Mildred Parten (1932) describes social play in early childhood as developing from *solitary play* to *parallel play* to *associative play* and finally to *cooperative play;* thus play shows young children's increasing ability to coordinate their own perspective with those of others.

These two types of classification can work together, especially when the structural criteria are used to define what develops in a particular play medium. Replica play (the more general term for doll play) and block play are two examples.

Replica play develops as simple representations of events (for example, a mother doll feeding a baby doll) evolve into full-blown stories or narratives (for example, a story about a mother rushing a sick baby to the hospital, where a doctor performs an operation). Even during the preschool years, these narratives come to depict fairly elaborate story worlds with characters appearing to resolve problems on their own (Scarlett & Wolf, 1979).

Furthermore, in the development of replica play, at first actions alone carry the narrative's meaning, but with development, language takes over. A child begins to speak not only for and about story characters but also to the audience, who need help in interpreting what's happening in the story—what is called *meta-narrative* ("Pretend that . . ." and "Let's pretend . . .") (Scarlett & Wolf, 1979; Winner & Gardner, 1979).

The structural development of replica play presents an interesting paradox that many adults do not appreciate: The realistic replica play of toddlers indicates that toddlers have yet to clearly distinguish fantasy from reality, whereas the fantastic, unrealistic replica play of older children indicates that older children have made a sharp distinction between fantasy and reality. This is illustrated by what unfolds in early childhood in replica play.

The play of toddlers is apt to be realistic and imitative, as when toddlers reenact familiar scenes such as driving a car, ironing a dress, or feeding a baby. By age 3 or 4, scenes may be combined to form simple narratives, but the narratives lack the devices that make a story world appear to happen on its own. For example, young children sometimes become characters in their own stories, directly commanding doll figures where to go and what to do. By age 5, however, they typically are able to create not only familiar scenes, but fantastic scenes as well. Furthermore, the characters in these scenes and worlds seem to act on their own. The replica play of older children creates story worlds that appear to function autonomously, as explained more fully in the text box.

Storytelling With Dolls: Creating Autonomous Story Worlds

Children begin the preschool years using dolls or replicas to enact familiar events and in ways that make clear that whatever the dolls are doing is the result of being pushed around by the children. However, with time and development, the dolls seem to take on lives of their own as children create devices to create the illusion that the dolls are making decisions and reacting to events within their own autonomous story world. Furthermore, in speaking about and for their dolls, children come to speak about things that are not visible, such as the thoughts and feelings of the dolls and the objects in the story world that are not part of the setting in which the story is being told. By the end of the preschool years, children often can create entire autonomous story worlds, complete with characters facing problems and resolving them "on their own" in scenes that are quite fantastic and distinct from the actual scene in which the play is taking place.

Paradoxically, the autonomous story worlds of older children indicate that they have greater awareness of what is real and what is pretend. By creating fantasy worlds separate and seemingly autonomous from the real world, children gain a firmer grasp of the distinction between real and pretend. This is perhaps nowhere better expressed than in the older preschooler's use of *meta-narrative,* or speech intended to inform an audience or co-player about what is or should be happening within the story world. Visit any group of 5-year-olds playing together, and you are apt to hear a chorus of "Pretend that . . ." and "Yeah, pretend that . . ."

It seems, then, that as play with dolls develops, getting lost in some fantastic world is not a problem. What could be a problem is just the opposite, getting stuck in the real world (Scarlett & Wolf, 1979).

In sum, the structural development of replica play indicates an important structural development in the child's thinking: the development of the distinction between fantasy and reality.

As another example of play's development in early childhood and in a specific medium, block constructions usually begin as linear constructions—linear

Photo 3.2   The content of young children's make-believe is very much determined by gender. Here, a young boy plays with his wagon.

because they are made up of lines of blocks. They develop when their overall contours have defined and constructed tops, sides, fronts, and backs as opposed to being randomly placed blocks or just heaps of blocks. Block constructions become more developed also when the spaces between blocks are deliberate, not random, as when a child creates a series of arches, each with a space roughly equivalent to the spaces making up the other arches. These constructed (that is, nonrandom) spaces give to a construction a sense of having an inside or of having passageways. Even simple constructed spaces represent a significant achievement for the child, because space or nothingness has taken on meaning. In early childhood, then, a great deal develops structurally in block building. Furthermore, observers believe that this structural development reflects a developing understanding of space and shape (Forman, 1998; Wellhousen & Kieff, 2001).

To summarize, classification systems are for organizing observations and for making careful observation possible. At times, they are for describing play types regardless of development. At other times, they are for explaining what is developing both within children and within their play.

How Should We Describe, Evaluate, and Explain Group Differences?

Group differences can obscure the fact that children are children. This is as true for the way young children play as it is for other activities. The similarities outweigh the differences. Nevertheless, group differences need to be noted and understood because they indicate important variations in children's experience and in how they develop. We begin with gender differences in the play of young children.

Gender Differences

As mentioned in the introduction, before the early childhood years, not much differs in the play of girls and boys, which may explain why girl and boy toddlers often play together. However, sometime between ages 3 and 4, girls and boys often separate themselves into different play groups, even when adults wish they would stay together (Pitcher & Hickey-Schultz, 1983).

There may be a variety of reasons for this (Goldstein, 1994a). Some suggest biology, noting that boys are naturally and generally more active and aggressive than girls. Others suggest socialization, noting that in most societies there are plenty of pressures for girls and boys to play differently. For example, when one teacher showed a father of a 3-year-old boy the picture she had taken of the boy pushing a baby carriage, the father became upset and demanded that this type of play be forbidden. Still others suggest the influence of television advertising, noting that it uses obvious gender stereotyping.

Whatever the reasons for gender segregation, the fact remains that by age 4, young children usually have grouped themselves according to gender. Little boys play with little boys and often with themes of power and aggression. Little girls play with little girls and often with domestic themes of caring and connection. These and other gender differences catalyze further divisions, so that by elementary school the division between the genders is wide and stable (Maccoby, 1998).

However, as previously discussed, if one looks not just at the themes and content of young children's play but also at its structure, little girls and boys do not differ. The play of both groups follows the same general lines of structural development and develops at the same rate, as described by Piaget, Vygotsky, Parten, and others. Boys and girls move from nonsymbolic to symbolic play and from parallel to cooperative play at about the same rates. Furthermore, if given equal opportunity to build with blocks, draw with markers, tell stories with dolls, and so forth, boys and girls perform at the same level. When it comes to ability and development, then, there are no significant gender differences.

Culture and Socioeconomic Status Differences

In contrast, observations about the play of young children from different cultures and different socioeconomic classes have focused on differences in abilities, and these differences have sometimes been taken to indicate deficiencies. For example, in so-called traditional societies, which are largely rural, collectivistic, and not tied to technology and the printed word, the play of young children has sometimes been described as imitative, less imaginative, and dull (Ariel, 2002). However, the problem may be in the way observers have observed rather than in the way children have played.

In traditional societies, young children help with chores and so have less time for play. Furthermore, work for these children seems to serve functions we ordinarily reserve for make-believe play (Gaskins, 2003). Also, the adults in traditional societies are more apt to discourage make-believe as being of little value, sometimes even as being immoral or sacrilegious. In short, children from traditional societies aren't deficient in their play so much as they have less opportunity and support for it.

Nevertheless, when observers have followed children from traditional societies to their secret places away from adults, they have sometimes found that these children play much like children from industrialized societies (Ariel, 2002). Again, we need to be cautious about drawing conclusions about children from different cultures, especially when those conclusions label one group as deficient.

Keeping these cautions in mind, we can still say there are important cultural differences in how young children play. The main ones have to do with parental attitudes and with whom young children play. In North American culture, most parents see children's play as essential for their development, so many North American parents retain control over their children's play—over what kinds of toys they buy, over what kinds of play environments they play in, and over whom they play with. Furthermore, young children generally play with siblings or peers, not with nonsiblings of different ages.

This is not the situation in other cultures. As mentioned before, Italian mothers view children's play as something natural, not as something needing adult control. When young Italian children play, they are more likely to be unsupervised and in mixed age groups, with older children looking after their safety (New, 1994).

What these cultural differences suggest for young children's long-term development is not clear. Some have suggested that, from an evolutionary perspective, it makes more sense for young children to play in mixed-age groups (Konner, 1976). Many have argued for less adult interference in children's play (Sutton-Smith, 1995). These and other interpretations suggest that North American ways of supporting young children's play may not be the best. However, once again it is difficult to draw conclusions.

As for socioeconomic status (SES) and preschoolers' play, as mentioned in the introduction, Sara Smilansky (1968) conducted a study of children differing in SES and concluded that lower-SES children's play was less imaginative, more repetitive, more imitative, and, overall, less developed. For a while, research on SES and young children's play seemed to confirm Smilansky's results, but more recently those results have been questioned.

The main question has been about the research results being based solely on observations made in the classroom. These results could be more about a particular setting's effects on poor children than they are about poor children's abilities to play. Indeed, this seems to be the case, as the following example makes clear.

In one middle-class day care center, a boy from an economically disadvantaged home seemed quite lost. He spent much of his time indoors wandering around, getting into trouble, not playing much, and not playing well. But when he was outside on the playground, everything changed. Outside he became a leader in highly imaginative superhero play. Apparently, the classroom, with its activity corners and play materials had little to do with his experience at home.

This example and many more like it suggest that future research on culture, SES, and play in early childhood needs to be more cautious about interpreting abilities on the basis of play in one setting only. If we aren't more cautious, we end up stereotyping whole groups of children and treating them as being deficient when they are not.

Cultural differences and differences related to socioeconomic status will continue to raise concerns about possible deficiencies, but without good research and an eye toward the big picture, we should be cautious and not treat these concerns too seriously. This brings us to our fourth and final question for understanding what scholars have to say about young children's play.

How Valid Are the Common Concerns About Young Children's Play?

Adults, especially adults who are parents, often have concerns about young children and their play. Two examples are concerns about children playing with imaginary companions and concerns about children engaging in war play. Scholarly discussion and theory on this point have practical implications for important areas such as parenting.

What does it mean when a child creates an imaginary companion? Is the child losing touch with reality? Should we be discouraging war play? Might war play foster real violence or insensitivity to violence? These are a few of the questions raised by adults when observing children playing with imaginary companions and with themes of war.

These concerns have two things in common. First, they connect early play with later problems on the basis of some surface similarity. For example, having an imaginary companion at age 4 has a surface similarity with a symptom of schizophrenia, a disease that usually does not show itself before adolescence. Second, these concerns focus mostly on the content and themes of play (for example, the theme of death and destruction in war play) rather than on its structure (for example, whether the war play depicts elaborate battle scenes or simply isolated acts of pretend shooting).

For the most part, the results of research on these issues have been quite positive. Although children with and without imaginary companions do not differ significantly, there is some evidence that those who play with imaginary companions are more advanced in their social understanding, less shy, and more able to focus attention (Taylor, 1999).

The main finding, however, is not that having imaginary companions makes young children better but that there is nothing wrong or harmful in having imaginary companions and probably a good deal that is right and helpful. Imaginary companions seem to serve the same positive functions as make-believe in general.

Despite these positive findings, some parents and certain groups actively discourage play with imaginary companions. Often they do so out of religious belief, as the text box describes.

Imaginary Companions and Religion

Most parents in Western cultures look on make-believe and imaginary companions as positive expressions of children's imagination. However, this view is not shared by everyone in the world. For example, many Indian parents from Hindu traditions see in children's communion with unseen companions a connection with real beings that inhabited their children's past lives, and they become concerned that their children may not be oriented enough in the present. In certain fundamentalist Christian groups, parents see playing with imaginary companions as being deceitful and associating with the devil. How these diverse views influence children and children's play is unclear. It may be that imaginary companions live on in children's lives regardless of parental beliefs and attitudes (Taylor & Carlson, 2000).

Of all the concerns that adults have about children's play, concerns about war play outweigh the others, so we will review the debate on this issue. Over the past 15 years, this debate has heated up, fueled no doubt by increases in the number of movies and television shows exposing children to violence. For whatever reasons, parents, teachers, and some researchers have raised concerns and, in some cases, taken action. For example, not too long ago, one parent organized a campaign to have the children of Worcester, Massachusetts, exchange war toys for toys without war as their theme. But is this concern about possible harmful effects of war play legitimate? Is it true that war play might stimulate real violence or inure children to violence?

Like so many issues pertaining to play, there is no hard evidence suggesting that war play has long-term effects, good or bad. However, there are considered arguments among scholars on both sides of the issue. On one side is the argument that today's war play is so influenced by television that it has become unimaginative play that probably stimulates bad actions if not overt violence (Carlsson-Paige & Levin, 1987). On the other side is the argument that war play is natural to childhood and may well help children make sense of the world they live in (Wegener-Spohring, 1994).

There is, however, a third argument or perspective that may offer a way out of the war play dilemma. This is based on data suggesting that structurally undeveloped play in general and undeveloped war play in particular may well be associated with behavior problems (Gould, 1972; Lynch, 1997). All war play is not the same structurally, and as we have already seen, structural differences matter.

Consider, for example, the war play of the 4-year-old in the following box. By attending to its structure (that is, to the way characters, actions, and scenes are developed) and not to its theme or content, who would argue that this play is anything but wonderful?

One Child's War Play

Between ages 3½ and 5, Evan immersed himself in war play, reenacting with miniature figures scenes from early American wars. The American Revolutionary War in particular fascinated Evan. Almost daily and for over a year, with his blocks and with little figures of Redcoats and Minutemen, Evan built and rebuilt the Old North Bridge and carried out his version of the battle fought over 2 centuries ago. Not surprisingly, at first Evan's "Battle of the Old North Bridge" play was mostly make-believe. But out of it, Evan developed a genuine interest in history and in depicting the various characters, actions, and scenes that make the Battle of the Old North Bridge such a fascinating story.

(Continued)

(Continued)

In the course of 1 year, Evan used his battle play to process all kinds of information he sought outside his play: through having books read to him and videos shown to him about the American Revolution, through visiting and revisiting museums dedicated to colonial history, and through witnessing reenactments. Always Evan was the initiator, the one who sought out further information, from information about the names of the Minutemen and Redcoats to what the Minuteman fifer played on the way to the Old North Bridge, to exactly how the Minutemen wore the buckles on their shoes. By age 5, Evan was not a bad historian, at least with respect to his knowledge of early American wars. And what's more, he was a pacifist, confessing to his father one evening, "I wish there were no wars."

It seems, then, that banning or curbing war play makes little sense, both for reasons of evidence (or the lack of it) and for reasons of theory and common sense. War play, like any play, may best be judged not by its content but by its structure.

● SUMMARY

In this chapter, we have shown why most young children are highly motivated to engage in make-believe play. We have also shown why scholars generally have seen make-believe play as providing support for young children's cognitive, emotional, and social development. We have seen how classification systems are used to describe, evaluate, and explain young children's play, noting, in particular, classification systems that attend to play's structure. We have discussed group differences associated with gender, culture, and SES, noting how differences can be misleading by falsely interpreting differences to mean deficiencies. Finally, we have discussed why common concerns about young children's play are often unfounded, noting how, on the basis of surface similarities between children's play and problems later on, adults wrongly see play as having long-term causal effects. Furthermore, we have seen that it is more play's structural development and not its content that should be the focus of assessment.

In this chapter, we have emphasized make-believe play to the exclusion of purely physical play, in part because make-believe is the hallmark of young children's play but also, in part, because physical play is more prevalent in late childhood. In the next chapter, we will discuss physical play, along with the games with rules that typify play later on.

KEY WORDS, NAMES, AND IDEAS ●

Anxieties

Assimilation of reality to interests

Associative play

Compensate

Content vs. structure

Cooperative play

Embedding and expressing feelings

Expressing emotions

Feeling and thinking

Friendships

Games with rules

Gardner, H.

Gender segregation

Harris, P.

Horizontal vs. vertical classifications of play

Joint construction of make-believe

Liquidating

Make-believe play

Managing anxieties

Meta-narrative

Multiple intelligences

Narrative as a framework for thinking

Paradigmatic and narrative frameworks

Parallel play

Piaget, J.

Practice games

Replica play

Solitary play

Symbolic games

Symbolizing

Thinking tool

Vygotsky, L.

War play

Wishes and fantasies

Wish fulfillment

PLAY IN LATE CHILDHOOD

Rule-Governed Play

In the previous chapters, we explored how play develops in infants, toddlers, and preschool-age children. We also looked at how young children develop, both cognitively and socioemotionally. Now, we continue our journey through play in childhood by looking at what happens when children grow up a little bit more.

How is an 8-year-old's play different from that of a 2- or 5-year-old? For one thing, at least according to the boxes of most board games, 8-year-olds are granted access to games that younger children are not considered ready for. Yet, these same 8-year-olds might still have a collection of teddy bears, Barbie dolls, or toy cars. We will come to understand this seeming paradox by looking closely at how children play in late childhood, or during the elementary school years. Jimmy presents one example (see text box), which we will refer to throughout the chapter.

Jimmy's Play

Jimmy is an 8-year-old boy living with his mother and two siblings. He loves playing outside, especially with his older brother and the neighborhood children. Together, they often throw balls, play Frisbee, and roller skate. On rainy days, or when his mother worries that the streets are not safe, Jimmy also enjoys playing inside. He has an ever-growing collection of stuffed animals that have piled up in his bedroom since he was born, and occasionally he plays with them. On other days, the stuffed animals go back to being inanimate objects meticulously lined up on Jimmy's shelves next to his schoolbooks. On other days still, Jimmy invites friends over to play board games such as Risk or Monopoly. Although Jimmy tries to listen to his mother when she says, "Be nice to your little sister," he often becomes frustrated with Janet (age 5) when she becomes involved in the games. She keeps cheating, he says, though to an outsider, it is hard to tell.

SOCIALIZATION, RULES, AND "BAD PLAY" ●

Play and Socialization: Beyond the Classic Distinctions

Throughout the elementary school years, children refine their social skills. They spend less time with their parents and more time with their peers, both at school and during free time. In the process, *peer groups* are created, groups that usually develop in four main ways: first, children engage in regular interactions with each other; second, they develop a sense of belonging to the group; third, they share a code of conduct (dress, behavior, etc.); and fourth, they participate in a hierarchical group structure that often mirrors children's temperaments and skills (Shaffer, 2000). Throughout this process, play acts as an important catalyst. Indeed, children initiate contacts with each other through play. In several ways, then, play serves as an arena in which children can progressively master the social skills they need to experience a positive sense of belonging to their peer group (Hartup, 1983; Pellegrini, Blatchford, Kato, & Baines, in press).

Play and Gender

Play does not happen with random playmates, nor do peer groups form randomly. Gender often defines whether children play or do not play together, as the previous chapter made clear. In the elementary school years, maybe more so than at any other age, boys and girls usually play at different things and in separate groups (Goldstein, 1994a).

In late childhood, boys tend to maintain or even increase their preference for stereotypically masculine play (Moller, Hymel, & Rubin, 1992) by engaging in chase games (racing and tag games), ball games (soccer, baseball, basketball, catch), and rough-and-tumble play (Pellegrini, 1988). Generally speaking, boys, more than girls, engage in active and physical types of play (DiPietro, 1981; Moller et al., 1992; Posner & Vandell, 1999).

Girls, on the other hand, engage in more diversified types of play. They often engage in verbal and jumping games (hand clapping, chanting, and rhyming games; jump rope, skipping and "dipping"; hopscotch), games that many observers view as more quiet and sometimes more sedentary (Maccoby, 1998). Yet a considerable amount of physical energy can be spent in games such as jump rope, and an increasing number of girls also play at other, traditionally masculine, types of play (e.g., soccer). Girls' play, it seems, is far more active than has been traditionally assumed. Researchers have also suggested that girls who engage in opposite-sex stereotyped activities experience less negative feedback from peers and parents than boys who do the same (Green, 1977; Reckers, 1981). When it comes to breaking gender stereotypes, girls may have it easier—at least in play.

Play in late childhood also seems to hold a different function for boys than it does for girls. Whereas boys seem to value an activity most for the activity itself, girls seem to value the surrounding social context (McHale, Crouter, & Tucker, 2001). For both boys and girls, however, the overall goals remain the same: to have fun, to belong to a group, and to make friends (see Garvey, 1977, and Opie & Opie, 1969, for a rich description of the many types of games that both girls and boys play).

Photo 4.1 Play is determined by locale and socioeconomic status. Here, two urban boys are playing on a playground structure.

Play and Socioeconomic Status

Socioeconomic status (SES), because it often influences where children live and which schools they attend, is another criterion determining how peer groups are created.

Sadly, many adults do not encourage play in late childhood. Some fear for their children's security when left unsupervised. Others, because they want their children to perform at a higher level in school and in other domains (sports, music, etc.), fill their children's schedules with so many activities that little time is left for children to relax and play (Elkind, 1981). The children who do have free time, then, are often the ones whose families cannot afford the many costs that these other activities entail (Posner & Vandell, 1999). Because the amount of free time available to children has become a result of social class differences (Medrich, Roizen, Rubin, & Buckley, 1982), free and unsupervised play in late childhood has often been connected to problems (McHale et al., 2001). We suggest that problems in late childhood may result from other core problems (e.g., poverty), not from unsupervised play per se.

All too often, the differences in how or where children play seem most important, usually because they are most striking. In this chapter, we choose to emphasize the similarities in the underlying structure of all children's play rather than the most apparent but often superficial differences. This is not to say that gender and SES do not affect the type, frequency, and quality of children's play. But all children also have much in common when at play. In the next section, we explain why.

Play by the Rules

Rules and Age

During the elementary school years, children's increased cognitive and social maturity creates the conditions for a new kind of play based on rules. In this child-controlled play, children take charge of the rules, and whether they develop their own rules or choose to follow ones already established, they are the ones who decide what is acceptable and what is not, what is fair and what is not.

In his study of children's moral development and his analysis of the game of marbles, Piaget (1965) explains that four successive developmental stages can be distinguished in the practice and application of rules. Because our focus is on late childhood (between the ages of 6 and 11), we concentrate on the transition from Stage 2 to Stage 3. However, a short description of all four stages will allow us to briefly revisit some of the important topics discussed in Chapters 2 and 3. Doing so will help us better understand the developmental progression at stake in late childhood.

Stage 1 is purely motor and individually driven. During this first stage, which roughly corresponds to the first 2 years of life, children handle objects such as marbles according to their desires and capacities. In the first phase of Stage 2 (approximately between the ages of 2 and 5), children start receiving codified rules from the outside, but they play in an *egocentric* manner, meaning they invent their own rules without realizing they are doing so.

In the example of Jimmy given at the beginning of this chapter, Jimmy felt that his little sister was cheating because she was not following the official rules. But Janet probably thought she was following the rules because they applied to everyone. Her "cheating" was an expression of her age-appropriate egocentricity.

This is not to say that younger children do not follow rules when playing with others. As was explained in Chapters 2 and 3, young children are able to follow basic rules as they progressively learn about taking turns and playing roles (to play "mommy" entails acting one way; to play "daddy" entails acting another way). But in early childhood, the rules in play are not set a priori (Fein, 1981; Pellegrini et al., in press). They can be modified as the play unfolds, so the child who plays a monster one minute can suddenly turn into a prince. The other children are not annoyed if the pretense keeps going and if the other children are satisfied with their own roles.

The gap between Janet's and Jimmy's respective understanding and use of rules is not a matter of gender. It is a matter of age or, more precisely, of stage. The somewhat naïve flexibility toward rules that characterizes 4- and 5-year-olds is slowly replaced by a much more rigid adherence to rules as children develop both cognitively and socially. This transition, which often takes place around age 6 or 7 (end of Stage 2 and beginning of Stage 3 in Piaget's model), is characterized by a radical change in how children view rules: Rules are now for cooperation and competition, which explains why Jimmy gets upset at his sister's behavior.

As happens with so many other developmental changes, the pendulum often swings too far in the opposite direction before it returns to a more balanced position. Janet's and Jimmy's respective attitudes toward rules are strongly opposed to each other, but still older children develop a more balanced, flexible attitude. By age 10 or 11 (end of Stage 3 and beginning of Stage 4 in Piaget's model), rules can be changed if everyone agrees.

In late childhood, then, there is a new interest in rules per se. This new interest leads children to be flexible, but in a much more mature and informed way than when they were flexible as preschoolers. Among older children, rules can be transgressed or modified, but only when the transgressions or modifications are justified and accepted by all. In the process, the rules of any game become increasingly complex and precise, and many different versions may develop. "Which way do we play?" becomes a common preliminary question, and children often settle on a specific "way" before any game can actually start. This is the stage at which Richard, Jimmy's 11-year-old sibling, is most likely to be.

Rules and Familiarity

However, when older children do not know each other well, they sometimes choose games with simple rules, such as chase games. These offer a safer environment because the potential for disagreement is minimized. Therefore, at the end of late childhood, what may appear to be a regression to simpler games is really an adaptive strategy for playing with relative strangers. Then, as the level of familiarity with other children increases, so too does the complexity of rules. For children who know each other well, simple chase games become boring, and more complex games such as ball games take over (Blatchford, 1998; Pellegrini et al., in press). When friendships are well established, children are better equipped to deal with disagreements that occur over complex rules.

In late childhood, such apparent regressions may also happen when children play in different, less familiar locations, where the rules of more complex games may be different (Blatchford & Sumpner, 1998). Because more complex games usually require repeated exposure and practice, children who are unfamiliar with the rules followed in a particular setting initially feel more at ease playing simpler games, where the risk of unintentionally breaking a rule is not so high.

Although most of the studies cited here were conducted with boys, similar trends can be observed among girls. Girls are equally concerned with issues about the rules in play. As they become more familiar with a setting and with one another, girls too develop increasingly complex rules for their rhyming, chanting, and jumping games (Goodwin, 2002).

Rules and the Socialization Process

In following established rules, designing new rules, discussing rules, and having fun with games defined by rules, older children enrich their existing peer relationships and develop new ones. In this process, they develop their sense of fairness and what makes for good play. However, this sense of fairness and good play varies from child to child, causing some to engage in bad play.

"Bad Play" in Late Childhood

Bad play, in late childhood as at any other age, is play that is underdeveloped or dysfunctional. As we have already explained, friendships become increasingly important in late childhood as children progressively spend less time with their parents and more time with peers, and games with increasingly complex rules usually accompany this development. Bad play, then, is play that does not allow for the socialization process to take place in positive ways for all children involved. Play that excludes or ridicules other children and play that is destructive qualify as bad play.

Distinguishing good play from bad play is sometimes difficult, especially for adult observers who do not necessarily grasp all the subtlety involved in children's interactions with one another (Boulton, 1996b). For instance, rough-and-tumble play among older children generates concerns among adults even though the evidence suggests it should not. We discuss these concerns to show, once again, what scholars have to offer.

Is Rough-and-Tumble Play Bad Play?

Children's play sometimes carries the potential to turn into aggressive acts. Like war play, rough-and-tumble play concerns many parents, teachers, and psychologists who think that such play will trigger instances of real aggression (Miedzian, 1991). However, others feel that rough-and-tumble play, far from leading to aggression, acts as a positive force in children's development by contributing to their social and emotional development (Pellegrini, 1995; Sutton-Smith, Gertsmyer, & Meckley, 1988). Pellegrini (1988) explains that these disagreements around the potential consequences of rough-and-tumble play in late childhood may result from a blurry definition of what rough-and-tumble play really is: play, not an act of aggression. The following examples illustrate this distinction.

> It is late at night, and David's bedtime has already passed. David's friend, Thomas, is sleeping over. The two boys are so happy to be together that they have a hard time turning the light off. When Thomas starts "attacking" David with a pillow, and David returns the favor, nobody gets hurt. The pillows lose a few feathers, and all that David's parents can hear from the living room is laughter and excitement.
>
> The following day, David goes to school. At lunch break, another child pushes him aside, grabs his sandwich, and runs away laughing. Because David does not want this to happen again (and because he is hungry), he runs after the other child and grabs the sandwich back. This time, there will be no fight.

Clearly, these two play episodes are not the same. The first is rough-and-tumble play; the second is one-sided teasing play that could be classified as mean-spirited.

However, even when this distinction is clearly established, and maybe because rough-and-tumble play is quite frequent in late childhood (up to 10% of children's play time, according to Humphrey & Smith, 1987), rough-and-tumble play still generates a lot of debate. Happily, there is information to provide a resolution. For example, Anthony Pellegrini (1995), in his review of his own and others' studies, concludes that rough-and-tumble play in late childhood is mostly positive. In adolescence, it can be a different matter: "For children, it is a playful, affiliative category, while for adolescents it is used as a way in which to exhibit dominance" (p. 123).

Still, some of the most frequently asked questions include these: Is rough-and-tumble play more frequent among boys than it is among girls? and Does its frequency increase or decrease with age? Several scholars have investigated these questions (e.g., Boulton, 1996a; Humphrey & Smith, 1987; Pellegrini, 1988, 1995).

Humphey and Smith (1987) conducted a cross-sectional study with 7-, 9-, and 11-year-old boys and girls. While observing these children in the context of school recess, they found that boys spent significantly more time in rough-and-tumble play than girls did at ages 7 and 11, but not at age 9. They explain this somewhat surprising finding by the fact that games such as soccer often took an increasing amount of boys' play time at age 9 (up to 60%), thus leaving less time for rough-and-tumble, whereas the same trend was not observed in girls. Interestingly, they also found that girls initiated rough-and-tumble play with both boys and girls, whereas boys initiated it only with boys. Finally, Humphrey and Smith found that the children became increasingly selective in the choice of their rough-and-tumble partners as they grew older. Whereas children of all ages chose partners that they liked for rough-and-tumble activities, thus clearly indicating that rough-and-tumble play and aggression are two distinct types of behaviors, older children were more selective and chose partners who were slightly weaker than themselves.

Boulton (1996a) conducted a similar study with 8- and 11-year-old boys and girls, but he subdivided rough-and-tumble play into six distinct behaviors: boxing/hitting, brief rough-and-tumble play, chasing, chase initiation behavior, restraining, and wrestling. He found that although boys engaged in much more overall rough-and-tumble play than did girls, there was no significant difference in how boys and girls engaged in specific subtypes of rough-and-tumble (e.g., wrestling). One of Boulton's major contributions, then, was to emphasize the complexity of rough-and-tumble play and to encourage the differentiation between its subtypes when making comparisons between children on the basis of gender or age.

Clear Instances of "Bad Play" in Late Childhood

We have seen that rough-and-tumble play is usually good, not bad play. Yet clear instances of bad play do exist in late childhood. For example, who has not witnessed, if not participated in, the exclusion of a child from a play group?

Here again, boys and girls often behave differently, at least on the surface. Among boys, bad play is often linked to competitive games. A typical instance is when captains of sports teams choose members of their respective teams and always pick the same boy last. In boys' play, then, exclusion or the attempt to exclude is often connected to performance in games, where the opportunities for overt competition and for establishing rankings are many (Goodwin, 1990).

Girls compete in less overt ways. Because girls often evaluate their peers on the basis of how well they fit in and relate to others, social exclusion and ridicule are conveyed differently. For instance, girls who are viewed as "tagalongs" are often excluded from the group's conversations and informal activities.

Peer Victimization and Aggressive Play in Late Childhood

Peer victimization is broadly defined as "the experience, among children, of being the target of the aggressive behavior of other children" (Hawker & Boulton, 2003, p. 505). Peer victimization can refer to those behaviors that are perceived by one child (the perpetrator) as play, and by the other child as aggression. Yet not all aggressive play is the same. Some scholars (e.g., Crick et al., 1999) distinguish between physical aggression and relational aggression. Hawker and Boulton went further by distinguishing five types of aggression in play: (a) *indirect,* such as spreading rumors; (b) *relational,* such as excluding from a play group; (c) *physical,* such as pushing or hitting; (d) *verbal,* such as teasing or calling names in a malevolent way; and (e) *generic victimization,* such as constant bullying. Regardless of type, the impact of aggressive play on a targeted child is usually negative: The experience is unpleasant at best and devastating at worst (Goodwin, 2002). Hawker and Boulton found that peer victimization was often connected to depression, loneliness, anxiety, and poor self-esteem. Aggressive play, then, can be particularly harmful in late childhood.

Now that we have explored the ambiguities that sometimes surround play, we are better equipped to learn more about children's play in late childhood. We do so in the next section.

Photo 4.2   Older children love challenges. Here an older girl takes on the challenge of climbing a tree.

INDUSTRY, FANTASIES, AND MASTERY ●

In late childhood, children develop a new eagerness to learn, and their imagination is enhanced by their new knowledge and understanding of the world. Once again, play is intertwined with overall development.

Industry and Collections

Starting at around the age of 6 or 7, children develop a new interest in the world. Perhaps for this reason, this is also when they start going to elementary school. From Japan to the United States, and from Peru to Cambodia, children start going to elementary, or primary, school at the age of 6 or 7.

We have already explained that children start developing a new understanding of rules at around this same age. Something, then, is taking place in children's development. Different theorists have given different names to this "something." Piaget (1952) refers to it as the *concrete operational stage,* and Erikson (1963) refers to it as the *stage of industry.*

Whatever their terminology, most theorists mean that children in late childhood become increasingly eager to understand and learn about the larger world and how it is organized. Where once there was simply the neighborhood and Grandma's house, now there is a whole world organized into cities, countries, oceans, and continents. This almost compulsive drive to organize the world shows up in children's play. They spend countless hours collecting and organizing things such as stamps, dolls, baseball cards, and toy soldiers.

Collections and Playful Social Interactions

However, collections are not simply about children satisfying their interest in organizing. Collections also lead to playful interactions with peers through exchanges of collectible items in quite rule-bound ways, as the text box illustrates.

Do You Want to Trade?

Nathalie, Ayanna, and Joanne are 10-year-olds and "best friends." They spend countless hours together in the evenings and on weekends. All three collect stamps, particularly stamps representing animals. They spend quite a bit of time organizing their respective collections on their own; however, they also like to get together to exchange their doubles. In the past few months, they have developed a certain number of rules to organize their trades: a single stamp cannot be traded for more than three others, even when the face value of these three stamps is less than that of the one; stamps that are damaged in any way cannot be traded; and any trade can be called off within 24 hours—but not afterward—if one of the girls changes her mind.

In this example, we see how a collection can lead to pleasurable and playful interactions with friends. The objective for each child is to increase her personal collection, and a great deal of negotiation is needed in the process. Opportunities arise for learning about what is fair and what is not fair, for developing and following complex rules, and for taking already existing friendships a step further.

Here too, bad play can take place. We can imagine what would happen if Joanne tried to disguise the fact that one of her stamps was damaged in hopes of trading it for two other stamps, or if all three girls tried to convince Tom, Nathalie's little brother, that he should trade the stamp decorating the postcard he just received from his grandmother (a truly valuable stamp) for one that looks appealing to Tom but that does not have nearly the same value.

Through these examples, we see the ambiguity that sometimes surrounds play. Collections provide opportunities for both types of play—good and bad—at a time when children progressively develop their sense of morality. This play development accompanies children's development across all domains (cognitive, social, emotional, and moral).

Collections and Imaginative Play

That play with collections marks developmental shifts is nowhere better illustrated than in comparisons of how older and younger children use collectible items. The text box gives an example.

Two Brothers at Play

Carl's collection of toy soldiers has grown since he was 5, and now he can trace the origin of each piece: This one was found at a yard sale 2 years ago, these two were a present from Uncle John for Carl's last birthday, those he inherited from an older cousin who stopped being interested in collecting toy soldiers, and so forth. Carl is now 8 years old. Through the years, his collection has increased in value because each piece is truly a "collector's item": He knows how much effort, meticulous care, and time he has put into building up his collection.

Al, Carl's 5-year-old sibling, does not really appreciate the value of his brother's collection. What Al appreciates, however, is the collection's potential for imaginative make-believe. One day, when Carl is at school, Al decides to organize a battle among the soldiers. Some die, others get badly injured, and most will never look the same. When Carl returns that afternoon and sees the damage, he is very upset. But Al does not understand his big brother's reaction. "Why are you so upset?" Al says. "They had a war, that's all!" Carl wishes he could strangle his little brother.

In this example, we see how two children, 3 years apart, can use the same play objects in radically different ways. There is definitely something more serious and respectful in the way that Carl manipulates his soldiers. But this does not mean that Carl never engaged in imaginative play. When he was younger, he used to organize make-believe battles himself, alone or with friends. Now his interests and abilities lead him away from pretense and make-believe.

But is this really true? Is late childhood a rather sober, unimaginative time of life? Or do fantasy and imagination simply take different forms?

Fantasy and Imaginative Play in Late Childhood

Most observers and theorists link make-believe with the preschool years, mainly because it is during the preschool years that this propensity fully emerges (Singer, 1994). Many assume that make-believe play progressively disappears after the age of 5 as older children develop a better grasp of reality and so no longer need to pretend. In the words of Piaget (1951), "the more the child adapts himself to the natural and social world, the less he indulges in symbolic distortions and transpositions, because instead of assimilating the external world to the ego he progressively subordinates the ego to reality" (p. 145). The underlying assumption is that children who keep pretending in late childhood are behind in their development or behaving childishly.

This book provides an alternative and contrary view that several scholars have come to support in the past few years (Harris, 2003; Taylor, 1999). First, we show that pretense does not disappear in late childhood; it simply takes place in different contexts, away from observers. Second, the contents of pretense and make-believe play evolve and develop as children grow older. Third, children who pretend in late childhood are not behind. As for being childish, if "childish" means acting in a childlike fashion, then children between 6 and 11 who pretend behave in childish ways, but not by pretending as younger children do. They are, after all, still children.

A Different Context

In late childhood, make-believe tends to diminish in its most overt forms. Children seldom pretend at school, where new demands to pay attention and be serious are enforced. As we shall see in Chapter 9, children still play at school, but mostly during recess, when they usually play games with rules such as those previously described in this chapter (chase games, ball games, jump-rope games).

Outside of school, however, in the privacy of their homes or in small groups of trusted friends, children still engage in pretense or make-believe play (Singer, 1995). The text box gives an example.

Two Siblings Hide to Pretend

... Sandra are respectively 7 and 9 years old. They have a big
... of play mobiles that they have been playing with since they
... . They still enjoy playing with them occasionally, although
... wish they could have some of the new accessories, such
... ate boat or the cowboy ranch. But their parents tell them
... are too old to play with such toys, and they buy them books
... ortunately, Marc and Sandra have enough replicas and enough
... tion to still create elaborate play scenes. But they now keep
... ake-believe behind closed doors. And when Marc and Sandra
... e in an occasional argument, as all siblings do, they threaten
... their parents and school friends about the other's make-believe
... forgetting, as children often do, that they too could be betrayed
... he same basis.

An Evolving Content

In late childhood, the contents of pretense also evolve. As Singer (1995) suggests, when children engage in make-believe during the elementary school years, they often do so by incorporating pretense into their games with rules. This occurs with the game Dungeons & Dragons, where a player can be a knight or a witch. Children at this age also develop fantasies and alternative scenes to real life in the privacy of their minds. Both types of pretense, Singer explains, carry on into adolescence and even into adulthood, particularly in daydreaming.

In the elementary school years, children start fantasizing about alternative lives—not the lives of superheroes, but lives filled with adventure and romance nonetheless (Harris & Began, 1993). Pretense is tied to reality in ways not common among preschoolers. Becoming a pop star singer or a world-famous athlete are tangible options in the older child's imagination and in his or her play. There is serious pretense in hitting a baseball as one pretends to be a favorite baseball player, and serious pretense in singing as one pretends to be a pop star.

The Benefits of Imaginative Play

In late childhood, children who engage in imaginative play, be it in the form of floor play, board games, video games, storytelling, or drama, usually derive a lot of pleasure from such activities. This, by itself, is an important benefit, but not the only one. In imaginative play, children between the ages of 6 and 11 continue to develop more mature ways to express and control their emotions (Singer & Singer, 1990). This practice, when encouraged, may lead to important positive outcomes: more openness and thoughtfulness (Singer, 1994), more creativity (Russ & Kaugars, 2001), and a better understanding of the relationships among one's own and others' thoughts, behaviors, and emotions (Niec & Russ, 2002).

In addition, children who engage in imaginative play during the elementary school years seem less impulsive, less aggressive, and better able to discriminate between fantasy and reality (Singer & Singer, 1990). As we saw in the previous chapter, many adults fear that imaginative play, at all stages of the child's development, may lead to confusion between fantasy and reality. Yet the opposite seems to be the case. Leslie (1987) suggests in her "theory of mind" that playing imaginative games helps children develop the ability to think in a subjective manner, so that they can compare possibilities. In the process of comparing, she says, children develop a gradual awareness of the distinction between fantasy and reality. Imaginative play, then, is a good thing for children, whether it be in early or late childhood.

A New Meaning for Mastery

As much as there is make-believe in hitting a baseball and in singing, there is also a new sense of mastery in these activities. During the elementary school years, children not only develop a new eagerness to learn; they also develop a new desire to do well academically, socially, and in other ways (Freitag, 1998), including in their play.

Mastery Across Play Domains

Children want to do well in school, in sports, in arts and crafts, in drama, in playing music, and in a host of other areas, especially if their peers value the activity. Play is no exception. Children can now spend hours constructing and organizing miniature worlds that will feed their imagination. Consider any group of 9-year-olds constructing a décor for a puppet show. Younger children simply do not bother spending much time and energy preparing such scenes; they just want to play. For older children, however, setting up the stage is already imaginative play in which one's imagination and art and craft skills converge and reinforce each other.

The same holds true for games with rules, such as ball games, jumping games, and board games. We return again to Janet and Jimmy playing Monopoly. Before the game even starts, Jimmy usually spends quite a bit of time organizing his bills in some kind of orderly fashion (e.g., from highest to lowest). Once the game begins, he tries to accumulate as much property and money as possible. Clearly, his goal is to win. Janet also tries to win, but in her world, winning is easy, because one does not need to demonstrate competence; in fact, young children often have everyone winning, even though the official rules allow for only one winner. In late childhood, then, play provides an arena in which children practice and demonstrate their skills, and in which they often strive to become "winners."

Mastery Play Across Cultures

This new sense of mastery emerges in similar ways across cultures. All children want to perform and demonstrate their new skills during the elementary school years. How they do so may vary depending on the values most cherished and encouraged in their culture.

"Doing well" does not carry the same meaning in all families, in all communities, and at all times. For example, Freitag (1998) has shown that throughout American history there have been shifts in the meaning of "doing well" and of "winning." One important change took place during the Great Depression. At that time, Freitag explains, hard work and sacrifice stopped acting as predictors of success, and wealth became much more valued. As a result, the board games of that time deemphasized the passé values of hard work and sacrifice, and games emphasizing wealth increased in popularity, the most notable example being Monopoly. What is popular in play is a function not simply of age but also of what is going on in the greater society.

The meaning of "doing well" also varies across settings. In societies where competition is valued and encouraged, as in the United States and many Western societies, children compete in their play (Devereux, 1978). Other cultures put more emphasis on cooperation. In most Western cultures, "doing well" means surpassing other children's skills; in other cultures, it means working well as a team member toward reaching the same goal. Thus in playing, all children learn about the values most cherished in their culture (Sutton-Smith, 1986).

● SUMMARY

In late childhood, children are still children. They like to play. But their play keeps evolving and developing. Children now spend more time with peers and less time with their parents, and socialization becomes increasingly important. Boys and girls tend to play among themselves and at different games. Their play, however, has much in common. In particular, increasingly complex rules now frame the development of play. Late childhood is also a time when children develop a new eagerness to learn about the world. Some new play behaviors emerge, such as collecting and trading objects, while other types of play, such as pretense and make-believe, keep developing. In the process, a new meaning of mastery emerges, with children wanting to perform well in all they do, including in how they play.

● KEY WORDS, NAMES, AND IDEAS

"Bad play"

Collections

Concrete operational stage (Piaget, J.)

Cultures

Egocentric

Familiarity

Gender

Imaginative play

Mastery

Peer groups

Pellegrini, A. D.

Physical aggression

Play domains

Relational aggression

Rough-and-tumble play

Rules

Socialization

Socioeconomic status (SES)

Stage of industry (Erikson, E.)

Sutton-Smith, B.

CHAPTER **5**

CHILDREN'S HUMOR

Author's Note: This chapter was written by Jennifer Cunningham, long-time investigator of language development, humor, and early schooling.

Some might not include humor as a type of play. We do so for three reasons: First, humor is enjoyable—in the ways that most play is enjoyable. Second, humor constructs an unreal world—much as make-believe play does. Third, the enjoyable, unreal world of humor often performs the same cognitive, social, and emotional functions as play in general. Even the simple scatological "jokes" of a preschooler ("You poo in your pants!") are just instances of enjoyable pretense that observe the rules for ordering the real world by breaking them. Humor, then, is play, and humor's development throughout childhood affords us a recapitulation of all the general issues about play's development. We will, then, trace humor's development both as a way of understanding yet another medium in which children play and as a way of recapping main themes about play's development throughout childhood.

● DEFINING HUMOR

"You had to be there . . . Well, it was funny at the time . . . I don't know what came over us . . . We laughed ourselves silly."

Humor is not easily defined. What makes a person laugh depends on many factors, including personality, culture, and past experience. Think for a moment of things that make you laugh. A partial list might include

- *The Simpsons*
- Puns and wordplay
- Silly Internet sites, such as animated dancing hamsters or singing cows
- The way your dog sneezes
- Nature film footage of monkeys cavorting in the jungle

Your list of funny things probably includes a wide range of jokes and situations, some of which are highly idiosyncratic. It might be quite difficult to explain why certain items on your list are so amusing. Even a list of "typically" or "traditionally" funny things probably contains a wide range of types and situations. Lists of slapstick humor might include anything from *The Three Stooges* and *Three's Company* to the more recent equivalents of Ben Stiller in *Zoolander* or *Meet the Parents*. All of these feature physical comedy from the mundane to the outrageous—slipping on a marble, getting hit on the head, being kicked in the crotch, dangling from a rooftop. Other types of humor—such as jokes or riddles, character-driven humor, and mimicry of another person's voice and mannerisms—have their own quite extensive range of subtypes. The world of humor is indeed complex, and the different types of humor or, more precisely, humorous actions, which researchers often call (rather unhumorously) "humor events," do not seem to have much in common other than that they elicit laughter. But why, exactly, are they all funny?

Our attempt to define "funniness" is complicated further when we consider that *all* humor is contextually dependent in one way or another. For each of our examples (a pratfall, a knock-knock joke, and an imitation or impression), we can easily imagine a context in which it would *not* be funny. What if Ben Stiller was actually seriously hurt in attempting a comic stunt? What if we'd heard the knock-knock joke several times before? What if we found the imitation to be hurtful, mean-spirited, or offensive? Furthermore, what if any of these jokes simply failed to "click" with our own sense of humor? Clearly, as adults, we can see that there is nothing inherently and always funny to all individuals in all situations. Thus, in attempting to understand children's humor development, we must examine how children arrive at intuitions about not only *what* is funny, but also *when* it is funny.

We see, then, that though humor can occur in isolation, it is, as is most play, a social phenomenon—a way of connecting with friends and a way of understanding the world around us. Our description of context must take into account not only the relatively simple situational rules for humor (e.g., it's not funny anymore if someone gets injured), but also social variables: Are things as funny with strangers as with close friends? Acquaintances? Parents? Bosses? Do these variables affect whether something is humorous, or do they merely modulate our response to the humor?

These *insider-versus-outsider* humor distinctions take on increasing influence during children's social development, as their peer relationships become central to their self-definition. The trend is a familiar one: Four-year-old children frequently approach their preschool teachers with knock-knock jokes or funny stories, yet by middle school and high school, most students would not initiate these interactions. Indeed, it seems older children and teenagers frequently like to conceal from adults what they laugh about with their friends, as demonstrated by the typical "Teacher: 'What's so funny?' Student: 'Nothing.'" exchange.

As children grow, they begin to use humor not only for its intrinsic values but also for what it does for friendships and group bonds. Sometimes, the fact of sharing a secret or *in-joke* is more pleasurable than the joke itself. This realization might lead to many more realizations about how humor may be used to further social goals: joking to create solidarity and to relieve tension or conceal discomfort and avoid embarrassment. This growing awareness of social goals—of humor as a means to an end—is surely another key to humor development.

From childhood on, individuals vary tremendously in their responses to humorous stimuli. Indeed, as is the case with much of personal-social development, the developmental course may be looked upon as a journey from the universal to the idiosyncratic: As children play with each other and solidify friendships, they develop their own unique styles of humor, both in terms of what they find funny and in terms of how often they initiate humorous interactions. As a child progresses from shared laughter to in-jokes to a propensity to share joking mannerisms with friends, some basic individual differences are downplayed whereas others are amplified. In adulthood, our sense of humor becomes an integral part of the way we perceive our personality; as the saying goes, everyone thinks he or she has good taste and a sense of humor.

Thus, we may see children learning to use humor as working out three central questions: (a) "What is funny?"; (b) "When is it funny?"; and (c) "How is humor used in service of various social-emotional objectives?" Yet, as we also begin to marvel at the complexity of why some things are funny, we can begin to appreciate how each child might arrive at very different answers to these questions.

● WHAT'S SO FUNNY?

As we have seen by examining our own humor preferences, the question of what is funny can be extremely difficult to answer. Because humor involves the intersection of emotional, cognitive, and social dimensions of development, any theory that focuses on only one dimension provides an incomplete picture of how a child's understanding of humor develops. Humor depends not only on these three dimensions but also on making connections among them and testing these connections. Dimensions and connections, then, make it difficult to categorize what all things humorous have in common.

However, if there is one way to categorize what all funny things have in common, the answer is deceptively simple: *Funny things are not serious*. As in the case of make-believe play, slapstick and jokes do not belong to the realm of the real world, and real-world rules do not apply. A humorous event does not need to be assimilated into our knowledge about the real world: In the land of humor, the cartoon coyote can swallow dynamite, explode, and come back the next day to try again to get the roadrunner. A clown who falls down the stairs may get cream pie in the face, but more serious consequences such as broken limbs or concussions never result. Verbal jokes, in which dogs walk into bars or rabbis and priests take camping trips together, also create an alternative universe that need not be plausible, let alone real.

Other types of humor, such as taboo violation (for example, bathroom humor, as when 4-year-olds repeat the words "pee-pee" and "poop") also demonstrate this knowledge that things that are not okay in most situations are somehow safe to say when one is "only joking." Thus, all the expectations of the "real world" are somehow violated, whether in the unexpected punch line of a joke, or in regard to the consequence of a controversial act (such as violence, or the use of a taboo word). In the words of humor researcher Thomas Veatch, "Humor is (emotional) pain that does not hurt" (1988, p. 164).

This unreality is at the center of many theories of humor and of play in general. For some theorists, the pleasure of humor is in the cognitive realization that the situation is unreal and incongruous with the "rules" of the world as we know it. As children begin to use their perceptions and past experiences to formulate expectations about situations and events, they often react with laughter and surprise when these expectations are violated.

However, though humor appreciation is certainly dependent on cognitive abilities, the pleasure we derive from humor need not be cognitive; it may be more emotional or physiological.

As an example of a theory of humor focused on emotion, Freud (1905/1953) maintained that laughter was a means of releasing excessive amounts of *psychic energy*, energy that often results in rechanneling sexual and aggressive impulses into an acceptable, indirect form of expression. For Freud, the appeal of slapstick, *Three-Stooges* style, may lie not in the "unreality" of the situation per se, but rather in the pleasure of seeing someone else act out our own aggressive impulses (pokes in the eye, smacks on the head) free from real-world repercussions.

However, like most forms of play, humor necessarily involves the intersection of the emotional, cognitive, and social dimensions of development. Any theory of humor's development that focuses on only one dimension would provide an incomplete picture of how a child's understanding, appreciation, and use of humor change over time. Therefore, one of the best ways to understand humor is to examine "snapshots" across childhood, snapshots not only of how a child *comprehends* humor but also of how she learns to *use* humor as a playful way to facilitate social interaction and to test beliefs about the world.

Photo 5.1   Infants laugh most at spontaneous, unpredictable stimuli.

● HUMOR IN INFANCY AND THE TODDLER YEARS

The pleasure of realizing that something that might otherwise be considered threatening and scary is in fact fun and safe seems to be a key to early humor. Indeed, for very small children, the boundary between humor and fear is often fragile. Infants may laugh at peekaboo or other *surprise games,* but an unexpected noise such as clapping may result in either laughing or crying.

A child's first laughter often emerges between the 4th and 5th months, well before she exhibits a capacity for symbolic play. An infant's early laughter is usually a response to perceptual stimuli such as whispering, blowing on the infant's hair, or peekaboo. Pleasurable sensations, such as blowing, can elicit laughs over and over again, as can peekaboo (see Chapter 2).

However, even in these early interactions, laughter expresses more than just pleasure: Babies as young as 7 months have been noted to laugh more at spontaneous, unpredictable stimuli than at stimuli that are repeated or expected, even if those stimuli have produced laughter in the past. Even a game of peek-a-boo, which may seem to adults to be the same over and over again, is exciting to infants because of its spontaneity: When researchers attempt to standardize peek-a-boo games for experimental purposes (eyes covered for 3 seconds and then opened, repeated five times), they often find that infants laugh much less than they would in an uncontrolled, naturalistic context (Sroufe & Wunsch, 1972). Surprise, then, is a needed ingredient for there to be humor—even for the very, very young.

This preference for novel events suggests that some of the pleasure of experiencing humorous events stems from children not knowing what to expect. Children's first attempts at humor production reflect this understanding that unexpectedness elicits laughter. Often, the first "jokes" that a toddler makes are nonverbal attempts to create *incongruity*, such as placing a toy in her cereal or in her shoe or on her head.

Of course, in other contexts, unpredictable and unpredicted situations might produce the opposite: anxiety instead of pleasure. From very early on, individual differences in temperament and personality can determine whether an experience is pleasurable or anxiety provoking. A mother of twins reported that although one of her daughters was clearly afraid of the family's dog, her other child loved to bat her own face with the dog's puffy tail, laughing uproariously at the interaction.

This fluctuation between laughter and distress remains common throughout early childhood. It may be familiar to anyone who has witnessed 2- and 3-year-olds at play. In early childhood, the physicality in most play can elicit laughter even as it has elements of danger. Toddlers and preschoolers tend to laugh much more during exciting or dangerous running games than during more reserved imaginative or constructive play. Children playing "chase" may laugh exuberantly until the game becomes too real, at which point they may suddenly burst into tears. In some instances, the laughter-arousal-anxiety cycle may be repeated several times. This was true of one preschooler named Max, who would initiate a game of chase in which he and five friends ran around the play yard, shrieking with laughter. When it came to be Max's turn to be chased, his laughter built up to hysteria and then quickly changed to tears. Max would then run to his teacher for comfort. Once comforted, he would quickly jump back into the game.

The psychologist Mary Rothbart (1973) noted this phenomenon in what she termed the *arousal-safety model of humor*; the child experiences "fight-or-flight" physiological arousal (increased heart rate, blood flow, and sensory awareness) in a context that he or she knows to be non-threatening. Long before children can appreciate riddles, knock-knock jokes, or other explicitly cognitive humor, early humor and laughter result from sensory stimuli at the appropriate level—exciting but not overwhelming. One might also see this situation as a cousin of Freud's impulse-channeling theory: In this context, laughter acts as a safety valve to release otherwise distressing levels of social arousal.

As children mature, they increase the strategies they have available to process intense feelings. The laughter and anxiety responses become increasingly differentiated from each other. However, the inclination toward laughter during tense situations remains present in most adults, who might be unable to prevent laughing nervously even in situations in which they know laughter is inappropriate. The inclination to laugh during an overwhelming or tense situation might perhaps be a vestige of the earliest use of humor—as an outlet for intense emotions. This most primal need for laughter remains even as the humor response changes and evolves. Indeed, as children's cognitive and social capacities become more developed, this outlet may take on increased importance.

Children learn to laugh not only when they themselves experience arousing stimuli but also when they see others in similar situations. Likewise, the types of stimuli giving rise to laughter may also begin to expand exponentially. For example, one may laugh in response not only to low levels of fear or surprise but also to higher-level emotions such as embarrassment (either experienced or witnessed). The inclination to laugh when one empathizes with someone else's embarrassing situation is often exploited in televised entertainment, both for children and for adults, as the enduring popularity of television shows such as *Candid Camera*, *America's Funniest Home Videos*, and MTV's *Punk'd* attest. However, as we shall see in the next section, although the conception of humor as a prime outlet for complex and conflicting emotional reactions never disappears with development, humor becomes reorganized around two specific dimensions—the social and the cognitive.

● HUMOR IN EARLY CHILDHOOD

There are few things in this world that are as fascinating, endearing, and maddening as a 4- or 5-year-old comedian. The child usually begins with an opener such as "Let me tell you a joke!," but that is the first and last predictable utterance. The typical "joke" might be a simple statement such as "My peanut butter sandwich can talk!" or an elaborate story such as "One day, a clown was walking in the woods, and he met a Pikachu, and the Pikachu said, come with me to visit my mother, and they went to the cabin, and the mother came out, and she was a spaghetti elephant!" The joke may meander from character to character, from silly thing to silly thing, but no one, least of all the child, will know where the joke begins or ends.

A Preschooler's Meaning of Getting the Joke

One little boy, Abe, frequently volunteered to share a joke or a funny story, using his active imagination to come up with several characters and an elaborate plot, only to lose track of the story and announce he was starting over. Several of his favorite jokes took a full 5 minutes to tell. Although his teachers would often exchange quizzical looks with one another, his classmates clearly "got" the jokes. More precisely, they got what is important about the jokes—Abe had clearly figured out that, even in the adult world, a joke is frequently less about humor than about creating a context in which one can initiate social interactions, increase feelings of camaraderie and solidarity, and make others pay attention to you.

As children work to develop their own social identity, they begin to devote considerable time and energy toward establishing and maintaining friendships with peers. Educators and psychologists often regard this as the central task of the early childhood years. Not surprisingly, then, children's conscious *initiation* of humor events increases dramatically during early childhood (Masten, 1986; McGhee, 1980).

As children age and have more opportunities to interact with and identify with peers, the frequency and sophistication of their attempts at being humorous increase, as does their preference for sharing jokes with friends. One observational study of 86 children ages 3 to 5 found that the frequency of children's laughter increased as they grew older (Bainum, Lounsbury, & Pollio, 1984). In addition, laughing and smiling behaviors tended to become more differentiated over time, with smiling used as a more general-purpose response to incidental pleasurable events, and laughter used chiefly to accompany intentionally produced stimuli such as joke telling, silliness, or clowning. The only decrease observed in this study was in the older children's likelihood of laughing when they were alone. In other words, 4- and 5-year-old children assimilate the concept of *audience* into their working definition of humor. Things become less funny when alone and more funny when others are around to take part. Thus, children are progressing toward utilizing humor for what Foote and Chapman (1976) have called a sophisticated form of social communication at the group level.

Sharing laughter together often serves as the precursor to other forms of social intimacy. Laughter becomes one of the earliest and most enduring tools for getting to know one another. The humor context is so powerful that it breaks down even difficult social barriers, as the following example illustrates:

Knock-Knock Jokes to Enter a Play Group

In one early childhood classroom, a reserved little girl, Lucy, who spoke limited English, began sharing silly knock-knock jokes. She was so empowered by her ability to share that she began to initiate knock-knock jokes throughout the day. For the remainder of the school year (nearly 5 months) Lucy entered playgroups in the doll corner or block area by approaching her friends with "knock-knock!" to elicit the familiar "Who's there?"

Although the intent to establish and reinforce social bonds develops as a primary motive for humor interactions, there is some evidence that the underlying "primal" arousal-release urge continues to play a role. For example, though the instances of *incidental* laughter (such as laughter in response to chasing) decrease over time, individual differences in children's humor initiation correlate positively with frequency of aggressive behavior (McGhee & Lloyd, 1982). The fact that a kindergartener's level of agression is moderately predictive of how often she or he initiates humor could perhaps be interpreted as evidence that some of the observed humor might be instances of rechanneling aggression into socially acceptable humor.

Alternatively, the positive correlation between humor and aggression could be due to the fact that in preschool, most social children show high levels of all activities, both positive and negative. Prosocial behavior and aggression don't start to show a negative correlation until the child is older.

Yet, McGhee notes that this trend linking humor and aggression often continues throughout the elementary school years, perhaps because aggression, like humor, is a way for children to control people and situations. McGhee notes that "by consistently clowning or joking, a child remains in charge of the flow of conversation or interaction . . . by initiating a joke or comic behavior, the humorist puts others in a situation where they are obliged to react in some way" (1980, p. 233). The scatological stage of humor

Photo 5.2   The humor created by the way these school-age girls dance strengthens the bonds between the two.

development, which often makes its first appearance around a preschool lunch table, may also be interpreted as evidence of this deepening understanding, as children discover that words such as "pee-pee" and "poop" elicit strong reactions from adults and other children.

   As children learn about the social world that humor creates, they learn to set humor apart from its literal context. For example, intentionally mislabeling the names of objects or people such as by calling a cow a dog or a car a bus can be humorous. Recall 4-year-old Abe's silly stories. Although they may not quite correspond to our adult conception of a joke, Abe clearly determined that unreality is central to humor, why else would he have chosen a spaghetti elephant as a main character, rather than a fireman or his sister Jessica? For many young humorists, then, the sillier the joke is, the better. This is why Abe added a clown *and* a Pikachu to the spaghetti elephant; the more silliness, the better the humor.

Abe's stories also illustrate another vital cognitive prerequisite to humor development during the preschool years, what psychologists call *theory of mind* or the realization that beliefs do not necessarily match reality and that different people hold different beliefs about the world (Perner, 1991). As mentioned in the introduction, children begin to develop a theory of mind early on; for instance, 3-year-olds demonstrate an ability to distinguish among the mental-state verbs *think*, *guess*, and *know*. Their subsequent mastery of this ability becomes a prerequisite for adult comprehension of verbal jokes involving characters who have ideas that are contrary to reality as the listener understands reality. Theory of mind (or the relative absence of it) also explains why young children sometimes have difficulty understanding adults' jokes, as when one 4-year-old named Gus failed to understand his parents' joke about his actually having alien parents who dropped him off during a visit from outer space.

● THE ELEMENTARY SCHOOL YEARS: INTEGRATING SOCIAL AND COGNITIVE HUMOR

Listening to elementary school–aged children tell jokes is a markedly different experience than hearing the elaborate impromptu stories created by preschoolers. The jokes of older children are far more likely to make sense to us; in fact, we are very likely to have heard them before, and maybe even told them ourselves 10, 20, or 50 years ago. A casual glance through *1001 Super Silly Halloween Jokes* or any other popular joke book aimed at 6- to 10-year-olds is enough to reveal that many of the same chestnuts we recall from our youth are alive and well.

The fondness many 6-, 7-, and 8-year-olds have for memorized jokes and riddles may be seen as a direct result of cognitive development beyond the preschool years. Following Piaget, Paul McGhee (2002) proposed a comprehensive stage model of children's humor, with the last stage being in the elementary school years. As we have seen, a child progresses from being able to perceive incongruity in infancy (Stage 1) to producing incongruity nonverbally in toddlerhood (Stage 2) to producing incongruity verbally in early childhood (Stage 3). Also as we have seen, incongruity in early childhood often means being silly. In the elementary school years, the silly quality of humor gradually gives way as children see humor as involving more than what is nonsensical. By Stage 4, the final stage in McGhee's model, the "mature" humorist begins to prefer humor that presents not only an incongruity but also a *resolution* to the incongruity. This shift is evident in the following exchange, where the humor clearly functions on two distinct levels:

Knock-knock.
Who's there?
Potato chip.
Potato chip who?
Potato chip you!

(Liza, 4, to Sam, 7)

Knock-knock.
Who's there?
Olive.
Olive who?
Olive you! (I love you!)

(Sam, 7, to Liza, 4)

For Liza, these knock-knock jokes are funny because of the incongruity they present: In reality, an olive or a potato chip are equally unlikely to knock on a door, so the two scenarios are equally amusing. However, Sam recognizes that the second joke is funnier than the first because the absurd image gets resolved into a logical conclusion by reparsing "Olive" as "I love."

Stages of Humor Development
Taking a cue from Piaget's cognitive stages, leading humor researcher Paul McGhee first proposed a comprehensive stage model of children's humor in 1979. This model, last revised in 2002, maps the type of humor the child is likely fascinated with to underlying changes in her ability to perceive and make sense of her world.
Stage 0: Laughter Without Humor. McGhee dubs this pre-humor stage "Stage 0," although children may exhibit smiling and laughter.
Stage 1: Laughter at the Attachment Figure. In this stage, the child demonstrates an increasing awareness of her interpersonal surroundings and participates in social humor with a parent or other attachment figure through games such as peek-a-boo.
Stage 2: Treating an Object as a Different Object. At Stage 2, the child begins producing "jokes" nonverbally by performing incongruous actions such as putting her bowl on her head as a hat or pretending to talk into her shoe.
Stage 3: Misnaming Objects or Actions. Once the child's vocabulary hits a critical point, she can extend her incongruity humor to misnaming objects or actions. McGhee notes that children at this stage often enjoy calling things by their opposite name—cold as hot, boy as girl.

(Continued)

(Continued)

Stage 4: Playing With Words. As the child's verbal competence grows, she is less dependent on objects as the source of humor. She may experiment with rhyming words, made-up silly words, and other humorous play that does not directly link to concrete objects within her reach.

Stage 5: Riddles and Jokes. As the child develops, she begins to understand that humor has a meaning—that jokes must resolve from something absurd into something that makes cognitive sense. She often starts memorizing riddles and jokes and using them as a means of initiating social interactions with peers and adults.

Several experiments have demonstrated this developmental shift by comparing children's responses to "original" jokes with versions lacking either the incongruity or the resolution (see the next table). They found that preoperational children (ages 6 and below), though rejecting the incongruity-removed version as "not funny at all," did not rate the resolution-removed joke as significantly less funny than the original. Yet older children overwhelmingly preferred the original joke to alternate versions that did not contain a word or phrase with a dual meaning. This developmental change is consistent with the Piagetian model of cognitive development, in which the concrete operational stage is marked by a child's newfound ability to consider different aspects of a situation at once—in this case, two possible meanings for a word or phrase.

Original Joke	Resolution-Removed Version	Incongruity-Removed Version
Call me a cab. You're a cab.	Call a cab for me. You're a cab.	Call me a cab. Yes ma'am.
I saw a man-eating shark in the aquarium. That's nothing. I saw a man eating tuna in the restaurant.	I saw a ferocious shark in the aquarium. That's nothing. I saw a man eating tuna in the restaurant.	I saw a man-eating shark in the aquarium. That's nothing. I saw an octopus.

Source: Partial sample from Shultz & Horibe (1974).

As cognitive abilities increase, children find pleasure in humor not only for its incongruity, its novelty, and the social connectedness it creates but also, and perhaps mostly, for the challenge it presents. In one experiment, elementary school children asked to rate the funniness level of cartoons consistently found the cognitively challenging jokes to be funnier. Furthermore, research has suggested that among 8- to 14-year-olds, there is a significant correlation between measured IQ and both humor appreciation and humor production. No such correlation exists for either younger children or teens (Masten, 1986).

But why this interest in humor involving cognitive mastery? Some researchers (Berlyne, 1972; Masten, 1986)[1] believe that the dilemmas that riddles and jokes pose to their elementary schoolaged listeners create a cognitive tension that can result in a physiological response similar to the more sensory-oriented arousal of toddlerhood and early childhood. As an older child struggles to resolve a humorous dilemma into her logically consistent worldview, this *intellectual arousal* is heightened if the situation is especially difficult or complex. If the older child does not have to perform cognitively rigorous "work" to understand the joke (for instance, if she has heard the joke before or can guess the punch line), then she will perceive it as less humorous.

This last observation seems to contradict the observation that a 7-year-old child armed with a copy of *1001 Super Silly Halloween Jokes* may find its jokes and riddles hilarious even after many repeated readings. A parent, teacher, car-pool driver, or other captive audience may hear "*Where did the ghost get her hair done? At the boo-ty parlor!*" countless times before its teller tires. However, novel listeners are always approached with great zeal, and the teller's delight may be mostly about a new audience getting his or her old jokes than it is about cognitive mastery and tension.

In this way, the special social context of humor is essentially unchanged throughout childhood. Most typically, children view humor as an *act,* either deliberate silliness or a memorized joke, an act performed by or for peers, an act that reinforces connection through shared laughter.

As school-aged children develop the cognitive capacity to appreciate humor more fully, some of the subtler aspects of the social elements of humor appreciation begin to emerge as well. Unlike preschool children, school-aged children demonstrate the adultlike behavior of *modulating* their humor behavior to depend on social context.

As children mature, they become more likely to look at or consult a peer when asked to judge whether something is funny. Although we all seem to laugh more in the presence of others than we would if we were alone, as we get older we adjust our reactions to more closely match those of our friends.

By the time children reach preadolescence (ages 9–12), this combination of progressively more important social constraints on humor reaction and an increased emphasis on comprehension or "getting" the joke often converge in the form of a well-known middle-school phenomenon: the *inside joke*.

As humor increases the social connectedness among its participants, it highlights the differences among those who share in the understanding and those who do not. Rather than the central theme being a cognitive one, humor starts to transition to a more naturalistic way of looking at common experiences. Observational jokes, such as secret nicknames for people, are examples of this type of humor. Only a certain group knows why something is funny, and they are less likely to share it with others. Here is where we find the first occurrences of *metahumor*—joking about joking, a precursor to adolescent humor.

Charlie the Tuna

As a gaggle of sixth grade girls gather at their lockers at afternoon dismissal time, they compare notes about the day's events.

One girl asks, "Do you have any homework?"

"Yeah. Charlie gave us an extra chapter of review."

They both giggle. "Oh Charlie! We had a pop quiz from Charlie today. I hate how he always quizzes us on Mondays!"

At this moment, the math teacher in question (whose name is Josh) greets the students. Their friends have joined in the laughter, and they can barely contain themselves.

In the girls' invented language, their teacher is named "Charlie" after Charlie the Tuna, thanks to his tuna breath in their afternoon class. Yet however mean-spirited this may sound, the goal is not to openly mock him or hurt his feelings but rather to reinforce bonds of solidarity within their own social group; they are speaking in code about something they have in common and that they each can observe and comment on.

● SUMMARY

We see in humor's development, then, all the main themes about play and play's development. In particular, we see complexity in its many forms—from slapstick to sarcasm—and in its many functions, with functions being added as children develop. Furthermore, we see how humor both reveals and drives social, emotional, and cognitive development. We see humor starting out mostly with familiar caregivers and ending with inside jokes kept hidden from those very same caregivers. We see humor helping modulate difficult feelings such as fear and anger as well as the impulse to be aggressive. We see humor revealing thinking and reasoning about the world as children play at newfound cognitive abilities, such as the toddler's ability to match word to referent and the older child's ability to reason logically. Most important, we see humor developing as a wonderful alternative world to better appreciate and adapt to reality. Children's humor and its development does indeed mirror the main themes in play's development.

KEY WORDS, NAMES, AND IDEAS ●

Arousal-safety model of humor

Incongruity

In-jokes

Insider vs. outsider

Intellectual arousal

Metahumor

Modulating

Psychic energy

Resolution

Surprise games

Theory of mind

NOTE ●

1. See Berlyne, Rothbart.

PART II

Revolutions in How Today's Children Play

P art II is about revolutions in how today's children play. The first chapter is about electronic play. The second is about organized youth sports. In both chapters, we highlight the fact that *play is tied to history and to the economic, social, and technological transformations occurring in the larger society.* Play in nineteenth-century rural America was dramatically different than play in twentieth-century industrialized America. It should come as no surprise, then, that play in twenty-first-century America is dramatically different as well.

Part II also highlights the fact that *when we are in the middle of a revolution, it is hard to evaluate what is going on.* This is certainly true of the revolutions in electronic play and organized youth sports. We give these subjects their own section, therefore, to show how one can think about problems even without sufficient experience to solve them.

Finally, Part II highlights the fact that *dramatic changes in how children play challenge us to think of new ways to think about and define play.* Prior to electronic play, it was easy to think of play as being about jumping and climbing, about moving dolls around living-room floors, and about running to "capture the flag." Now, it is not so easy, because electronic play is about playing with virtual worlds. In a similar vein, prior to organized youth sports dominating backyard sports, it was easy to speak of play as being largely controlled by children themselves. Now, it is not so easy, because organized youth sports are largely controlled by adults.

CHAPTER 6

ELECTRONIC PLAY

Computer, Console, and Video Games

A s recently as 15 years ago, there was no reason to have a chapter on electronic play in a text on children's play. Electronic play existed only in rudimentary forms and only in a very few homes. How times have changed! Today, in most industrialized countries, electronic play is the preferred form of play for millions. It is important to remember, though, that electronic play is currently available to only a relatively small percentage of the world's population. However, in countries and cultures in which home computers are widely available, interest in and incidence of electronic play are increasingly widespread among children and adults.

Electronic play is the first qualitatively different form of play that has been introduced in at least several hundred years. With most forms of play, the essence of the game exists in the interactions between the players and the physical media—blocks, sticks, dolls, pinecones, paints, and so on. Unlike with most forms of play, the essence of electronic play exists in the interactions between the players and the distinctly intangible potential for a wide range of experiences, whose physical properties of hardware and software are less the essence of the game and more simply a means of accessing it.

Some might argue, though, that electronic play is just the latest expression of a human tendency that has far-reaching historical roots. According to Stafford and Terpak (2001), the desire to use media to distort our senses can be traced back to magic temples in ancient Egypt and includes such devices as the seventeenth-century multiplying spectacles and the eighteenth-century *camera obscura*—things that gave us the ability to explore in ways that seemed to go beyond reality. Electronic play may, then, be only the latest expression of this desire to distort. However, electronic play does more than distort the real world; it creates whole new worlds.

So the rapid expanse and widespread popularity of electronic play, along with the changes that this qualitatively different form of play brings, make it more than fair to say that because of electronic play, we are in the midst of a play revolution. Furthermore, because we are in the midst of and not beyond this revolution, there are more questions than there are research-based answers—questions about how electronic play affects children in the long term, whether electronic play promotes violence, the importance of the differences between the electronic play of girls and boys, and how the effects of electronic play will influence families and parent-child relations. Right now, these and other frequently asked questions have no clear, research-based answers that pinpoint causes and effects.

If, then, there are no clear research-based answers to questions about causes and effects, is there nothing we can say about electronic play? In fact, we can say a great deal, mostly by describing what is happening and by providing cautious evaluations and tentative answers to questions based on observations as well as theory. That is what this chapter aims to do—describe the current scene with respect to electronic play and offer cautious evaluations and tentative answers to questions.

In describing and evaluating, this chapter will describe who plays electronic games and where (in what countries) and when (at what ages) people play them. It will describe what kinds of games and game systems are being played and played with. It will describe the special features of game systems and electronic games, features that partially explain why so many children are so highly motivated to play electronic games. It will describe differences in the way different children engage in electronic play—differences that pertain to age and gender. Finally, it will discuss several of the more common concerns about electronic play and its possible negative effects.

This chapter will not focus on educational aspects of electronic play, although it is an important area with many questions of its own. Because there is often a great deal of overlap between electronic play that is designed simply for play and electronic play that has education as its main goal, this chapter will touch on educational uses of electronic play. However, the main discussion of educational uses of electronic play can be found in the chapter on play and schooling.

● DEMOGRAPHICS OF ELECTRONIC PLAY: WHO IS PLAYING? AND WHERE? AND WHEN?

Although it is difficult to give exact figures, most studies indicate that the majority of American school-aged children are playing electronic games—on home computers, console game systems (e.g., Nintendo, PlayStation, Xbox), or both (Jordan & Woodard, 2001). This is true for European and Japanese children as well (Beentjes, Koolstra, Cees, Marseille, & van der Voort, 2001). Finland ranks highest in terms of prevalence, with approximately 90% of Finnish children being regularly engaged in some form of electronic play.

In these industrialized countries, the older a child gets, the more likely the child is to play computer and console games and to play them for longer periods of time. By adolescence, the most common pattern is playing electronic games for half an hour to an hour daily (Phillips, Rolls, Rouse, & Griffiths, 1995).

Boys outnumber girls in terms of who is playing computer and console games. This is true throughout the industrialized world. The reasons for and implications of this gap are not yet well understood. It may be simply that more games are designed especially for boys (Cassell & Jenkins, 1998).

A family's socioeconomic status influences the access and exposure that children have to electronic games. As of this writing, most game consoles cost around $200, and computers that would support the current releases of games cost closer to $1,000, at minimum. Most games for both computers and consoles cost as much as $50 when they are first released.

Although these costs could certainly influence a family's ability to provide access to these games for their children at home, they do not necessarily prevent children's access and exposure to electronic games outside the home. It seems likely that as children's access and exposure to electronic games outside the home increases, particularly for children who cannot play them at home, parental awareness and guidance could decrease.

● DIFFERENT TYPES OF ELECTRONIC PLAY: WHAT IS BEING PLAYED?

Currently, the most popular types of electronic play are computer and console games. *Console games* are played through a special game console used with a television, for instance the Xbox, the PlayStation, and the Nintendo GameCube. *Computer games*, as their name implies, are played on a computer. However, this division becomes less distinct as the technology supporting each type merges, and as the same games are frequently produced for each type of technology.

As for the games themselves, there are several category systems for describing different types of games. No one system has emerged to provide a common language. The table below offers an example of one of these category systems, which is used by game designers. It will serve as our description system throughout the chapter.

Types of Electronic Games

Type of Game	Description	Examples
Real-Time Strategy	Fast-paced strategy games, often played online with other players	Warcraft, Starcraft, Command & Conquer, Age of Empires
First-Person Shooters	First-person perspective shoot-em-ups, often played online with other players	Doom, Quake, Unreal Tournament, Half-Life
Empire Builders	Slow-paced games that are played out over weeks; players begin with a small village equivalent and promote technological progress, expansion, conquest, and trade in order to rule the world of the game	Civilization, Alpha Centauri, Master of Orion
Simulations	Games that simulate reality, a period in history, a fictional setting, etc.; emphasis is not typically placed on winning or losing	SimCity, RollerCoaster Tycoon, Caesar-Pharaoh-Zeus, etc.
Adventure Games	Games that follow a linear story involving puzzles to solve	King's Quest, Space Quest, Prince of Persia, Myst
Role-Playing Games	Games in which players take on the role of a character and build on its knowledge and skills as the storyline progresses; often involves tactical combat	Baldur's Gate, Final Fantasy, Ultima, Diablo
Massively Multiplayer Role-Playing Games (MMRPGs)	Role-playing games that are played online with hundreds or even thousands of other players	Everquest, Ultima Online, Anarchy Online, Dark Age of Camelot
Sports Games	Games simulating various kinds of sports	Grand Turismo, John Madden Football, Tiger Woods Golf
Puzzles	Games that involve logic or reflexes in putting pieces together	Tetris, Crystalis

Source: Levin (2002).[1]

Computer and console games played in a stationary setting are what we traditionally think of when we consider electronic play, but electronic play has become increasingly portable—especially with the advent of Nintendo's Game Boy, and, more recently, with the inclusion of games that can be played on mobile phones and personal digital assistants (PDAs). Nokia offers games on all of its mobile phones, and some think that their complexity and sophistication will soon begin to mirror that of games for computers and consoles (Nokia, 2002).

Mobile phones in and of themselves are becoming a new type of electronic play in some cultures. Approximately 70% of Finnish adolescents and adults, and two out of three Finnish school-aged children, have mobile phones (City of Helsinki, 2002). Children and adolescents use them for instant messaging and for passing jokes and graphics to each other. However, it is too soon to tell whether mobile phones will be used for play in other cultures as they are in Finland.

● WHY DO CHILDREN PLAY THESE GAMES?

There are several striking features about today's video games that partially explain why they are played: (a) their *graphics* and *realism;* (b) their *levels* or graded challenges; and (c) their ways of encouraging *interaction*. Together, these features explain a good deal about why children find electronic play so appealing.

The graphics and realism in today's computer and console games are striking—marvels of technological achievement. What is more, the graphics and realism matter to the children themselves. Ask the average 10-year-old why he or she likes a particular game, and the answer you get is likely to include a reference to its graphics or realism. Sports games not only provide opportunities to play soccer, basketball, or whatever; they also provide realistic representations of well-known sports arenas, real-life "color" commentators (for example, John Madden plays himself in John Madden Football), and all the little gestures that help define a player as being linked to a particular sport (soccer players throwing up their hands when receiving a yellow card, tired-looking basketball players leaning over and gripping the bottoms of their shorts, and so forth). The graphics and realism are there for other types of games as well. Adventure and *role-playing* games draw children into fantastic worlds that momentarily feel quite real, and *simulation* games turn children into bona fide city planners, nineteenth-century pioneers settling the American West, and a host of other roles that children are eager to try on. The graphics and realism make computer and console games wonderfully exciting—as the example of Juan and Miguel's play clearly shows.

Juan: "Quick, go faster, before he catches up! QUICK!!!"

Miguel: "I'm going as fast as I can!"

Juan: (*With fear in his voice*) "He's getting closer . . . GO! GO! GO!"

Miguel: "Oh no, he got me, he got me!"

Someone who heard this conversation between Juan and Miguel out of context might think that they were in danger. In reality, these children are sitting in front of a television with a game console, playing a racing game. To these children, however, it is not just a console game, but a whole other world filled with fantasy and adventure—a world that is just waiting to be explored.

It is important to remember that the concept of realism does not refer to the degree to which a game accurately represents real life; in fact, many games that include realism are quite fantastic in their content. Realism describes how real the game feels to its players—how vivid the depicted world seems to be.

As of this writing, the latest technology to power realism (and interaction) in games is "real-time 3-D," which allows images to be created instantaneously as players progress through a game, unlike the "prerendered" images of earlier technology, whose limited range of possibilities rarely allow players to forget even for a moment that it's only an illusion. The enhanced graphics and freedom of movement of real-time 3-D can elicit physiological responses, such as motion sickness or even vertigo, to perceptions of realistic movement (Keegan, 1999).

As new technology is developed that increases games' realism, many game development companies are making it a goal to blur the line between fantasy and reality, to make it easy for players to forget that they're playing a game. As of this writing the games that exist are already pretty good at blurring fantasy and reality, but developers say that the line between fantasy and reality will get increasingly blurry in the coming years (Simon, 2002).

The blurring of the line between fantasy and reality poses questions for other types of games as well, including Electronic Arts' The Sims, which, as of this writing, has been the best-selling computer game of all time (Simon, 2002). The game involves players creating depicted characters and essentially living out their lives; from building a dream house to making friends to having children to taking out the garbage, The Sims can do it all. In fact, The Sims

Tips and Tricks Archives (http://thesims.ea.com/us/about/tipsandtricks/index.html) resembles the archives of an advice column, with categories such as "Time Management," "Making Big Bucks," "Social Motives," and "Jobs and Careers" that contain items such as "Catching the Carpool," "Neat Freak?," "Family of Eight," "Fading Friendships," and "In the Army Now." Special Expansion Packs allow players to give their Sims pets, take them on a vacation, set them up on dates, and throw house parties (Electronic Arts, 2001). Sims Online makes the game seem even more real by allowing players to put their Sims into a virtual Sim world (Simon, 2002).

The Sims co-creator Will Wright described the game by saying, "You get amazingly immersed in this world. When you're sitting there in the house and having an interesting discussion with other players, you . . . leave your body. I mean, you totally feel like you are in that environment" (Simon, 2002). The creators of The Sims agree that the game has great power to blur the line between fantasy and reality. Players create their Sims and then invest a great deal of time and energy into leading their Sims' lives. The average player of The Sims plays the game for 20 hours a week (Simon, 2002).

In addition to realism, another feature of computer and console games that makes them so attractive to children is their having levels or graded challenges. Take the example of Juan and Miguel's racing game: The goals of this game include passing several driving tests by racing around a track in a certain amount of time, participating in races to earn money, and handling business aspects such as buying new cars and improving existing cars. Players begin the game at a basic level, without a lot of strategy involved. Players pick their cars based on subjective judgments of how fast they might go, using trial and error to figure out how to make the car move. At the next level, players make decisions that solve simple, concrete problems having to do with more than simply going fast. Players now have to pick their cars based on tangible features such as type of tires, engine, and brakes—all to match the particular racecourse laid out before them. Furthermore, while racing, they now need to orient themselves by looking at a map and by changing their view of the track. Doing so helps them know where the competition is and when to speed up or slow down. To succeed at the highest level, players must use complex strategies and think abstractly in order to systematically evaluate different options and to carefully plan their approach to the game. At this level, players must figure out subtleties such as the best timing and speed of braking for particular track conditions so that their cars get around curves quickly and without crashing. To do so, they must think about several relationships simultaneously. Who says electronic play is mindless?

Still another feature of computer and console games that makes them so attractive is their way of encouraging interaction—both in the sense of interaction between the child and the game and in the sense of interaction between the child and other children. Games that are interactive change as a result of players' input (Strommen & Revelle, 1990), which enables them to seem more realistic even within their fantastic context. Interaction can also give children a sense of being in control, which is equally important.

As for games encouraging interaction among children, most console game systems provide ways for more than one player to play at the same time. For computer games, the Internet encourages much more. Right now, children on different continents who have never met can simultaneously play computer and console games together. In addition, the Internet also has created the virtually unlimited potential for players to trade tips and strategies, access demo versions of new games, and form friendships based on their shared interest.

However, interaction is one area in which a difference exists between computer and console game playing. Children are more likely to play console games with their peers physically present than they are computer games. As we will discuss later, there is increasing concern about solitary game playing and game playing whose interaction does not involve physically present peers, concern that this type of electronic play is replacing more interactive types of play.

Photo 6.1   For very young children, electronic play may not stimulate development as well as a good set of blocks, but this isn't true for older children, such as these two girls.

● CHILDREN'S DEVELOPMENT AND ELECTRONIC PLAY

Everything that we have presented so far—about games, game systems, and technology—serves as a context or backdrop for this next discussion of the developmental characteristics of the players themselves.

Infants and Toddlers

Six-month-old Pekka sits on his father's lap in front of the family's computer. Pekka seems interested in the shapes and colors on the screen, peering at the monitor with a fixed gaze. His father decides to move on to another part of the software, which he thinks might interest Pekka even more. A talking bear appears next.

Pekka hears a noise coming from the floor nearby and looks down at his 2-year-old sister Satu, who has just happily discovered the light-reflecting properties of a CD-ROM that she grasps tightly in her hands, still sticky from her forgotten apple slices. Play ends abruptly for both Pekka and Satu, as their father tries to gently pry the CD-ROM away from Satu without diminishing the pleasure and satisfaction she derived from her first independent exploration of technology.

Different shapes, colors, textures, and other physical properties have always been interesting to infants and toddlers; does electronic play make them any more interesting or make their exploration any more beneficial, or at least make their electronic exploration beneficial enough to outweigh the disadvantages?

Electronic play is progressively being developed and marketed with younger children, even infants, in mind. Most software designed for infants is *lapware*, which is geared toward parents and infants using the programs together. However, other than the social interaction and physical contact with their parents, what value does this kind of play have for infants? One study had infants up to 12 months watch either *Sesame Street* or random images with accompanying sounds. The results revealed that there was no difference between how infants attended to *Sesame Street* and how they attended to the random images (Anderson & Evans, 2001). The results of this study make it seem questionable that infants are ready for electronic play. It is important to keep in mind, though, that infants' readiness for electronic play is likely to depend on characteristics of particular games. Perhaps in the future, as we develop a better understanding of electronic play with infants, games may be developed that would be appropriate for these young players.

There is perhaps more potential for electronic play with toddlers, whose cognitive capabilities are expanding to include the ability to symbolize. It seems like ability to symbolize would be a basic requirement for electronic play because so much of electronic play has to do with appreciating the meaning of images or symbols. Time will tell whether enhanced programming and design can truly provide special advantages for toddlers. However, right now, there do not seem to be any special advantages of electronic play over traditional types of toddler play.

There are concerns that electronic play for toddlers may serve as only a negative distraction. An important developmental task for toddlers is the development of a sense of self, which allows them to recognize that they are separate from others and separate from the world around them. The world of electronic play may be too sophisticated for these young children, who are still unclear about the boundaries between themselves and the physical world around them, let alone a world of depicted illusions. Again, as we develop a better understanding of electronic play with toddlers, games may be developed that would be appropriate for them.

Preschoolers

As we have seen elsewhere in this book, the preschool years are in many ways the golden years for play and make-believe. Children have the cognitive ability to engage in make-believe. They can imitate models that are not present and so find in their play ways to reflect on reality (the inner reality of their feelings as well as outer reality). They can construct products in a variety of play media—from block forts, to pictures of home life, to stories using dolls about fairly elaborate fantasy worlds. They can, in short, engage in all kinds of play requiring symbolizing, organizing, and planning—both alone and in cooperation with others. All this makes for very rich play. Equally important, unlike school-aged children, preschoolers don't have to bother themselves with work, so they can focus almost entirely on becoming masters of play.

What special features, then, can electronic play offer preschoolers? The answers are not clear. There are indeed computer and console games for preschoolers, but most, it seems, do not come close to stimulating the mind the way, for example, a good set of wooden blocks can. Preschoolers are focusing on developing fine and gross motor skills through physical exploration, which also helps to facilitate their cognitive development, as they begin to make sense of the world around them. It seems like wooden blocks, with all of their tangible characteristics, would better enable preschoolers to do this than electronic play. Although most types of computer or console games provide children with an opportunity to practice hand–eye coordination, they tend to exclude gross motor skills, and they limit children's exploration to specific activities that are determined by the software and input devices, whereas virtually the only factor that limits children's exploration of wooden blocks is their own imagination. Furthermore, learning important concepts through everyday, real-life experiences provides a richer cognitive experience for preschoolers because this learning takes place within a naturally occurring environment (Lerner, Singer, & Wartella, 2001).

School-Aged Children

Because Juan is better at racing games than Miguel, they decide to switch to Super Mario World, a game that Miguel is good at and enjoys. Miguel has learned that by making Mario jump into one tube rather than another, he can immediately skip from Level 2 to Level 9. But Miguel wants to show Juan some of the other hidden aspects of the game, so he keeps playing without going into the secret tube.

At Level 4, Miguel doesn't make Mario jump soon enough, so Mario falls and Miguel's turn is over. Now it's Juan's turn to play. The two boys continue playing until Juan's older brother arrives to take them to the park to play soccer.

Juan and Miguel are able to figure out some of the more complex aspects of games through trial and error and are able to make decisions about which strategies to use, depending on their goals. Their electronic play experience is social, involving consideration and cooperation, and it is one type of play among many that they enjoy.

By the time children begin their formal schooling, they are ready to appreciate and take advantage of electronic play's special features. Their minds have developed to the point where they can appreciate the graphics and realism of electronic play. Likewise, school-aged children are mentally ready to take on these games' graded challenges and levels of difficulty. Specifically, their newfound capacity to consider two relationships simultaneously allows them to develop the strategies needed to solve the myriad problems posed by most computer and console games. Finally, school-aged children's newfound capacities for perspective taking and for collaborating with peers make them ready to take advantage of electronic play's opportunities for interaction.

However, there are more reasons why school-aged children are ready for electronic play than just those having to do with their cognitive development; the main additional reason is that computer and console games tap into school-aged children's specific interests. As an example, by 7 or 8, many children are passionately involved in organized youth sports, and by 9 or 10, a good many have become avid fans of professional sports. These children often turn to sports games in the realm of electronic play as another way to express their interest and passion.

Adolescents

Alejandro, Serena, and Paul went to Kisha's house after school to play the computer version of Dungeons & Dragons, a role-playing game in which players take on different roles and work together in order to accomplish the particular goals of a quest or adventure. The first step is for each player to decide what kind of character to play—for example, magic user, cleric, thief, fighter, and druid—as well as the character's race—elf, troll, hobbit, orc, human, dwarf, and so on. Players try to minimize the downsides and maximize the upsides of their characters by using points to gain relevant skills. Serena, who is playing a thief, decides to use a lot of her points to gain dexterity, which will help her to sneak into places undetected—an important skill for her character. Paul is playing a wizard for the first time, and he has decided to split most of his points between charisma and wisdom because he thinks these assets will be of great value as his character learns to use spells and manipulate magical powers. Play has already begun; in fact, this is Alejandro's and Kisha's favorite part of the game—balancing the number of points they can use with the types of skills they think their characters will need throughout the course of the game. Now that everyone has generated his or her character, it is time to set off on an adventure, in which the players will try to understand their characters' particular motivations and make effective combinations of their respective skills to accomplish the goals of the quest.

In this game, Alejandro, Serena, Paul, and Kisha are using their developing skills of hypothetical–deductive reasoning and systematic evaluation in order to generate their characters and navigate through the storyline. Dungeons & Dragons also gives them a chance to try out roles that are quite different from who they are in reality; this experimentation can be helpful as they navigate through their own storylines of identity development.

Adolescents, like school-aged children, are also attracted to electronic play for its graphics, realism, graded challenges, and opportunities for interaction. Furthermore, adolescents find in video games important ways to express their passions and specific interests. However, adolescents also are drawn to video games because they offer opportunities to play with identity and challenge authority—two themes that are central to being an adolescent. The example above of Dungeons & Dragons is an example of playing an with identity. Games such as Grand Theft Auto 3 and other seemingly antisocial games are examples of games that challenge conventions and authority.

Photo 6.2 Boys are more likely to play electronic games that feature action, individual prowess, and winning through competition than games that explore social interactions, story lines, and character development.

● GENDER DIFFERENCES AND ELECTRONIC PLAY

As already stated, on average, boys play video games more frequently and for longer periods of time than do girls. Furthermore, they choose different games and different strategies than girls choose (Kafai, 1996). The main differences follow gender stereotypes. Boys are more likely to play games that feature action (shooting, running, etc.), individual prowess, and winning through competition. Girls are more likely to play games that feature in-depth social interactions and character development through story telling—games whose content often features themes about fashion or dating.

There are also gender differences in how electronic play sessions continue and end. Girls, more often than boys, can name characters, describe storylines, and accurately articulate relationships among characters. While playing games, girls tend to work together and socialize, whereas boys tend to focus on competing. Girls also tend to prefer games that have more than one way to win. Girls are more likely to stop playing when they get bored, whereas boys are more likely to stop playing when they either win or lose a game, or when their depicted character runs out of lives (Swanson, 2001).

There are, then, gender differences in game interest, use, and performance. However, these differences are neither universal nor consistent. Fantasy and role-playing games, as well as the popular Where in the World Is Carmen Sandiego?, show equal appeal for boys and girls, and gender differences in performance disappear over time (Kafai, 1996).

The gender differences discussed so far have not been cause for concern. That has not been the case with all gender differences related to electronic play. For example, most popular games present stereotypic views of gender-appropriate behaviors, with female characters depicted as dependent and male characters depicted as dominant (Funk & Buchman, 1996; Swanson, 2001). In addition, a study of video arcade games showed that 92 games of a 100-game sample did not even incorporate female roles (Swanson, 2001). Further research is needed in order to determine the effects that female characters' representation (or lack thereof) may have on children.

COMMON CONCERNS ABOUT ELECTRONIC PLAY ●

Many parents, teachers, and other child development specialists have voiced concerns about possible negative effects of electronic play. Of these, concerns about violence and addiction have been the most pressing.

Violence

The problems that cause *violence* are complicated and many. They include factors of neurology, parenting, and cultural values (Fleming & Rickwood, 2001). Children bring these and other factors into their electronic play, so that any violence following such play cannot be easily attributed to the play itself.

That said, there is research suggesting that violent electronic play may promote violence among a small subgroup of children—those with a predisposition toward violence (Funk et al., 2002). No one yet knows just how and why this happens; further research is needed. But some theories provide explanations that seem to make sense.

So far, hypotheses have been largely based on studies of the effects of television, in which children who have watched violent television programs have imitated the behavior immediately after watching and, in some cases, gone on to display further aggressive or violent tendencies. But a child who simply observes a certain kind of behavior will not necessarily be led to perform the behavior; preexisting normative beliefs about the behavior will help to determine whether the child will in fact perform it (Fleming & Rickwood, 2001).

It appears that children's level of *arousal* may also help to determine whether a child will perform aggressive or violent behavior. Research has shown that electronic play can increase players' arousal, as players manipulate controllers, assume the role of the hero character, fight enemies, or compete for higher scores. Lab studies have shown that computer- and console-game players have increased heart rate, blood pressure, and oxygen consumption after playing. In addition, these effects are greater after engaging in electronic play than they are after engaging in more traditional activities such as watching television, reading, or listening to music (Fleming & Rickwood, 2001). Because heightened arousal can amplify predisposed responses, it is possible that even subtle effects of electronic play could have a greater impact on behavior than other types of play.

Anderson and Bushman (2001) have proposed the *general aggression model* (GAM), which explains this process of violent electronic play promoting aggression and violence in children through the "learning, activation, and application of aggression-related knowledge structures stored in memory (e.g. scripts, schemas)" (p. 355). Situational input variables, for instance exposure to violence through violent computer or console games, can promote aggressive behavior by affecting players' current internal states, which include cognition, affect, and arousal (Anderson & Bushman, 2001).

Exposure to violent media may also have long-term effects, and these effects may have a greater chance of influencing behavior than short-term effects, regardless of predisposing characteristics. Long-term effects of exposure to violent media occur through "the development, rehearsal, and eventual automatization of aggressive knowledge structures such as perceptual schemata (Was this bump accidental or intentional?), social expectations (Are other people expected to be cooperative or vengeful?), and behavioral scripts (insult? retaliation)" (Anderson & Bushman, 2001). So long-term effects result through a gradual increase of aggressive cognitions, which can promote the development of aggressive personality. Even so, such a development would still not necessarily lead to aggression or violence; it would be influenced by personality and situational variables (Anderson & Bushman, 2001).

Researchers are also seeking to understand why some children prefer violent computer and console games to others. Using a technique that employs peer nomination, Wiegman and van Schie (1998) found that seventh- and eighth-grade children who demonstrated a preference for violent games received higher aggression ratings and lower prosocial ratings from their peers. Another study demonstrated a relationship between the preference for violent games and lower self-perceptions in the areas of academic competence and social acceptance in sixth-grade boys (Funk, Buchman, & Germann, 2000). Although these studies do not imply causation, they do indicate that preference for violent computer and console games is associated with several fairly negative conditions.

One factor that complicates the search for causes is the factor of what actually interests children about violent computer and console games; is it the violent content, or is it something else? Games that utilize real-time 3-D tend to be the most popular because of their realism. But these games also tend to include violent content. It could be that a preference for violent games is actually a preference for more realistic games, regardless of their content.

The game Grand Theft Auto 3 (GTA3), released as a PlayStation console game at the end of 2001 and also released as a computer game midway through 2002, provides a good example: The main plot of the game involves "walking around the city mugging, maiming, killing, and car jacking" (Armchair Empire, 2002). However, a unique and particularly appealing aspect of the game is its "fully realized and dynamic" free-form design. This design allows players to entirely disregard the main plotlines and instead explore a virtual city complete with interactive details that make the game one of the most realistic games currently available. Furthermore, unlike many other games, disregarding the violent plotline does not result in play ending through a character's death. But although game playing can continue without following the violent plotline, depicted activities that do follow the plotline earn players more money, which leads to more success in the game. As games like GTA3 become more sophisticated and complex, violence tends to be but one element among many; consequently, the question of why children prefer these games becomes more complex.

Addiction

Is a child who runs home from school to play a computer game for several hours each day addicted? Is extreme frequency or duration enough to demonstrate *addiction*? The answers aren't clear—in part because there is no general agreement about how much is too much, and in part because heavy use of electronic play does not clearly lead to dysfunction. For example, one study conducted in the United Kingdom in the mid- to late 1980s followed a sample of adolescents (96% of whom were male) who identified themselves as having been addicted to video games for a minimum of 5 years. Five years later, most of the participants had been successful academically, had gone on to college, and were successful professionally (Shotton, 1991).

The relatively few studies on electronic game addiction tend to not make their models of addiction explicit, and the measures used are often of questionable reliability or validity. In addition, generalizations are limited by the studies' focusing on different kinds of games and different game systems (Tejeiro, 2001). Still, though current research may be too little and flawed, the concern about addiction seems a real one, warranting further study.

● WHAT ROLE SHOULD PARENTAL GUIDANCE PLAY?

Researchers are hard at work trying to find answers to all of the questions that exist about the world of electronic play, a world that is in a constant state of flux. New technology and new games continue to be developed at a rapid pace, exciting children and raising more questions for parents, teachers, and other child development specialists. Amid all of this, what should parents do? How can parents make effective, well-informed, appropriate decisions regarding their children's electronic play?

There are some resources for parents, who are certainly not alone in wanting to protect children. The Entertainment Software Rating Board (ESRB), a system created by the International Software Developers Association (ISDA)[2] to classify games based on their suitability for particular audiences, gives ratings including E for everyone, ages 3 and above (62% of titles); T for teens, ages 13 and above (25% of titles); M for mature, ages 17 and above (10% of titles); and AO for adults only (ESRB, 2003; Keegan, 1999). But the ESRB's ratings do not necessarily concur with the perspectives of the audiences themselves. Consumers tend to agree with ESRB ratings regarding games that are either obviously nonviolent or extremely violent.

Disagreements tend to occur regarding games that fall in the middle—for instance, games that depict violence among cartoon characters, which have been rated as appropriate for general audiences, a view that is not necessarily shared by all players and parents (Funk, Flores, Buchman, & Germann, 1999).

In 2003, the ESRB created new content descriptors in order to help parents make informed decisions about games that contain depictions of violence. These descriptors will divide violence into four categories: (a) Cartoon Violence, including violent actions involving cartoon characters (a content descriptor assigned to the Crash Bandicoot games); (b) Fantasy Violence, including violent actions of a fantastic nature in situations "easily distinguishable from real life"; (c) Intense Violence, including graphic, realistic depictions of violent actions that may involve weapons, gore, and human injury or death; and (d) Sexual Violence, including depictions of violent acts that are sexual in nature (Newman, 2003; ESRB, 2003). This step may help parents to make judgments that correspond with their values about the appropriateness of games for their children.

Some examples call into question the potential for game developers to inappropriately get around ESRB rating standards. With the current standard, it is possible for a violent game to get a T rating if the red pixels that represent blood are removed. There are other similar loopholes; note that BMX-XXX, a game that features a player bonus of entering a virtual strip club, received a rating of only M.

In addition, though these ratings do exist, they do not guarantee that parents of game players will check the ratings before allowing their children to purchase a game (Walsh, Gentile, Van Overbeke, & Chasco, 2002), and not all retailers have implemented policies that prohibit children and youth from purchasing games rated for adults (Markward, Cline, & Markward, 2001). This is further indication that parental awareness, involvement, and guidance are necessary in order to ensure that children of any age play games that are suitable for their cognitive, emotional, and motor development as well as their emotional maturity and attention span.

It seems like the ESRB is at least off to a good start in developing a fairly reliable tool for parents to use in evaluating their children's game choices. After all, 8 of the top 10 games on the National Institute on Media and the Family's MediaWise Parent Alert list were rated M (the other two were rated T), which means that anyone under 17 years of age should not be playing them. The reality, of course, is that plenty of kids under 17 are playing these games.

It is important to remember that the electronic gaming industry is increasingly focusing on an adult market; the average electronic gamers are in their midtwenties. Electronic play certainly does not present the first incidence of children gaining access to things meant for adults. The gaming industry itself, including game developers, the ESRB, stores that sell or rent games, and companies like Microsoft, whose Xbox game console has parental control capabilities, should be held responsible for only part of the battle. There is no way for children to be kept away from material that is inappropriate for them if parents, teachers, and other child development specialists are not involved; and involvement should mean not only censoring inappropriate material but also providing guidance when exposure to inappropriate material inevitably occurs. We hope that we are moving toward a partnership between the gaming industry and those interested in serving the needs of children.

● CONCLUSIONS

> Almost 5-year-old Sam is preparing to build a sailboat. "This looks like the bottom of a boat," mumbles Sam, eyeing [a] wood scrap speculatively. . . . "But it needs a stick—here," indicating a mast. He rummages further and comes up with a small length of dowel. He smiles. Sam holds the dowel in place, pushing down hard, with the superb confidence of almost-five that it may somehow magically stick. It doesn't. Sam looks puzzled. [After a teacher's suggestion,] Sam applies some glue, inserts the dowel and now has to wait until the glue dries a bit. He is fidgety, but he manages (attention and self-control areas of his brain hard at work). When the boat is completed, the expression on his face is wonderful to behold. . . . Two visitors from the central [school] office enter the room. . . . [T]hey stop to examine some computerized printouts in a wall display. These are "drawings" comprising mostly clip art selected from a menu and "pasted" on with a quick click. They admire these fruits of technology. "Isn't it amazing what today's kids can do?" one comments. Sam watches them. He clutches his boat (Healy, 1998, pp. 216–217).
>
> It is amazing what today's kids can do—both through modern technology *and* through more traditional kinds of play.

Whenever a new type of media has been introduced—radio, film, television, and computer and console games—there has been concern regarding its effects and its suitability relative to other types of media that are viewed as more traditional. Even thousands of years ago, when the written word was first introduced, people were skeptical about what its effects would be: Wasn't conversing better than writing? Would we continue to think as well if we wrote down our thoughts? Through the centuries that followed, we learned that spoken and written language complement each other—that in normative human development, one does not replace the other, and that in questioning which is better, we limit our queries of suitability to specific situations rather than sweeping generalizations. We may discuss whether written or oral examinations are more appropriate for certain topics in academic study, but we do not argue that either written or spoken language is better than the other and should replace the other.

As we have discussed, there are developmental issues regarding the suitability of electronic play for children in different stages of development, and different types of electronic play are more or less appealing for preschoolers versus young adolescents. There are aspects of more traditional types of play—physical, tactile exploration of blocks or trees or baseballs—that are not possible in electronic play. But exploring an Amazon rain forest in a computer game increases the possibilities for a child growing up above the artic circle in Finland. Electronic play offers a great deal in the areas of building and exploring imagined worlds. But more traditional types of play can enrich a child's experience of building and exploring an imagined world in ways that electronic play cannot. Each kind of play has contributions to make to children's enjoyment. Traditional types of play and electronic play can complement each other quite well when play is appropriate and suitable to children's developmental stages and contexts.

SUMMARY ●

Electronic play is a qualitatively different kind of play that is increasing in prevalence around the world. It is particularly common in North America, Europe, and Asia. There are several different types of computer and console games, and it is important to consider their sometimes vastly different characteristics when conducting, analyzing, or interpreting research.

Computer and console games that are currently available, for the most part, are probably not appropriate for infants and toddlers. They become increasingly appropriate for preschool children, whose symbolic thinking, motor skills, and attention span make electronic play more suitable and accessible. Due to their increased cognitive abilities and understanding, school-aged children can truly begin to benefit from the rich world of electronic play. Electronic play can provide a great deal of enjoyment for young adolescents exploring issues of identity and developing more sophisticated cognitive abilities such as hypothetical-deductive reasoning.

Gender differences have been demonstrated with regard to preferences for types of games and frequency of play, as well as in the marketing of games toward boys and girls.

There are several controversial issues that pertain to electronic play. Aggression and violence appear often in game content, and their presence has the potential to exacerbate predispositions for maladaptive behavior. There may be long-term consequences as well. Addiction to computer and console games has been demonstrated, although further research is needed to help identify and define addictive behaviors and their effects over time.

Parental guidance and involvement in children's electronic play is important for children of all ages. Although industry rating systems do exist, they often do not match parental views and concerns. It is important for parents, teachers, and other child development specialists to develop methods of guiding children and being involved in electronic play in ways that satisfy the needs of both parents and their children.

Electronic play has indeed revolutionized the way today's children play, and all signs indicate it will continue to do so. Where electronic play will lead to, no one knows for sure. But one thing is for certain: It will lead in a variety of directions, some good and some not so good. We need, then, to understand its effects on children and how we can help electronic play support children's development.

● KEY WORDS, NAMES, AND IDEAS

Addiction

Affect

Aggression

Arousal

Computer games

Console games

Empire builders

ESRB

First-person shooters

Graphics

Interaction

Levels

Massively multiplayer role-playing games (MMRPGs)

Realism

Real-time strategy

Role-playing games

Simulations

Violence

NOTES ●

1. Personal communication; Levin is a Senior Game Designer for Impressions Software, Cambridge, MA.
2. The ISDA recently changed its name to the Entertainment Software Association (ESA).

CHAPTER 7

ORGANIZED YOUTH SPORTS

W hy have a chapter on organized youth sports in a book on children's play? After all, aren't organized sports more like work than play? And wouldn't a chapter on backyard and alternative sports (for example, skateboarding) be more relevant?

These are legitimate questions. There is indeed a lot about organized youth sports that qualifies as work, not play: drills to promote skills and commands from both coaches and parents to pay attention, get in the ready position, pass the ball, and so forth. The list is long, and of course, there is risk of physical injury. No matter what coaches and parents may say, organized youth sports are never simply about having fun. In fact, for many, organized youth sports are mostly about skill development and winning—what has come to be called the *performance principle* (Coakley, 1998).

In contrast, backyard and alternative sports are almost always about having fun. Children may argue and bicker; some may feel rejected, and occasionally a child will get hurt, but overall, there is no question that child-run, backyard, and alternative sports are play. The made-up rules, the timelessness, the focus on remaining active and having a good time with friends, all suggest that backyard and alternative sports are not just play but are wonderfully rich and meaningful play (Devereux, 1978).

Nevertheless, we focus here on adult-organized youth sports for three reasons. First, the ambiguous status of organized youth sports provides an opportunity to sharpen our understanding of the boundary conditions that define what is and is not children's play. It is all too easy to limit discussion to doll play, rhyming games, *backyard sports*, and other activities that are clearly play. However, in doing so, we never explore the boundaries of where play stops and something else begins. So, we lose an important means for sharpening our definition and deepening our understanding of children's play. Furthermore, by taking on the ambiguous example of organized youth sports, we gain a new perspective on a number of issues, including the issue of whether children have to initiate and control their games in order for them to experience what they are doing as play. And, as the following example indicates, even if it isn't the game itself that children experience as play, it can be the *extra-game activities* that make the whole experience play.

Extra-Game Antics—One Person's Experience

"I took Little League seriously, but I never viewed it as my job. My fondest memories are not of the competition of the games, but rather of the more humorous moments: having a conversation with a fellow outfielder as the ball sailed past, inventing trick plays, and, of course, unsupervised trips to the snack bar."

A second reason for our focusing on organized youth sports is that they have grown and changed tremendously over the past few years. In America, it is estimated that over 35 million children, ages 5 to 13, are now enrolled in youth sports programs (Ewing & Seefeldt, 1996). This is a significant number, but what is most significant is what the number means in terms of what kinds of sports children now play and who plays them.

As we will discuss, organized youth sports in America date back to the Civil War, but until recently, they have always taken a backseat to backyard sports. Furthermore, until recently, organized youth sports meant sports tied to particular seasons and sports mostly for adolescent boys. Today, however, organized youth sports have crowded out backyard sports, have been extended "downward" for children as young as 5, and have secured commitments from families and children to play one sport throughout the year. Add to this list the dramatic changes since the 1960s with respect to girls' involvement in organized sports, and it is clear that organized youth sports constitute a second revolution (besides electronic play) in how today's children play.

A third reason for our focusing on organized youth sports is because they raise legitimate concerns. In previous chapters, we discussed how parents and teachers often worry about children's play when they should not. Well-developed war play and play with imaginary companions were two examples. However, in the case of organized youth sports, there are legitimate concerns about the degree to which adults have taken control. Of particular concern is the degree to which the values emphasized by many adults, those about winning and developing skills, have crowded out the values emphasized by most children, those about players remaining active and being with friends. We focus on organized youth sports, then, because we think readers should become better informed about the problems associated with organized youth sports.

For all these reasons, we discuss organized youth sports as another way of understanding how today's children play. We begin with a historical perspective because history teaches us what is new in the present and what are the enduring issues.

● A HISTORICAL PERSPECTIVE

The Nineteenth Century and Character Development

The development of organized youth sports in America began in earnest following the Civil War (Reiss, 1989; Berryman, 1996; Wiggins, 1996). The Civil War shifted power from the rural South to the industrial North. This shift fueled the American industrial revolution, which, in turn, transformed a rural nation into a nation of cities. The development of organized youth sports was initially promoted to address problems associated with urbanization, problems having to do with youth's character. Nineteenth-century youth leaders worried that urban American youth were going "soft." They saw organized youth sports as substitutes for healthy farm work and, regardless of socioeconomic class, as ways to socialize boys and turn them into men who knew how to work hard, cooperate with others, and pay the price to achieve. Furthermore, they saw character building as having a religious or spiritual meaning and spoke of organized youth sports as promoting "muscular Christianity" (Reiss, 1989).

The clearest example of the muscular Christianity movement occurred with the development of the Young Men's Christian Association (YMCA) and Luther Gulick's leadership of the YMCA Training School in Springfield, Massachusetts. The Training School and other YMCA programs openly promoted organized youth sports as a way to raise boys to become what they defined as Christian men—who combined character traits such as self-control and courage with spiritual values and a healthy, fit body. In many ways, this ideal was not very different from the classic Greek ideal developed thousands of years before.

The Twentieth Century and Nonprofit Agencies

By the beginning of the twentieth century, public school educators had taken the lead in promoting youth sports, and they followed their religious forebears by linking youth sports to *character development*. For example, the educator William Maxwell wrote, "The substitution of controlled athletics for uncontrolled, erratic contests is different only in degree from substituting pure, clean, valuable exercises and sport for the undesirable amusements to which a city subjects a child" (Reiss, 1989, p. 46).

Maxwell's sentiments were those that prompted school systems to sponsor organized youth sports programs such as New York City's Public School Athletic League, founded in 1903. However, schools lost their commitment to organized youth sports as progressive educators questioned the appropriateness of competition for children. By the 1930s, elementary schools had backed away from sponsoring competitive team sports. Instead of school-sponsored competitive sports, children were given programs in physical education. In retrospect, this may have been an ironic mistake because it left a vacuum soon filled by private, nonprofit agencies that, later on, promoted competition to an extreme. Nowhere is this better illustrated than by the immediate success of Little League Baseball.

Interesting Facts: The Beginnings of Little League Baseball

Little League Baseball began as the brainchild of Carl Stotz, a lumber company employee in the small town of Williamsport, Pennsylvania. According to Stotz, the idea of offering a league for children fashioned after the professionals grew from his being dissatisfied with backyard baseball. As a youth, he said, he would sometimes stand in the outfield, bored, as his fellow players argued about whether runners were out or safe. In 1939, when his nephews complained that older boys kept them off a team, Stotz set about finding a sponsor for an adult-run baseball league. After a fall and winter of searching, he found his sponsor, Floyd Mutchler of Lycoming Dairy Farms, whose response to Stotz's inquiry was, "We'll go along with the boys." The real uniforms and other trappings of professional baseball made Little League an immediate success, and today there are over 200,000 teams in all 50 states and in over 100 countries throughout the world (Fine, 1987).

Little League Baseball and Pop Warner Football significantly increased the interest and participation in organized youth sports, though during this time, they never replaced backyard sports, nor did they offer widespread opportunities for girls.

Prior to the 1960s organized youth sports meant organized sports mostly for boys. Girls' bodies and the prescribed roles for women made the rigors and risks of most sports unsuited for girls, or so it was assumed. Yes, there were sports for girls, but the rules often slowed the sports down and robbed them of excitement. For example, in girls' basketball, a girl could dribble only twice before she had to shoot or pass the ball.

The civil rights era of the 1960s and the feminist movement of the 1970s brought significant changes to organized youth sports. Through legal battles and shifting public opinion, girls joined boys to play on the same teams or on teams in competitive leagues of their own. The general public gave up erroneous views about girls' bodies not being suited for rigorous sports, and as more and more mothers joined the workforce, parents found that the reasons for promoting sports for boys applied to girls as well. Finally, Congress enacted legislation to ensure that college women athletes had equal opportunities to those afforded men, thus giving parents added incentive to encourage their daughters to get involved in team sports.

Interesting Facts: Allowing Girls to Play Little League Baseball

In 1973, the New Jersey Division of Civil Rights brought a lawsuit against Little League Baseball on behalf of Maria Pepe, a girl from Hoboken who had been kept from playing Little League Baseball. At the trial, an expert witness for Little League Baseball argued that girls' relatively weak bone structure could not take the rigors of baseball. Later, an expert witness for Maria Pepe demonstrated how girls' bone structure is actually stronger than that of boys and that the League's witness had relied on data drawn from the study of adult cadavers! Legal proceedings continued until Congress amended the National Little League Charter to allow girls to participate (Wiggins, 1996).

Organized Youth Sports Today

New Sports, New Schedules, New Pressure

For previous generations, sports for children were tied to seasons, typically football and field hockey in the fall, basketball and ice hockey in the winter, and baseball and softball in the spring. Now, more and more children are playing one sport throughout the year. This means that children today are being trained to perform at higher skill levels than ever before. Furthermore, most children who play one sport year-round also play other sports, which means sports now compete with one another. Children today often have to choose between participating in a "very important" baseball playoff game and a "very important" soccer tournament. There is, then, a pace and pressure about today's organized youth sports not experienced by previous generations of children.

Another recent development has been the popularity of comparatively new sports, soccer being the prime example. As recently as 1980, books on organized youth sports hardly mentioned soccer. Yet today, in many communities across America, soccer rules. Soccer's meteoric rise can be explained in a number of ways, two in particular. First, soccer is a sport that even very young children can play. Given a ball to kick and a field with a couple of goals, children as young as 5 can achieve the semblance of soccer. The same cannot be said for sports such as baseball and football, where the skills required and the risks of injury prevent small children from playing the game. Second, soccer emphasizes what children want most from sports— constant action and full participation. That is, soccer allows lots of children to participate and remain active for most of the game. This contrasts sharply with other sports such as baseball, where a young child waiting in the outfield is apt to "space out" and lose interest in the game. Of course, the rise of organized youth soccer would probably not have happened had backyard sports continued to dominate. In backyard sports, the rules and equipment can be changed dramatically to accommodate even small children in games of baseball, football, or whatever.

In fact, the most significant change in youth sports today may be the change to emphasizing organized sports over backyard sports. Dramatic decreases in outdoor play space, decreases in the number of mothers at home to attend to children playing outdoors, and decreases in the perception that neighborhoods are safe—all these decreases help explain the shift in emphasis from backyard to organized youth sports (Coakley, 1998; Rivkin, 1998).

Sponsoring Programs

To fully understand organized youth sports, one needs to understand the differences among the kinds of sponsoring programs. Today's organized youth sports programs come in three main types. They are (a) community-based *recreational programs;* (b) *Nonprofit agency-based programs;* and (c) *club programs.* The key differences among them have to do with the level of intensity and commitment.

Community-based recreational sports programs are what their title suggests. Town and neighborhood leaders set up a sports program for children from the community. Compared with other types of sports programs, community recreational programs are the least intense and make the fewest demands. However, this is not always the case, especially when communities set up divisions and when community leaders and parents become intent on winning and developing champion teams. This can happen especially on Division 1 teams.

By far the most popular type of youth sports program is the nonprofit agency, such as Little League Baseball and Pop Warner Football. Nonprofit, agency-sponsored youth sports programs are run by volunteers. There are volunteer commissioners, volunteer boards of directors, and volunteer coaches—usually the parents of children on the teams they coach. Nonprofit, agency-sponsored sports are run according to national rules that pertain to both playing the games and choosing the teams.

In nonprofit, agency-sponsored youth sports programs, teams are usually chosen through a draft. Coaches take turns selecting players, sometimes with ratings from previous seasons to guide their selection. Drafts help ensure that teams are comparable with respect to ability. Unfortunately, they often fail to ensure that children play on a team with friends.

Club sports are the most intense and demand the greatest commitment. These are for-profit agencies that charge fees for professional coaching. To develop more competitive teams, club sports keep children together on the same team from year to year. Because club teams are all about skill development, they are in constant search of top competition. This means traveling—usually within state but sometimes out of state as well. Club sports programs are especially common for soccer.

Youth sports programs of all types sponsor regular season games, which can have a relaxed atmosphere. They also sponsor play-offs and tournaments where the atmosphere can be anything but relaxed. For many coaches and parents, play-offs and tournaments are serious business, and the children know it.

We have described these various types of youth sports programs for two basic reasons: First, how children experience organized youth sports is deeply affected by the type of program they are in. Second, there are critics who argue that many of the negative excesses in youth sports programs should be addressed first by examining the way youth sports programs are organized. For example, Bigelow, Moroney, and Hall (2001) argues that the best way to achieve true reform is to start by eliminating elite teams and drafts.

Bigelow also questions the validity of the performance principle, the principle that drives parents and coaches to promote skill development and winning even if it means keeping children stuck in undesirable positions or inactive and on the bench, or excluding children altogether. He notes that there are many superstars in professional sports who, as children, were neither coached nor good athletes. However, Bigelow's questioning gains even more credence when we take a cross-cultural perspective—as when we compare youth baseball as it is played in America and as it is played in the Dominican Republic.

On a per capita basis, the Dominican Republic may well turn out more professional baseball players than any other country in the world, and yet adult-organized baseball for children is virtually absent. What is even more remarkable is the fact that boys in the Dominican Republic play the backyard game of *vitalla* rather than baseball, as the boxed example describes.

Playing *Vitalla* in the Dominican Republic

Vitalla refers to the plastic cap on a 5-gallon glass water container used in the Dominican Republic. The game of *vitalla* is played with one of these plastic caps and a sawed-off broomstick. Pitchers throw the *vitalla* much like one would throw a small Frisbee, only overhand. Throwing it fast allows it to move with lots of curves and surprises. As for the rules of the game, it is much like the American game "three flies in." Runs are scored when a hit *vitalla* rolls to a stop before an opponent grabs it. Three swinging strikes, and the batter is out.

Boys play *vitalla* almost every day of the week—and in their own barrio. The closeness of the houses, the fact that everyone knows everyone else in the barrio, and the fact that traffic on the streets is light and slow moving mean the children can play *vitalla* unsupervised. When they are 14 or 15, the boys might switch to baseball, but even then, *vitalla* remains a favorite.

AGE CHANGES AND ORGANIZED YOUTH SPORTS •

Accommodating Children's Age and Stage

When discussing age and organized youth sports, one issue in particular is likely to come up, namely the issue of *readiness* for competition (Passer, 1996). A second issue is what coaches should teach children of different ages. The concern here is that children be challenged but not so much that they are overwhelmed.

In their backyard sports, children become masters at matching their games to different ages and levels of maturity. If it is a younger, less-skilled child at bat, players may give him an extra strike. If a child is much older, they may make him bat lefty. Such dramatic accommodations do not occur in organized youth sports because adults keep the games as close to the "real thing" as possible. In this practice, one might well ask, "Who is more confused about fantasy and reality: adults or children?"

However, in most organized youth sports, there is some accommodation to age. We see this in the special equipment for younger children, in the smaller playing fields, and in the modification of rules. For example, for games with young children, soccer balls and basketballs are much smaller. Baseballs are much softer, and fields and courts are shortened and narrowed. In general, the games are miniaturized.

As for rules, organized sports for younger children may include new rules and exclude old ones so as to keep the game moving. For example, in organized baseball for younger children, stealing is not allowed because catchers can't throw accurately to second, and in organized youth soccer, off-sides is allowed because young children have a hard time keeping track of where they are in relation to others.

The Issue of Readiness

Perhaps the greatest challenge to match the game to a child's age and stage comes in deciding when and how to teach skills. Anyone coaching children has to have at least an intuitive sense of what children at different ages can and cannot do. At 7, children playing soccer can be taught to keep their distance from teammates and not swarm around the ball, but few 7-year-olds can be taught to touch pass.

From a psychological point of view, much about readiness has to do with how many relationships and perspectives a child can consider simultaneously. Younger players let their perceptions control their actions, as when, in soccer, a moving ball pulls them in its direction—what Coakley (1998) refers to as *beehive soccer* (to capture the way young children swarm around the ball). Older players are more likely to let thinking control their actions, as when they resist heading for a moving soccer ball in order to position themselves to receive a pass from a teammate. In the first instance, there is only one relationship considered, that between the child and the ball. In the second instance, there are at least two relationships, one between the child and the ball and the other between the child and her teammate. This example shows just how cognitively challenging team sports are for children.

As for the more social-emotional challenges, players in competitive team sports need to be motivated to focus and attend, and they must have enough self-control to tolerate the anxieties and frustrations that accompany competitive team sports (Magill & Anderson, 1996). This is a lot to ask of young children, which is why they need lots of support to play organized team sports. But what does it mean to provide support for the more social and emotional challenges in organized team sports? Two examples may clarify.

The first example is one in which the coach used *strategic positioning* to help a child focus and attend. One 9-year-old on a Little League Baseball team stood out for having only minimal ability to pay attention. If positioned in the outfield, he spaced out, sometimes by turning his back on the game. To address this problem, the coach moved the boy to catcher. At catcher, the boy had to attend because thrown pitches were coming right at him.

The second example is one in which the coach used a technique known as *reframing* to prepare children to handle anxiety, frustration, and losing. Noting that his players might be overwhelmed by the intensity of the upcoming end-of-the-season play-offs, one baseball coach sat players down beforehand and renamed the play-offs "off-season play."

Age and maturity, then, figure into how organized youth sports should be coached and how coaches can help make children ready. We see here just how important a coach can be. We turn, then, to the role of the coach.

COACHES ●

The focal point of organized youth sports, the point where everything comes together, is the coach. The coach makes it all work well or poorly. The coach sets the tone, the overall climate for the team, and which values get emphasized—whether winning and performance will be paramount or whether participating and having fun will be enough. The coach determines what and how skills are taught and when and where players will be positioned. A good coach can make a bad system work well, and a bad coach can make a good system work poorly. To understand organized youth sports, then, one needs to understand what makes for a good coach.

Here, we focus on three essentials of *good coaching;* First, good coaches know how to teach requisite skills to children of varying abilities. Second, good coaches know how to manage the *value conflicts* that are inherent in organized sports for children. Third, and most important, good coaches know how to cultivate positive relationships with children. Add to this list the ability to foster family and community involvement, and you have a composite picture of an excellent coach.

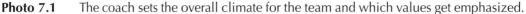

Photo 7.1   The coach sets the overall climate for the team and which values get emphasized.

Most head coaches are parents with experience playing high school sports. Most have one of their own children on their team. Furthermore, contrary to the negative stereotypes in the media, most receive positive evaluations from players and parents (Fine, 1987; Coakley, 1998). This does not mean, however, that most coaches for children are good or even adequate.

Especially with regard to teaching skills, coaches today have a lot to learn. Bigelow et al. (2001) points out that those coaching children often assume that their high school athletic experience is enough to qualify them to coach children, even though these same coaches do not assume that their high school academic experience qualifies them to teach English, math, or history. No wonder, then, that there are often subtle and widespread deficiencies in the way amateur coaches teach skills.

To teach the skills needed to play sports requires an ability to break down complex skills into their component parts and to explain these parts using words children can understand. Take teaching defense in lacrosse as an example. One key to good defense is having defenders come at an attacker from opposite sides, what one clever coach referred to as "making an attacker sandwich." Unfortunately, such cleverness is not common in teaching skills to children.

Soccer 101: Coaching Over Children's Heads

Before the soccer game, the coach corralled his 10-year-olds to give them last-minute instructions. With a small chalkboard, he made X's indicating different positions on the field, and in less than a minute he covered several different possible offenses and defenses for the children to consider during the course of the game. Even experienced onlookers had trouble following what he was explaining. As for the 10-year-olds, they seemed totally nonplussed.

Take another example from baseball. One of the *component skills* in hitting a baseball has to do with the batter putting weight on his or her back foot before and throughout most of the swing. This is not an impossible skill to teach. However, not many parent coaches teach it because not many know it needs to be taught. Instead of learning this component skill, children are told to "Keep your eyes on the ball" and "Swing hard"—not very helpful. The result is that many children fail to develop as hitters and so become frustrated, lose interest, and quit.

The second essential in coaching children is having the motivation and ability to manage value conflicts. Unlike high school sports for adolescents, organized sports for children need to balance the values of skill development and winning with the values of everyone participating and staying active in the game. Achieving this balance is harder than one might think. No child wants to be on a team that constantly loses, so coaches have to keep the team competitive. However, no child wants to sit on the bench or be stuck in undesirable positions, so coaches have to get children into the game as much as possible and put them in positions that satisfy them.

This tension between staying competitive and having everyone participate calls for creative strategies and compromises. For example, before stealing is allowed in Little League Baseball, the key positions for keeping a team competitive are pitcher, shortstop, and first base. Furthermore, the only positions children generally do not like are positions in the outfield. So, a coach can manage the *competitive-participation conflict* by having the better players at shortstop, first base, and pitcher while rotating the rest in and out of third base, second base, and catcher. This compromise may not work for everyone, but it works well enough.

Of the three essentials for coaching children, knowing how to relate to children is by far the most important. Coaches can be weak on teaching skills and not so good at managing value conflicts, but they must be good at relating to children. This means they must know how to encourage and guide rather than command and direct, and they must know how to communicate that they care more about the child than about winning. Bigelow et al. (2001) suggests an 80% rule stating that all coaches should be smiling at least 80% of the time. His point isn't meant to be taken literally. Rather, it is meant to underscore the need for coaches to remain positive in their relationships with children and not act like the coach in the following example.

When Fear Strikes

On a Little League team, one shy 11-year-old had a particular fear of getting hit by the ball. The coach seemed almost outraged. Pulling the boy aside, the coach handed him the ball and demanded that he throw it at the coach's stomach as hard as he could. The boy threw the ball, which struck the recommended target. Without flinching or showing emotion, the coach then handed the ball back to the boy and in a stern voice said, "See, it doesn't hurt. Go back and stop being afraid." Now, the boy was no longer afraid. He was terrified—not so much of the baseball, but of his coach, who he thought was crazy.

● PARENTS AND ORGANIZED YOUTH SPORTS

It is impossible to fully understand what organized youth sports mean to children without mentioning their parents. Parents not only determine whether children get involved in youth sports. To a great extent, they also determine how their children will experience youth sports. Will sports be emphasized and valued? Will there be someone to pay for equipment and agency fees, someone to provide transport to games, someone to practice with at home, and someone to talk sports with at the dinner table? These and other questions all have to do with *parental involvement*.

What are the issues with respect to parental involvement? Two in particular warrant special attention. The first has to do with the fit between parents' interests and those of their children. The second has to do with the degree to which parents become involved.

Parents with more than one child often remark about how different their children are from one another and from themselves, as well. From the very beginning, each child has his or her own temperament, personality, and identity. The differences lead inevitably to parents and children developing different interests. Good parents find ways to support their children's positive interests, despite possible differences between their own interests and those of their children. However, it is not always easy. When there isn't a match, it is all too easy for parents to push or neglect.

The issue of involvement is not so easy to evaluate. Some parents remain relatively uninvolved. They do not play sports at home, talk sports, or attend their children's games. Others get so involved that their lives revolve around their children's games. Most parents fall somewhere in between.

At first glance, the extremes may seem problematic. However, this is not always the case. As Bigelow et al. (2001) points out, for years parents were relatively uninvolved in their children's sports compared with parents today, and their children did just fine. On the basis of this observation, Bigelow advises parents to become less involved so that children can take back some of the control lost to them when parents became involved. As for the opposite extreme, some families become especially close by using sports as a way to connect to one another. Finding the right degree of involvement is, then, something relative to each family. That said, overinvolvement can indeed be a serious problem, as we will discuss shortly.

SERIOUS PROBLEMS IN ORGANIZED YOUTH SPORTS ●

If the only problems in organized youth sports were those mentioned so far, the situation would not be too serious. The fun and excitement of the games would outweigh the problems. However, there are serious problems that do, unfortunately, outweigh everything. There are serious problems having to do with putting so much pressure on children that they burn out and quit sports. There are serious problems having to do with coaches and parents treating children poorly, and there are serious problems reflecting the larger societal problems of violence, discrimination, and poverty.

Burnout: One College Student's Autobiographical Account

I put on my first pair of ice skates when I was 2 years old. I took tons of lessons, spent countless hours at practice, and spent even more time practicing off the ice and watching ice-skating on TV. When I got older, I joined the local precision team. I also skated competitively as a soloist. I had a team of adult managers, choreographers, coaches, instructors, costume designers, and my mother. The equipment and fees were tremendously expensive. The skates alone were at least $700, and I needed new skates every new season.

At first competing and performing was fun, but after a while, I didn't know what or whom I was doing it for. I was on a routine where I had to get up at 5:00 in the morning, skate for 2 hours before school, go to school all day, skate after school from 2:30 until 6:00, go home and do my homework for a few hours, eat dinner, go to bed, and start the cycle all over again. It was grueling. After a while, I hated going to the rink. I was rude to my coaches. I was sloppy in my routines. I skipped practices. When I turned 12, I had to start watching my weight because I had to wear tight spandex outfits and skate next to all these skinny girls. So when I turned 13, I quit.

I miss it at times, but I don't want to do sports like that ever again. There was too much pressure. I felt that if I messed up, I let everybody down. So my experience with ice-skating was not all fun and games.

One of the root causes of serious problems such as burnout has to do with adults living *through* children rather than *for* them—what has been called *achievement by proxy*. Achievement by proxy can lead to coaches and parents treating children poorly. Coaches treat children poorly when, in order to win, they keep less-skilled players sitting on the bench or stuck in undesirable positions. They treat children poorly when children are drafted onto teams without any of their friends. They treat children poorly when they yell and push children beyond their limits, and they treat children poorly when they submit children to endless, boring drills.

Parents treat children poorly when they overcoach from the sidelines, when they bark out directives that cause *cognitive overload*. Watch any child playing basketball trying to find someone to pass to, and watch what happens when a parent or coach starts yelling out directives. Often the child freezes—leading to the ball being stripped by an opposing player. This is what is meant by cognitive overload, and because it means a bad experience for children, it is an example of treating children poorly.

Finally, coaches and parents treat children poorly when they fail to protect children from overuse injuries. Today's equipment does a reasonable job of minimizing the kinds of injuries that are inevitable in sports—ankle sprains, bruises, and the like. However, equipment cannot protect children from developing overuse injuries—chronic inflammations caused by the kinds of repetitive activities associated with skills training and keeping children at some particular task (e.g., pitching a baseball) that their growing bodies are not able to support (Lord & Kozar, 1996).

The other types of severe problems, those stemming from larger societal issues, can be even more serious. One such serious problem is violence. For example, not long ago outside Boston, Massachusetts, one father killed another who was coaching and refereeing a game—because the first father thought the second was encouraging the children to be too rough!

However, despite what the newspaper headlines report, violence in organized youth sports is rare, and focusing on rare acts of violence may mask a far more common and insidious problem: namely, the problem of coaches and parents being uncivil. On playing fields and in arenas everywhere, it is not uncommon to see coaches and parents yelling at young referees and at the children playing. Such behavior may not constitute physical violence, but it is verbal violence that makes for an uncivil society.

Racism is another of societal problem that causes serious problems in organized youth sports. Racism in youth sports used to mean segregated sports. Today, racism shows up in different ways. It shows up in how African American children are sometimes stereotyped—as when they are assumed to be interested in basketball and assumed to have natural talents for sports. It shows up in the added pressures on children of color to gain respect through sports. It shows up in the undue demands for poor minority children to become professionals. It shows up, then, in the way sports for children of color can become serious business rather than simply fun (Coakley, 1998).

Case Study: Segregated Youth Sports

In 1956, an all-black Little League baseball team in North Carolina came in first in its division because the white teams had forfeited their games rather than play against them. Their being first qualified them to

(Continued)

(Continued)

go to the Little League World Series in Williamsport. When they arrived in Williamsport, they were allowed to practice with the other teams but not to compete. The Little League directors said they were disqualified because they had won their division through forfeits. The boys could only watch the others play and then return home after a long and very hard bus ride.

The societal problems of poverty and disability are also problems effecting youth sports. Poverty does so because the registration fees and expensive equipment needed to support organized youth sports often prevent poor children from participating. This may be especially true for today's children from low-income families because organized youth sports have become so privatized (Coakley, 1998).

Having a disability also presents a serious problem with regard to children participating in organized youth sports. Without programs such as Special Olympics and wheelchair basketball, children with disabilities would be largely relegated to the sidelines. However, with such programs, children with disabilities can experience the same joys of participating and competing that typical children experience.

Special Olympics

In the early 1960s, after starting a day camp for people with mental retardation, Eunice Kennedy Shriver developed the concept of Special Olympics; she saw then that individuals with mental retardation were far more capable in sports and physical activities than many experts thought them to be. In 1968, she organized the First International Special Olympics Games, held at Soldier Field in Chicago, Illinois. One thousand athletes with mental retardation from 26 states competed. Since then, millions of children and adults with mental retardation have participated in Special Olympics track and field events, bowling, basketball, football, and aquatics. At the start of the games, each participant takes the Special Olympics oath: "Let me win. But if I cannot win, let me be brave in the attempt."

Photo 7.2   Adults continue to think of organized sports in terms of skill development and character development and not simply in terms of sports being played.

ORGANIZED YOUTH SPORTS AS PLAY? ●

We opened this discussion with the promise that organized youth sports helps us explore the boundaries of play. So how has this discussion delivered on that promise? Are organized youth sports play? We think our discussion answers this question with "It all depends." It all depends on the experience of the child. If the experience is one of fun, excitement, and connection, then organized youth sports are indeed play, regardless of how they are controlled. If, however, they are boring, hurtful, or unduly stressful, then they are not even bad play.

For most children, it appears that organized youth sports are play. The excitement of playing the games, of developing and showing off new skills, of competing successfully, and of being with friends and friendly adults makes for a very positive experience. Add to this list the extra-game antics that often accompany youth sports, and one can't help but agree with the children that, for the most part, youth sports are play.

It all depends, then, on a child's experience, which, as we have learned, depends on how adults organize that experience, how skills are taught, how value conflicts are managed, and how relationships are formed. It all depends on whether adults organize and direct with children in mind, whether they meet children's needs and support children's wishes, whether they attend to what the ball does to the child and not just to what the child does to the ball.

● CONCLUDING REMARKS

Throughout this book, there has been a lot said about play rhetorics, particularly about the *rhetoric of progress*. Once again, the rhetoric of progress sees play as preparing children for the future by promoting their cognitive, social, emotional, and physical development. And as discussed in the introduction, though the rhetoric of progress may look like the friend of children's play, at times it can be the rationale for adults wrongly taking control of children's play. Nowhere do we see this more clearly than in organized youth sports.

As we have seen in this chapter, adults have taken control of youth sports for a good many reasons having to do with children's development. The muscular Christianity movement took control to promote children's spiritual development. The Public School Athletic League of New York City took control to promote children's character development. Carl Stotz started Little League Baseball because he thought child-run baseball was not good for children.

Today, the rhetoric of progress continues to justify adults keeping control of the games—especially in the way youth sports continue to be thought of as character building—through their demanding discipline, commitment, teamwork, and good sportsmanship. To the adults involved, organized youth sports are, then, not simply recreation. They are moral endeavors.

But how much of this rhetoric about character building is a cover for adults stealing the games for their own goals? How much of this rhetoric of progress masks adults' arbitrary disdain for the diffuse organization of children's games? How much masks adults' need to be entertained? How much masks adults' need to achieve by proxy? These and other questions must continue to be asked as a way to monitor the games, as a way to ensure that the games exist not for the benefit of adults but for the benefits that children get from their play.

In closing, so as to keep organized youth sports in perspective, it might be worth recalling how much can be learned in backyard sports run by children. Here is Edward Devereux (1978) reminiscing about his own childhood experience:

"We learned a lot of other kinds of things which are probably more important for children between the ages of eight and twelve. Precisely because there was no official rule book and no adult or even other child designated as rule enforcer, we somehow had to improvise the whole thing; this entailed endless hassles about whether a ball was fair or foul, whether a runner was safe or out, or more generally, simply about what was fair. We gradually learned to understand the invisible boundary conditions of our relationships to each other. Don't be a poor sport or the other kids won't want you to play with them. Don't push your point so hard that the kid with the only catcher's mitt will quit the game. Pitch a bit more gently to the littler kids so they can have some fun, too; besides, you realize that you must keep them in the game because numbers are important. Learn how to get a game started and somehow keep it going, as long as the fun lasts. How to pace it. When to quit for a while to get a round of cokes or just to sit under a tree for a bit. How to recognize the subtle boundaries indicating that the game is really over—not an easy thing, since there are no innings, no winners or losers—and slide over into some other activity . . . mostly on to the endless variety of other games, pastimes, and interests which could so engage a young boy on a summer afternoon or evening." (p. 122)

Maybe, then, we should think less about how adults, in organizing youth sports, can teach skills and build character and more about how adults can give the games back to the children.

KEY WORDS, NAMES, AND IDEAS ●

Achievement by proxy

Backyard sports

Character development

Club programs

Cognitive overload

Community-based recreational programs

Competitive-participation conflict

Component skills

Extra-game activities

Good coaching

Nonprofit agency–based programs

Organized youth sports

Parental involvement

Performance principle

Readiness

Reframing

Rhetoric of progress

Strategic positioning

Value conflicts

PART III

Major Settings
for Children's Play

P art III is devoted to major settings for play. Here we look at home and outdoor play as well as play in schools. In this part more than in the others, we see cultural-ecological perspectives at work. Here, we explore how different physical and social environments have profound effects on children's play. Here, too, we see how development never occurs in a vacuum, and how impossible it is to separate children's development from children's participating in particular environments.

CHAPTER **8**

HOME AND
OUTDOOR PLAY

An Adult Remembering Her Childhood

When I was young, I would visit my friend's house and play outside in their backyard. Each of us had a horse that lived there, invisible to all except us. We would spend hours grooming, feeding, and training our horses. Then we would gallop around the backyard for hours. When my friend's mother would occasionally step out the back door, we would instantly stop our play because it was too personal to share.

Homes and neighborhoods have always been the most important settings in which children play, simply because they are where children play the most. In homes and neighborhoods, children spend countless hours playing with their toys, friends, and siblings. Sometimes they even play with their parents, though not so often as one might expect (Bloch & Pellegrini, 1989).

Of course, *home* and *neighborhood* can have different meanings to different children: a rural farm, a suburban mansion, a two-family dwelling outside a city, or an apartment in the heart of an urban center, to name a few. Regardless of meanings, play can take similar forms, such as an infant's banging on kitchen pots and an older child's playing ball outside.

However, with respect to how children play, the differences between different homes and different neighborhoods can matter a great deal. They can matter in physical ways. For example, wealthy homes supply more expensive toys, and crowded urban neighborhoods restrict outside play (Garbarino, 1989). Neighborhoods can matter in social ways as well. For example, children from wealthier homes often have less time for free play because of their being placed in so many adult-organized activities (Elkind, 1981). In this chapter, we discuss the ways in which homes and neighborhoods generally support play and also discuss how differences in home-neighborhood environments produce differences in how children play.

Talking about homes, neighborhoods, and their influence on play provides an opportunity to adopt a cultural-ecological perspective, one that equips us to ask the right questions about settings. What are those questions? We suggest that there are three.

First, there is the question about how the physical attributes of homes and neighborhoods influence play. Second, there is the question about how the social attributes of homes and neighborhoods influence play. Third, there is the question of how homes and neighborhoods are themselves influenced by other settings (e.g., school and workplace) and by the historical era and culture in which they are found. Here, we explore all three questions as well as questions about designing homes and neighborhoods to support play.

Throughout this chapter, we are concerned with what cultural-ecological psychologists refer to as *environmental press* (Garbarino, 1989) or the combined and interacting forces in a child's environment that partially account for how a child plays. The key words here are *combined* and *interacting*, because no one force acts alone or is unaffected by the other forces, including forces from within a child.

Concerning this last point, the words *setting* and *environment* are to be thought of here as outside children, but only for the sake of discussion. In reality, and from a psychological standpoint, it is difficult to say what is outside the child. The same settings and the same environments from an observer's perspective can be experienced quite differently by different children. For example, one 4-year-old may experience a large, knotty tree as something to stay clear of because it looks scary, whereas a 7-year-old might experience it as something to climb. In one sense, the tree is the same tree regardless of child. In another sense, it is two trees because of the different experiences of each child. We must keep this in mind when speaking about home and neighborhood environments and never assume they are experienced the same way for every child.

THE HOME SETTING AND CHILDREN'S PLAY ●

In this section, we look at the home setting in terms of how space is designed, what toys and play materials are provided, and what kinds of practices encourage or discourage play. However, issues of space, toys, play materials, and practice all exist within a particular culture and historical time. It is impossible to understand these issues without first understanding something about family life today and how it has changed so much from family life in previous generations, at least in many industrialized societies.

One of the main overarching issues today is how families are handling the age-old dilemma of balancing children's needs with those of adults.

As David Elkind (1994) has argued, today's families have, in many ways, accommodated adults at the expense of children. Divorce is acceptable, so fewer unhappy couples are staying together "for the sake of the kids." Many homes, then, are single-parent homes or homes with blended families where the stresses to make home life work well are often greater than when there is more than one amicable caregiver to share the load. And, of course, family life has changed as women have taken up careers (Belsky, Lerner, & Spanier, 1984). It is telling that one popular parenting book today is titled *The Family Manager's Guide for Working Moms* (Peel, 1997). All these changes have changed homes as places to play.

Commercialization of Toys

The changes present a paradox. On the one hand, the changes are about added stress and an erosion of the old commitment to creating for children a protected niche, that is, protected from adult subjects such as marital troubles and work pressures—a niche that lends itself to play. On the other hand, and perhaps to compensate for these recent developments, children in industrialized societies (at least children from families who are not poor) have an incredible array of toys, children's TV programs, and child-centered activities to entertain themselves and to use to play. The result has been the creation of conditions in which play is more solitary than it used to be. Nowhere is this more evident than in the commercialization of toys.

Today, toys are big business, as any glance at children's television shows and toy superstores reveals. With respect to supporting children's play, this would seem to be a good thing, and indeed, children seem eager to explore the variety of available toys. However, some worry that the commercialization of toys has changed the function of toys in ways that may not be good for children. Stephen Kline (1995) worries that today's toys suppress autonomous imagination in favor of children using toys to connect to peers around themes, stories, and characters seen on television. David Elkind (2003) agrees and adds that unlike toys in the past, today's toys have little to do with introducing young people to adult life (superhero play, violent video games, etc.). He writes,

> They now create toys to please children without regard to their relevance to adult life or to their congruence with parental values and morals. In effect, toymakers have employed a child centered approach to attain adult centered goals, namely to turn children into consumers. It is just this practice which can be called the commercialization of childhood. (p. 3)

Finally, with respect to scholars who worry about the commercialization of toys, Brian Sutton-Smith notes how the giving of toys by parents has become a way to keep children occupied and alone (Sutton-Smith, 1995). He writes, "In effect, the parent says, 'I give you this toy to bond you to me; now go and play with it by yourself'" (p. 141).

But lest thoughts about the commercialization of play get us too depressed, consider the following examples, which suggest that, thankfully, children do not always use toys in prescribed ways. In fact, the way children use toys suggests that there may not be a true educational toy, for it isn't the toy itself that is educational but the use to which the child puts the toy—a sobering thought for those who feel that the toy industry has too much influence on how children play.

It was Christmas and my parents had been up all night assembling a child-sized kitchen play set. It had a mini microwave that made sounds, a coffeemaker, an ice dispenser, and a light that turned on in the little fridge. My parents were so proud of the toy. But when the time came to open toys, I ran down the stairs to find the most wonderful of all the toys. It was the cardboard box that had come with the kitchen play set! For the next hour or so, that cardboard box became my castle and fire station.

Construx was a popular Lego-style toy in the late 1980s. It was popular with parents because they thought of Construx as stimulating spatial thinking and leading children to become budding engineers. Children, of course, thought of Construx in other ways. For example, in one western Massachusetts town, two brothers used the Construx to make highly attractive Construx swords, which they then proceeded to play fight with.

But are today's homes less well designed for quality play than they used to be, as the critics suggest? It's hard to tell. On the one hand, everything that the critics of change say is true. On the other hand, there is today a focus on designing homes and outdoor spaces where children can play in rich and enjoyable ways that is unparalleled in history, as the rest of this discussion will attest.

Designing Play Space in the Home

In the "good old days" alluded to by the critics of today's family life, homes were not designed or organized with children in mind. For one thing, children generally were not given free access to play in major living areas (Johnson, 1987). For example, in many homes, living rooms were kept as showplaces for special occasions such as adult parties.

Today, however, there is at least a heightened awareness that access to major living spaces is valuable for children (Weinstein & David, 1987). Today's architects and designers understand that children, especially very young children, need to be in proximity to their caregivers if they are to play (Pollowy, 1977). They know too that for their optimal growth, babies and toddlers need to explore. Therefore, the old restrictions, such as the use of playpens, need to be removed so that babies and toddlers can roam freely and safely. Furthermore, this new breed of child-wise architects and designers are suggesting innovative ways to turn kitchens and living rooms into spaces for both adults and children (Cohen, McGinty, & Moore, 1979).

This heightened awareness of designing home space with children and their play in mind is not just a middle-class phenomenon. In the 1950s and well into the 1960s, cities built high-rise apartment buildings for low-income families. By a good many estimates, the result was the impoverishment of children's play, because a family on, say, the eighth or twelfth floor was, in effect, a family trapped in a small apartment where children had no place to go to play. Even the balconies as they had been designed proved unsafe (Allen, 1968), though with a little more thought they might have proven excellent and safe places to play.

In several respects, this heightened awareness about designing homes for play has benefited from the thought that has gone into designing early-childhood education centers. For example, the same ideas about activity centers, bounded spaces, and pathways (see Chapter 9 for a more extended discussion)—ideas initially developed in research on early-childhood centers (Moore, 1987)—are perfectly applicable to the home. Indeed, as Laura Johnson reports (1987), it is possible to provide all the major shared living spaces in the home with activity corners furnished with appropriate toys and play materials for easy access—just as one finds in good early-childhood centers—without the home turning into something other than a home.

For the majority of homes today, the design features that make homes places for rich and varied play have not been incorporated, according to Johnson's (1987) review of the research. However, the existence of good research and good models for designing homes for play should be encouraging, because knowing better makes it at least more probable that the majority of homes in the future will be better places for children to play.

● PLAY IN OUTDOOR SETTINGS

Children seek access to a place where they can dig in the earth, build huts and dens with timber, use real tools, experiment with fire and water, take reallygreat risks and learn to overcome them. They [children] have an irresistible urge to build houses and dens, dig holes, make gardens, trot after pets, make bonfires and cook meals out-of-doors. These are delightfully messy occupations and they make the planners, who are mostly tidy-minded people, unhappy. (Allen, 1968, p. 1)

For all the reasons discussed in the previous section, children today have far less access to outdoor play spaces than did children in previous generations (Rivkin, 1998). Compared with previous generations, many children do not spend much time playing out-of-doors, at least not in industrialized societies. This too suggests that today's children are getting shortchanged with respect to opportunities to play.

Consider the rather idyllic description of backyard play in a previous generation that concluded the last chapter to understand why, with respect to outdoor play, the family critics are mourning not just losses within the home but losses outside as well. Devereux's analysis would have us believe that without the kind of backyard sports that children commonly played in previous generations, today's children are at risk of not developing morally.

Even the ecology movement has negative implications for the fate of today's children and their play, as children today are pictured as being removed from nature and therefore denied opportunities to satisfy a basic genetic need for nature (Kellert & Wilson, 1995).

However, once again, what seems to be an undermining of the quality of life for children and especially for their play has been offset by a new thoughtfulness in the designing of outdoor play spaces. The best examples are today's playgrounds.

Playgrounds Today

Over the past 15 years, playgrounds have undergone a transition from highly structured play spaces to more open and flexible settings. One impetus for this change has come from the architectural community, whose interest in design has resulted in structures that are interesting and visually

Photo 8.1   The best examples of the new thoughtfulness in the designing of outdoor play spaces are today's contemporary playgrounds. Here, though, is a more traditional playground.

pleasing (Pellegrini, 1995). Furthermore, a number of landscape architects (Moore, 1987) have involved children themselves in the design of playgrounds and outdoor play spaces, suggesting that children are having at least a modicum of control over what goes into designing their outdoor play spaces. As a result of these efforts to design new and better playgrounds, there are in neighborhoods today two relatively new and interesting types of playgrounds called *contemporary* and *adventure playgrounds*, along with what remains of the few old-fashioned playgrounds that, in the literature, are called *traditional*. To help us understand why contemporary and adventure playgrounds were designed in the first place, we begin with a discussion of traditional playgrounds and their deficiencies.

Traditional Playgrounds

Traditional playgrounds are made up of fixed metal structures such as swings, slides, jungle gyms, merry-go-rounds, seesaws, and concrete "flooring."

The climbing structure is located in the periphery of the yard. It is marked by a ground covering of tan bark, which separates it from a cement portion of the yard. The climbing structure includes a seven foot high, two-tiered deck supported by brightly painted poles from which attach a number of slides, chutes, sliding poles, and ladders. (Perry, p. 7)

The traditional playground design dates back to the early 1900s and still is the most common type in America (Brett, Moore, & Provenzo, 1993).

There are four serious deficiencies to the traditional playground. First, in traditional playgrounds there are virtually no materials adaptable for creative purposes; all of the toys and climbing structures are fixed to the ground. Second, traditional playgrounds encourage only one type of play, namely, gross motor play. The level of social play on traditional playgrounds is low, meaning that traditional playgrounds encourage mostly solitary and parallel play or rather uncreative cooperative play such as that which occurs on the seesaw. Third, the climbing equipment on traditional playgrounds is often mismatched to the size of the children. For example, traditional playgrounds have climbing structures that are too high for kindergarten children. Fourth, and most significant, traditional playgrounds are unsafe. Every year there are an estimated 200,000 playground injuries, and 80% of these injuries are caused by children falling on the hard surfaces of traditional playgrounds (U.S. Consumer Product Safety Commission, 1991). No wonder, then, that one study found that during peak play hours, traditional playgrounds were empty more than 88% of the time (Hayward, Rothenberg, & Beasley, 1974). In fact, given a choice, children seem to prefer playing in the street!

In order to fully understand the current negativity toward traditional playgrounds, consider one common play structure, the seesaw. For children, the seesaw is functionally narrow as a vehicle for play. What can children do on the seesaw? They can go up or down or fall off sideways. The seesaw inhibits dramatic play and creative play in general.

Contemporary Playgrounds

In the early 1960s, much more thought was given to developing playgrounds. Designed by architects and built from a variety of natural materials (e.g., wood, stone), railroad ties, and recycled materials, contemporary playgrounds are the most aesthetically pleasing. They usually blend in with the natural environment and are much more flexible for play. For example, on many contemporary playgrounds, the structures and equipment are arranged for the integration of play across space and between pieces of equipment. The following is a description of a child's experience in a contemporary playground:

> Ashley contemplates the complex structure. An enormous castle of wood stands before her. Where she should go first? Should she crawl through the door, use the chain ladder, or climb the cargo net? Maybe a quick ride on the zip line? There are so many options for her movement!

Adventure Playgrounds

Unlike traditional and contemporary playgrounds, adventure playgrounds have loose materials for children to play with as they wish. Adventure playgrounds use a variety of materials that children can independently use to create their own play space. The London Adventure Playground Association (LAPA) describes adventure playgrounds as places where children are free to do many things that they cannot easily do elsewhere in a crowded urban society. The idea, then, is to offer a playground that to some extent compensates for the artificially constructed environment that surrounds the city child.

Adventure playgrounds had their beginning in postwar Denmark. Experienced playground architect C. T. Sorensen noticed that children seemed to enjoy playing with the extra materials left behind at abandoned construction sites. In fact, the children played with these extra materials longer than they played with the playgrounds built especially for them! It was this observation that led him to create the first "junk" playground. Included were extensive areas for cooking, building, animal care, and climbing.

Adventure playgrounds are the most flexible in terms of having open-ended materials, such as sand, water, large wooden blocks, and woodworking tools. Open-ended materials are materials that can be used in many different ways, not just in one or two ways as is the case with the seesaw.

Although from this description the adventure playground may seem the most successful for creative play, giving children control over such items as nails and hammers, saws, open flames, live animals, large walls, water sources, and sharp garden tools understandably generates concerns about safety, although adventure advocates point out that their safety record is no worse than that of traditional playgrounds (Frost, 1992).

In addition, adventure playgrounds are costly. Despite the low start-up cost, play leaders must be hired to supervise, and the liability insurance can be considerable. Finally, as one might imagine, the "junk" for play does not make for a playground that is aesthetically pleasing. Because of all these shortcomings, and despite their appeal to children, adventure playgrounds are rare.

Successful Design Features of Playgrounds

Attempts have been made to identify the specific properties of playgrounds that hold children's interest and lead to good play. The following discussion includes a partial list of these properties and the resulting criteria that today's playground designers use for designing and evaluating playgrounds.

A Range of Experiences

Playgrounds must provide children with a range of experiences. One major concern for parents and educators is that today's technological society provides children with fewer natural sensory experiences. For this reason, playgrounds should offer as many sensory experiences as possible—for example, rough and smooth objects to touch; heavy and light objects to lift and move; wet materials as well as dry; cool materials in the shade as well as hot materials in the sun; soft and hard surfaces to run and jump on; things that make sounds (e.g., running water, chimes); smells of all varieties (e.g., flowers, bark, mud); high and low places; materials that are natural and synthetic, thin and thick. The list could go on and on. The richer and more varied the materials, the better.

Providing Control

Once there are plenty of materials to see, touch, smell, hear, and taste, children must feel invited to take control and explore and use what playgrounds provide. For example, playgrounds must invite children to move over, under, around, and through the various structures and to choose which direction they want to go. With regard to giving children control, sand and water are powerful playground materials to have available because they can be manipulated in any way the children choose.

Providing Challenges

Playgrounds should contain challenges ranging from those appropriate for toddlers to those appropriate for older children. By providing these challenges, playgrounds give children the option of trying things they have already mastered or taking on new challenges. For example, balance beams, crawling tunnels, stairs, and tire climbs could be "old hat" but still fun for most 9-year-olds, while the higher monkey bars, swaying balance beams, and zip lines provide new and interesting challenges.

Photo 8.2   There is something in children that makes them play regardless of where they play or what has been provided for them to play with. Here, children play tug-of-war.

Another advantage of playgrounds that incorporate a broad spectrum of activities and challenges is that children of different ages can work and play together in the same environment; as a result, younger children learn from the older and older children learn how to care for the younger. This can happen if playgrounds are designed in such a way as to keep the younger children safe—for example, out of the way of big kids on the slides or jumping from high places.

Choice

Playgrounds should provide children with choices. Children should be able to decide whether to play alone or in a group, on a particular climbing structure or on another, with sand or water, and so forth. These options can be created by the spaces built into the playground, such as small, sheltered areas for solitary play, ample space for small groups, and large open spaces for large groups. Spaces also need to provide multiple entrances and exits to climbing structures and multiple routes through structures so that children constantly have the opportunity to choose their direction.

Fantasy Materials

Playgrounds should provide support for make-believe play. Playground equipment can be built in the shape of fire engines, horses, submarines, rocket ships, and other objects from the real world that can stimulate make-believe play. Children can create fantasy play with natural materials such as a mound of dirt or a tree branch.

● CONCLUDING REMARKS

There are, then, two ways of looking at home and outdoor play today. On the one hand, home and outdoor play seem impoverished compared with the home and outdoor play of the past. Children are swamped with toys they don't need and toys that fail to stimulate imagination and connect them to traditional values. In addition, outdoor play space has diminished to the point that children stay indoors or go out only for adult-controlled organized youth sports. On the other hand, more thought is now given to designing good play spaces for children, and this trend has turned homes into places for children to play and made playgrounds full of opportunities for diverse forms of play.

However, while posing the present situation with regard to home and outdoor play as a paradox inviting irreconcilable views, we should remember one point made throughout this book—namely, that children and their development trump other developments, including the developments having to do with change in family structure and change within the larger society. What this means is that despite the impact of their environment on how children play, there is something in children that makes them play regardless of their environment. Perhaps these recent changes are but tiny bumps on a very long evolutionary road that is moving like an escalator. But such speculation takes us too far afield. It is enough to note that children have an inner strength that shows up in their capacity for play almost without regard to changing circumstances.

KEY WORDS, NAMES, AND IDEAS ●

Adventure playgrounds

Commercialization of toys

Contemporary playgrounds

Environmental press

Traditional playgrounds

CHAPTER 9

SCHOOLING AND PLAY

Early Childhood Education and Play
The Built Environment
Programming
Teachers Relating Directly to Children
Play in Elementary Schools
Games
Technology
Recess
Misbehaving Play
Summary

Mentioning schooling and play in the same sentence might well be likened to announcing the contestants in a boxing match. In one corner is schooling with its mission to have children learn. In the other corner is play with its mission to have children enjoy themselves. Indeed, the two are often at odds with one another, and nowhere do we see this more clearly than in the misbehaving play that occurs in every classroom. However, schooling and play have not always been contestants battling one another, and more and more educators are seeing *play as an ally to learning*. This chapter explains why.

We begin with developments in educational philosophies in the nineteenth century and the first half of the twentieth century because they frame discussions of education today. Before the nineteenth century, education in Europe and America was mostly authoritarian and divorced from children's everyday activities. If a child attended school (and most did not), he or she was expected to follow a curriculum in which the goals and methods had little to do with a child's world. Rather than moving about freely, children sat still in desks or stood to recite. Rather than pursue their interests, children pursued the interests of their teachers. Rather than being inventive and inquisitive, children followed prescribed processes to get "right" answers and acquire "right" habits (Beatty, 1995). If children did not conform, they got punished. Here is a quote from one early-twentieth-century educator caught in the midst of educational reform and change.

> I find one party strenuously maintaining that improvement in our schools can advance only so far and so fast as bodily chastisement recedes, while the other party regards a teacher or parent, divested of his instruments of pain, as a discrowned monarch. (Harris, 1928, p. 48)

Of course, there were always notable exceptions. However, the sketch at the beginning of the chapter defines the context from which later educational movements developed. These movements were as much against the old authoritarian and mechanistic ways as they were for what they advocated.

The new movements focused on four concepts: *interests, activity, structure,* and *mentoring.* With regard to *interests,* the progressive movement led by John Dewey advocated that teachers find ways to build curriculum around children's interests (Jones & Tanner, 1981). An example might be noticing that some children are interested in baseball and then promoting a math project for children to develop their own measures, statistics, and graphs to evaluate and compare ballplayers.

Building Curriculum Around Children's Interests

In my fourth-grade classroom, I noticed that my boys would talk incessantly about baseball. I wanted to find a way to channel this interest into our math lessons. I decided to start using a free fantasy baseball service. This was a game available on the Internet, where the children would choose players each day and then calculate their rankings based on the players' statistics. The game was a total success. Children would come into class each day having computed their players' statistics from the morning paper. Soon, the entire class got in on the act, and everybody seemed to have fun, boys as well as girls. I was happy because my students were learning valuable math skills and finding a way to apply them in their everyday lives.

—Tom Banazewski, Head Teacher, Lexington, MA

With regard to *activity,* the new movements followed a *constructivist* philosophy of knowing, which says each of us must question, problem-solve, and act if we are to understand and know. Constructivist philosophies of education, such as Dewey's, Piaget's, Kohlberg's, and Vygotsky's, all advocate that teachers find ways to help students actively question and reflect, whether that be in traditional academic domains or in social domains such as figuring out alternatives to quarreling (Glassman, 2001). For example, two preschoolers quarreling over a limited supply of blocks might be encouraged to figure out a solution that would avoid quarreling, either on their own or with prompting from their teacher.

With regard to *structure,* the new movements redefined what it should mean to provide structure for optimal learning. In the old, authoritarian meaning, teachers structured children through their directives, lectures, and assignments requiring rote learning. Teachers' control was obvious. The new movements had teachers structuring in more subtle ways, such as by the way they organized time, space, and the built environment (DeVries & Kohlberg, 1990). For example, a shelf with art materials organized meticulously to display markers, paints, paper, and scissors is a shelf organized to structure children to initiate their own, constructive play. Similarly, timing a recess to relieve the mounting tension of fidgety children helps structure the school day to maximize learning. In both examples, we see teachers structuring but in indirect and subtle ways.

With regard to *mentoring,* the new movements advocated a very different vision of the teacher's relationship with children. Rather than being an authoritarian instructor, the mentor was a caring guide, someone who worked to facilitate and stimulate. For example, in progressive early-childhood classrooms, teachers kneel to carry on dialogues with individual children in a way that stimulates thinking (one needs good knees to teach in these schools). The mentor may suggest new goals, but the relationship remains collaborative rather than authoritarian (Katz, 1998; Rogoff, 1991; Scarlett, 1998).

Even with this very brief overview, one can sense how different the new movement's overall approach is compared with the approach that dominated schooling before and throughout the nineteenth century. Perhaps, too, one can sense how this new approach opens up possibilities for linking play to learning, especially for young children.

When we value children's interests, we value their play. Furthermore, to structure indirectly and to mentor is to give children enough control so that they are free to play. With the new approach, play came to be seen not as a diversion from schooling but as an indispensable ally.

Since this has been especially true for early-childhood programs, the remainder of this chapter will separate discussion of play in early-childhood programs from discussion of play in elementary schools. However, for both younger and older children, the new movements linked play to learning.

● EARLY CHILDHOOD EDUCATION AND PLAY

When we say early-childhood education, we mean education for children between 2 and 5 years of age. In most North American and European early-childhood programs, play *is* the curriculum. Programs differ with respect to how play is supported, but not in whether play *should* be supported.

However, most programs do not support all types of play. In fact, in most there is a selective bias toward supporting *constructive* play, or play in which a child is trying to construct something, such as a fort made with blocks or a

Photo 9.1　　In most North American and European early childhood programs, play *is* the curriculum. Here a child engages in constructive play in preschool.

picture of a house made with paper and markers (Forman & Hill, 1980; Forman, 1998). Although dramatic play and constructive play are usually treated as separate types, dramatic play becomes constructive play when the object is to create a full-blown story. In constructive play, then, children construct some defined product.

Educators focused on constructive play because it provides the clearest example of play that requires thinking. Anyone witnessing a child constructing a castle or trying to paint a picture of a house will see immediately that there are problems to solve, that there is thinking needed. How, for example, is the drawbridge to be built, and what about adding a roof, and how can the walls be shaped to convey the spaces from which archers shoot? By supporting constructive play, then, early-childhood programs see themselves as supporting thinking and learning (Forman, 1998).

To accomplish this goal, early-childhood educators have focused on (a) ways to design the physical or *built environment,* (b) *programming,* and (c) *relating directly to children.* Let us look at each of these in turn.

The Built Environment

Most of us give little thought to the environment's organization and how it affects children's play. But early-childhood educators have found that the design of physical environments has a profound effect on whether and how young children play (Pellegrini & Perlmutter, 1989). We will look at probably the two most important concepts that early-childhood educators have used to design environments to support constructive play. The first is the concept of *activity areas.* The second is the concept of *pathways* (Moore, 1987). To illustrate these two concepts, we will concentrate on describing typical classrooms in center-based (as opposed to home-based) early-childhood programs.

As one enters the typical early-childhood classroom, one might be first impressed by the organization of the space into defined areas. There may be an area with rug and mats where the group holds meetings and another space with books, carpeting, and pillows where children can read picture books. The other defined areas are apt to be for play. There is the blocks area where blocks are stored on low shelves so that they are accessible to even small children. There is the dramatic play area where dress-up materials and replicas of real-world items such as telephones and irons are kept. There may be a separate area for a water or sand table and another for painting. There may be a loft or some cave-like space where children can get away from the main group to continue their make-believe. And somewhere in the room, there may be large round tables that double as spaces for crafts and for eating.

The text box describes typical activity areas. Of course, each classroom is apt to be different, so one or two of the areas mentioned may be missing, or areas not mentioned may be added. There is no prescribed list of activity areas in an early-childhood classroom; however, what we have provided is an illustration of how early-childhood settings support constructive play.

There are two major devices at work in the classroom environment: bounded areas and accessible materials. Bounded areas separate the classroom both visually and physically so that children can readily see what each area has to offer and can play within any given area without too many distractions. Accessible materials provide an independent venue for the child to use and store supplies.

Besides deciding which activity areas to have in a classroom and what to stock them with, early-childhood educators are also careful to locate them wisely. For example, research shows that placing the block area next to the dramatic play area invites crossover play between the two so as to enrich all the activity (Block & King, 1987). In contrast, placing the relatively noisy block area next to the reading area can disrupt reading and lead to conflicts that ultimately disrupt play.

Crossover Play Between Adjacent Activity Corners

Mark and Liz decided to pretend to be dogs in the pet store. The two children happily barked and played fetch with a ball in the dramatic play area. "We need dog houses!" explained Mark. Then, spying the blocks in the adjacent block corner, Liz said, "Oh! I will get those big blocks and we can make walls and a roof!"

The other main concept early-childhood educators use to design the built environment is the concept of *pathways,* the physical infrastructure for moving from one activity area to another. Experienced teachers usually have these pathways curve and wind so that children aren't tempted to run. Sometimes a teacher will purposefully put a sand table or climbing structure in the middle of the room just to slow children down.

Stepping back and looking at the classroom as a whole, early-childhood educators have come upon another important insight having to do with the built environment, namely, that bounded areas and pathways must work together to create *modified open classrooms*. In open classrooms, activity areas are not clearly bounded, and there are long and often straight pathways. Children in open classrooms are likely to initiate play, but their play is less likely to be constructive play and more likely to be disruptive.

Open Classrooms and Disruptive Play

Having plenty of open space to run in, two 4-year-old boys refine their hurdling technique by racing down the room, then hurdling the low shelf marking off the block corner. Wonderful play for the outdoors, but not so wonderful in the classroom.

In contrast to open classrooms, closed classrooms have activity areas bounded off from one another so that when children are inside one area, they are cut off from the other areas. The result is that children are less likely to move around and more likely to need an adult assistant for them to initiate and continue to play.

Modified open classrooms have bounded areas, but the areas are never so bounded as to make children feel "cut off." Often this is accomplished using low shelves that even a very small child can see over.

Photo 9.2   Early childhood educators have sought to create activity corners where children can play constructively. Here, preschoolers are in one such activity corner of the classroom.

Programming

Programming refers to the many decisions that teachers make to get themselves and a group of children from the start to the finish of the day. In supporting constructive play, the most important decisions have to do with curriculum, the sequence of activities, and what kinds of rituals and rules to impose (Scarlett, 1998; Steinsieck & Myers, 1998).

Curriculum can be defined loosely as virtually anything planned or narrowly as a course of study. Early-childhood educators seem to define curriculum somewhere in between. Though planned, snack time is not generally considered part of the curriculum, but children helping to construct the rules governing appropriate behavior might well be.

With this fairly broad notion of curriculum, early-childhood educators have sought to build curriculum around children's interests and to have them link play to learning. A simple example occurs in many centers around young children's natural interest in construction machinery such as diggers, bulldozers, and steamrollers and the process of repairing roads and putting up buildings. It is not uncommon for young children to be taken on field trips to construction sites, to be shown films featuring construction sites, and be read to about construction projects, all as sources for learning and to material for play. If given appropriate play materials (toy diggers, bulldozers, steamrollers) and opportunities to play, young children will use play to consolidate their learning (Block & King, 1987), as described in Chapter 3. The key concept here is *linking*. Linking play to sources of learning ensures that play functions not simply to amuse but also to consolidate learning.

Another and more recent strategy for helping classroom play become linked to learning has been *documenting* children's play projects (New, 2003). Documentation can occur in many ways, one being photographing the steps in the process of carrying out a project. (Note that there is no requirement that the photographer be the teacher; the child as documenter can also create a successful experience.) Not only does the documentation make the process of playing more reflective, but it also proves to be quite motivating. Children love to see themselves and their projects reflected in the documentation.

However, perhaps the heart and soul of programming is the thoughtful way that teachers prepare play materials and match play activities to the developmental stage of children. Doing so not only helps capture children's interests but also avoids many problems that can disrupt play. For example, young children love to play with modeling clay, but if teachers have not mixed the clay beforehand with just the right amount of water, what should be a fun and meaningful play experience can turn into a messy and contentious disaster. Similarly, if a play activity requires children to cut materials with scissors, then teachers should provide child-friendly scissors that can do the heavy duty of cutting materials.

Early-childhood educators are generally mindful that the way time and transitions are organized and managed can determine whether there is harmony or discord in play. In some classrooms, the sequence of activities is not clear to the children, so they feel at a loss for what to do, or worse, they find things to do that they should not. And in some classrooms, there aren't the right rituals for managing transitions, resulting in an overall negative classroom climate that inhibits constructive play (Scarlett, 1998). For the most part, however, early-childhood educators have mastered the art of programming: planning thoughtfully so as to engage children in meaningful activities that link learning to play.

Teachers Relating Directly to Children

Early-childhood educators have to take on a more personal role as well. Small children demand and need teachers who do more than manage. They need teachers who know them, who are available to them, and who make them feel approved of, safe, and secure. In the eyes of small children, teachers are second only to parents.

With respect to play, this more personal role gets expressed in three main ways: by the way teachers *mark* what children are doing, by the *dialogues* teachers initiate with children to stimulate their thinking around play, and by occasional *co-play*.

One of the primary needs of young children is to feel known and approved. This shows up in the many times that they call attention to themselves by making known what they are doing and accomplishing: "Look, I'm drawing a horse!" "See, I built a humongous fort!" Experienced teachers do more than offer praise; they also mark or reflect what the children have accomplished or are attempting to accomplish: "I see you are drawing a horse." "My, what a humongous fort you have built." This pleases children and makes them feel known, as well as reinforcing their constructive play (Forman & Hill, 1980).

The second personal way teachers support children's play is by initiating dialogues that help children reflect on their play so that they can become more self-aware. For example, when young children start to draw, they create designs out of their scribblings made of dots, lines, and colorings. Initially, they draw without planning because they don't have the words or concepts needed to plan. So, teachers engage beginning drawers by describing what they have drawn: "Oh, I see you used a brown marker to make this all brown." "Oh, over here you made a curvy line, and over here you gave your picture lots of dots." To the untrained observer, these conversations seem pleasant but insignificant. However, they are enormously significant because they give children words to plan and organize their drawings. The best early-childhood teachers take an extra step by inviting the children to take an inquisitive look at their work. The phrases "Tell me about your work" and "Tell me more" have astonishing power because they make children feel that their teacher has a genuine interest in their work, and they also gently nudge children toward reflecting on the creative process.

A third personal way teachers support play is by co-playing. Throughout the history of early-childhood education, there have been times when teachers have been discouraged from playing with children because doing so was thought to restrict a child's natural creativity. However, more recently, co-play is seen as another potential tool to stimulate constructive play, especially for children who have problems playing.

When Culture Prevents Teacher–Child Co-Play in the Classroom

"We have to maintain roles in the classroom," said one teacher from Beijing, China. "American teachers create an atmosphere of the teacher as a friend, which I believe is completely confusing to children." When asked about the distance perceived between her students and herself, she continued, "Here in China it is vital that the child understands that I have complete authority over the classroom, which fosters a sense of safety and security."

In every early-childhood classroom, there are apt to be one or two children who spend a great deal of time wandering and watching other children rather than playing on their own. These "watchers and wanderers," as they are sometimes called, remain relatively isolated because they don't play much, and on those rare occasions when they play with others, they seldom initiate ideas. In co-playing with these children, teachers help them by asking them for help (e.g., "Where should I put my block?"), that is, by getting them to lead, even if that means simply imitating the child. In other words, teachers help foster in these children what they need to do if they are to succeed in playing with their peers (Forman, 1998). This is but one example of how teachers use co-play selectively to foster constructive play.

There are, then, a good many ways that early-childhood educators support constructive play and link play to learning. We have not mentioned outdoor play because the kind found in early-childhood programs is covered in Chapter 8's discussion of playgrounds. We can turn now to discussing play in elementary schools.

Photo 9.3   Play is an ally to learning in schools, particularly through games, technology, and recess. Here, a teacher uses play to teach something about measurement.

● PLAY IN ELEMENTARY SCHOOLS

When we leave early-childhood education programs and enter elementary schools, we no longer find play featured. In fact, despite the newer educational approaches described earlier, in the minds of many, play is a distraction from formal schooling. However, it need not be. It can be an ally to learning, even for older elementary school children. Here we will describe three important ways that play promotes learning in elementary schools: through *games*, through *technology*, and through *recess*. We will end by discussing misbehaving play, for in elementary schools, play can sometimes be a distraction as well.

Games

Academic learning is hard work for children. However, like medicine and a "spoonful of sugar," it can be swallowed more easily when it is made into a game. Indeed, games permeate the elementary school curriculum, and sometimes they are pleasurable enough for children to consider them play. Often games are organized and evaluated by the teacher with the goal of teaching academic lessons. Examples are playing vocabulary games, writing stories from a picture provided by the teacher, listening to stories and guessing the endings, or putting on a class play. These types of play are not self-directed, and they serve goals beyond the purposes of the participants (Block & King, 1987).

A game of Hangman (where children fill in the missing letters of a word), for example, serves the larger goal of teaching children how to spell complicated words, but to the child, it may just be a game. Another popular game, Five and One, can be good for math and for just plain fun. In this game, all of the numbers on the first five cards picked have to be used (by adding, subtracting, multiplying, or dividing) to arrive at the number on the sixth card picked. Active games, brainteasers, and crossword puzzles are all examples of how teachers use games to facilitate learning (Hollis & Felder, 1982).

Often these games are what children remember best from their entire school experience. Even as the years pass, we can still remember the games that our teachers allowed us to play, games that may have seemed "just for fun" but had a deeper purpose.

Remembering Spelling Bees

What I remember best about elementary school are the spelling bees. The whole class loved them. The teacher would instruct us to put our books away and stand in a straight line against the wall. We would each be called forward by name. I could feel the excitement turning inside my stomach each time she called on me. I can still hear her saying, "Please spell library," and me responding with, "L-I-B-R-A-R-Y." I can still hear her saying, "Correct," and I can still feel the pleasure and pride from seeing my classmates be impressed. But what I remember best was one girl, Sally, who would always win. The whole class came to expect Sally to spell any and every word correctly; it was just as sure as the sun would rise and set. So, I will never forget the day Sally got a word wrong. For one fleeting second, our world was turned upside down.

—One middle-aged man recalling his spelling bee days

Many educators today are concerned that competitive games such as spelling bees and math races could be negative experiences for children. They fear that children cannot cope with the stresses of losing or the pressure placed upon them by competitive games. However, we must ask ourselves if we're projecting our own fears onto children. Perhaps it is a positive experience for children to feel the rush of victory as well as the sorrow of defeat.

There is evidence from research that games can be both successful and unsuccessful as a teaching tool. One study found that children who played games requiring them to use multiplication skills improved on posttest scores. Other studies have discovered that games are unsuccessful in teaching children academic skills. And one study showed that the use of games and play materials actually hindered children's learning (Baker, Herman, & Yeh, 1981). These results suggest that the need may be for developing quality games rather than disguising poorly planned activities as games.

On the surface, games seem to offer a lot to the young learner. They provide a fun, interactive way to motivate students and liven up the classroom. However, despite the potential, pitfalls remain. First, games are not playful if the children do not enjoy them. This is a point so obvious that we feel it would go ignored if unsaid: Games are supposed to be fun. If not fun, children will view them as nothing more than classwork.

This presents a challenge for teachers who choose to implement games in their curriculums. The balance between playful and academic elements requires careful planning. Too much weight placed on academics creates a boring game, but too little creates a breakdown in classroom order. Further complicating the matter is the fact that children can walk away from games with quite different reactions. In sum, when it comes to games in the classroom, there is much work in making games function as both play and learning.

Technology

In the 1980s, Apple Computer Corporation began selling a device known as the personal computer, a device that worked on the principle that a computer could exist on a desk and provide a credible alternative to mainframes occupying entire rooms. Soon after, Apple IIe's began to dot the classroom landscape. Today, most classrooms in technologically endowed societies are equipped with computers, with schools in America averaging one computer for every five students. Clearly, the computer revolution has affected education, but exactly how? How are computers being used in schools, what is the software, and how do computers in schools connect to our topic of play?

Software for children to play and learn with predates the advent of personal computers. In the late 1970s, Seymour Papert (1980), a student of Piaget and cofounder of the MIT Media Lab, developed a programming language he called LOGO to enable children to create their own "microworlds" (as the virtual worlds created on computers are sometimes called).

LOGO created opportunities for children to experience their work on computers as play. As in most play experiences, children were put in control; they became *tutors* and computers were their *tutees.* And just as with most play experiences, programming with LOGO was enjoyable and allowed children to pursue their personal interests. However, for schools and schooling, the most important aspect of LOGO was that, in playing with LOGO, children learned.

For example, a young girl has taken an interest in gymnastics and wants to create a virtual acrobat. Making the acrobat "jump" straight up and down provides the girl with a computer programming and math problem that is easy and fun for a while. But to sustain interest, she might want to make her acrobat "leap" with great arching leaps, which will require a different, more sophisticated math than for jumping straight up and down. Suddenly, the child has gone from working with linear geometry to a crude form of calculus by trying to recreate the parabolic path of a leap. We don't expect the child to spontaneously start calculating derivatives and integrals, but the child's interest in making her acrobat leap may well drive her to learn more sophisticated ways of programming and possibly to learn more sophisticated math.

This open-ended approach to computer use is rooted in a *constructivist* educational approach. However, Papert prefers the term *constructionism* to capture the idea that children build their learning environment from the ground up. In programming the computer, the child is actively solving problems, and in doing so is constructing new knowledge.

In contrast to this constructivist approach, in which the computer is a *tutee,* the *instructionist* approach has children using the computer as a *tutor.* Most of what goes by the label of "educational" electronic games falls under this instructionist category.

For many years, MathBlaster[1] has been the number one example of educational electronic play following the instructionist approach. With MathBlaster, a child is presented with a math problem—such as adding a series of numbers—that he or she has to do as quickly as possible. At the end of each problem set, the child is rewarded with a game to play, for example, shooting at virtual garbage floating in virtual outer space.

Given the opposing nature of constructionist and instructionist philosophies, it's not surprising that each is open to criticism from the opposite camp. Many claim that constructionist programs such as LOGO do not address the need for teachers to meet state guidelines and prepare students for state and national tests. Though this is not necessarily true, the only way a teacher can successfully implement a constructionist curriculum is through careful planning to create a balanced curriculum.

In contrast, instructionist programs such as MathBlaster are open to the criticism that they are little more than electronic work sheets with electronic reinforcers. There is no creativity fostered on the part of the child and often no sustained motivation over time. Finally, because these programs are so closed-ended, they follow, in effect, the principle that "one size fits all." When it comes to teaching groups of children, we know that one size almost never fits all.

There are other electronic playscapes that have obvious educational value and that fall somewhere in between the open-endedness of LOGO and the closed-endedness of MathBlaster. These other playscapes are most often used at home, but sometimes they make their way into classrooms and are used in less structured times of the classroom day, such as right before class officially begins. They include games such as Oregon Trail and Where in the World Is Carmen Sandiego?—simulation games that resemble real-world problem solving (such as that used by the American pioneers moving west) and puzzle games that require children to acquire useful information (such as information about the capitals of countries and states). What is attractive about these games is that their play format motivates children to learn. What is unattractive is that they share some of the limitations of electronic work sheets. In particular, with these games, it is the adult programmer's creativity and not the child's that matters.

Cutting-Edge Technology: A Window on the Future?

We could not end a discussion of computers, play, and learning without saying something about cutting-edge technology that may influence future play and learning in the classroom. One example is the Lego programmable brick, also known as the RCX.

The RCX is a self-powered Lego brick that contains a small computer with three outputs for attaching motors and lights, three inputs for attaching sensors, a small liquid crystal display (LCD), and an infrared (IR) port for communicating with a computer. Children control the actions of the bricks using one of two pieces of software, either ROBOLAB (developed at Tufts University) or Lego Mindstorms (developed at MIT). Using this software, children can become engaged in a number of fun and educational projects.

For example, in one classroom, children built their own robotic animals that moved exactly like their real counterparts. In doing this, the students had to be creative and solve engineering problems. One student chose to build a robotic coyote, but in the process he had to figure out a way to slow the effect of the fast-moving Lego motor so that his coyote could move properly. To solve this problem, he discovered he could slow the coyote if he had a large gear fitted between the Lego motor and the small gear attached to the coyote. Two girls in the same class had an even greater challenge to slow movement down, for they had built a robotic snail. In addition to making good use of different-size gears, they used small wheels on the snail. Needless to say, these insights into basic mechanics came within the supportive context of having fun. For these children, learning was play.

But perhaps the most inspiring examples of cutting-edge technology are projects that stimulate what Csikszentmihalyi has called *flow.* This is the term given to experiences of intense and satisfying concentration, to times when there is a release from dissatisfying self-consciousness, and to times that are intrinsically meaningful and motivating. Certainly *flow* captures something of what happens when children are deep into their play. But it also captures what happens when adults are deep into their work. Flow, then, blurs the distinction between play and work.

All these concepts have a great deal to do with learning and play. The following school project can serve as an example. After becoming fascinated with the idea of making a "marble machine" that would lead a marble snaking its way along a path, one preadolescent girl decided to create her own marble machine in preparation for the school's science fair. The student's teacher wasn't so enamored with the project because it didn't seem to support the scientific process of posing and testing a hypothesis.

Undeterred by her teacher's lack of enthusiasm and support, the student completed a design that sent a marble down a series of ramps. In doing so, she utilized a device similar to the Lego RCX, a device called the cricket, to build and program a basket that lifted a marble back to the beginning after it had completed its course. The girl received one of the two top honors given out at the science fair (Resnick, Berg, & Eisenberg, 2000).

There are lessons to be learned here about technology and play's role in the classroom. First, this girl, when able to pursue a project and goal of her own making, brought far more energy than she would have if she had had to follow some prepackaged set of instructions for carrying out someone else's project and achieving someone else's goal. Second, as can happen with many projects that adults see as "just play," there was more science to this project than there seemed to be at first glance. For example, marbles racing down ramps provided for microstudies of gravity. Third, students often need the right technology if they are to learn. The technology available to this student (the cricket) allowed her to take on the traditional physics topics of motion and gravity in nontraditional ways.

In conclusion, technology such as the personal computer and ROBOLAB has a place in the classroom, in part because it provides new opportunities to link learning to play. However, most schools are more eager to purchase computers than they are to invest time, money, and energy into training teachers to make the best possible use of this technology. And most schools, though they may be positive settings for children to learn and play in traditional ways, are not yet settings for linking play to learning in nontraditional, technological ways. However, changes are occurring.

Recess

The most obvious examples of play in elementary school occur during recess. But how does recess link play to learning? Research suggests it does in at least two ways. First, recess provides a much-needed respite from tension-producing seat work and academic tasks. Second, productive play on school playgrounds predicts academic success in the classroom, suggesting at least the possibility that recess play has a positive influence on learning (Pellegrini, 1995; Pellegrini & Davis, 1993; Pellegrini & Smith, 1993). More research is needed to establish whether there are indeed causal connections.

Independent of this question is the question of how children play at recess. Recess is the only time when children have an opportunity to engage in spontaneous play, unhindered by adults (Pellegrini, Kato, & Banies, 2002). Children use this time to foster connections with their peers that are for the most part based on mutual interest in common play activities. Girls are more likely to play at jumping (skipping rope) and singing or chanting games ("A my name is Alice . . ."), and boys are more likely to play at sports (soccer, touch football). However, two things unite girls' and boys' recess play. First, it is often governed by complex rules, and second, it is the group that regulates the play, not adults. Adults (teachers and special recess monitors) remain on the sidelines.

In recent years, some educators and parents have advocated reducing the frequency and duration of recess so as to create more time for study. They use three main arguments. First, recess detracts from the needed instructional time in an already crowded school day. Second, recess disrupts children's work patterns. "It distracts them from their work. They are focused and then the recess period gets them hyper. It's so difficult to bring them back down," explains one teacher. Third, recess encourages aggression and antisocial behavior.

However, research on recess shows that recess helps children by reducing tension. Furthermore, at recess play is generally quite positive, not overly aggressive or antisocial. It seems that when children sit for long periods of time they accumulate surplus energy; therefore, physical activity at recess is necessary to use up this energy so that the children can then concentrate on the more sedentary tasks (Pellegrini & Perlmutter, 1989). In fact, the only negative findings have been about boredom among girls, mostly in school systems where recess occurs quite often, as in English public schools.

Misbehaving Play

We could not discuss play in elementary schools without discussing misbehaving play, because there is always illicit or misbehaving play when children are asked to sustain attention and work hard. Children are, after all, children. Misbehaving play is a relief from work, a tension reducer, and sometimes an attention getter. The fact that educators rarely study misbehaving play does not diminish the significance of this play phenomenon.

Misbehaving play is important to children because it provides them with a sphere of autonomy within the structure of the classroom (Weisz, Chaiyasit, Weiss, Eastman, & Jackson, 1995). Favorite examples of misbehaving play include playing "field goal kicking" with tiny paper footballs (usually paper shaped into triangles), blowing spitballs, and cracking jokes during work time. Children also create songs that ridicule their teachers and challenge authority, such as "Mrs. Dylan is a villain! She will eat your children!" These parodies are especially popular in elementary school because they enable children to freely express their contempt for school and their resentment of individual teachers. One can imagine the verbal fluency as well as the social skills required to create these rhymes. Unfortunately, these skills are easily overlooked when they occur in the context of misbehavior.

Although children's misbehavior can be disruptive, it is also "playful." The school is a socially constructed space where children have to go by the schedule, listen to teachers, pay attention to lessons, and obey rules. All children feel more or less confined by school, so much so that they sometimes need to "go against the grain." The text box gives three cross-cultural examples of misbehavior in school.

Culture and Misbehaving Play in the Classroom

In Japan a boy stands on his chair pronouncing that he is the king of the toilet. "I will make the biggest poop in the world!" he says. The other children in class hear his announcement and beg to join in. The teacher nearby hears the commotion, smiles, and turns back to the attendance book.

On the other side of the world in the United Kingdom a girl sits at lunch with her chocolate pudding cup. "Look! It's like poop!" she exclaims as she mixes it with her spoon. "Ha ha! Let me see!" says the girl sitting next to her. "Now I am going to eat it!" she announces. Just as the situation begins to escalate the teacher walks over. "You are using lots of bathroom words; do you need to go to the bathroom?" the teacher asks her. The girl puts her head down and shakes her head. "I'll stop," she says.

At the same time, in Taiwan, a boy yells from the bathroom, "Everyone come here and see what I put in the toilet!" A few of the children run from the classroom to see. The teacher immediately follows. Upon entering the bathroom the teacher is startled to see some snack cookies thrown into the toilet. As the children became hysterical the teacher also begins to laugh. Unexpectedly, she shouts in a stern voice, "Everyone back into the classroom; this behavior is unacceptable." The boy spends the next 15 minutes standing on a chair with his hands on his head.

In these examples, we see a similarity in the children's behavior and differences in the reactions from the teachers. Different cultures bring different meanings to the definition of misbehaving play (Roopnarine, Johnson, & Hooper, 1994). This is especially evident in the classroom.

In moderation, misbehaving classroom play in elementary schools need not be a bad thing. Most misbehaving players go on to do well enough. However, for a few the misbehavior is symptomatic of deeper and more pervasive problems. The class clown, for example, may be a child who is lousy at making friends and who feels desperate to gain his classmates' approval, even at the expense of his relationships with teachers. Experienced teachers know this and work to get these children the help they need.

SUMMARY ●

From the beginning of this chapter, we have exposed the tension between teaching academics and allowing children to have fun. Newer approaches have attempted to resolve the tension by linking play to learning. We have seen how play takes form in the early-education classrooms through the greater goal of selectively supporting constructive play, through the *built environment,* through *programming,* and through *teachers relating to children.* We have seen too how play takes form in elementary schools through games, technology, recess, and misbehaving. However, we acknowledge that our discussion of play and learning in the classroom is heavily skewed by research on what works best and not on what is typical. For example, only a very few teachers are fortunate enough to have RCXs in their classrooms and the training to use them. Also, we have adopted a culture-specific notion of play in the classroom.

We know, for example, that Chinese early-education programs emphasize academics over play and that their Japanese counterparts do just the opposite. Technology too varies from country to country and from community to community. In the United States, it is typically more available in schools in richer neighborhoods. In Ireland, however, the telecommunication company EIRCOM has brought technology even into schools in poor and rural areas.

Finally, we should point out that many teachers who try to implement play in their curriculum are attempting a Sisyphean task. Just as research began to promote play in elementary schools, a new wave of standardized tests placed new demands on the teachers to increase nonplay time.

This does not mean that linking play to learning in elementary schools is a lost cause. Regardless of the high demands on the teacher, we believe that play has a place in the classroom. The cleverest educators will find ways to build play into their programs to enhance both learning and the quality of life for students.

KEY WORDS, NAMES, AND IDEAS ●

Activity areas and pathways

Bounded areas and accessible materials

Competitive and cooperative play

Constructionism vs. instructionism

Constructive play

Constructivist

Documenting

Flow

Linking

Microworlds

Modified open classrooms

Progressive movement

Teacher marking, dialogue, and co-play

● NOTE

1. Broderbund Software.

PART IV

Therapeutic Uses of Play

P art IV discusses therapeutic uses of play. The first chapter discusses how play is used to reduce stress in environments where children are at risk for developing psychological problems. We call this restorative play to indicate how infusing play into stressful environments can restore them to a more natural and child-friendly state. Here, the problem is more in the environment than in the child.

The second chapter focuses on play therapy. It explains how play therapy changes dramatically when going from its use within one theoretical tradition to another. In changing theories, we see how play is used to solve very different clinical problems. But, unlike the problems in the chapter on restorative play, the problems addressed in play therapy are mostly within the child—although, of course, those problems may stem from problems in the child's environment.

Chapter 10

RESTORATIVE PLAY IN STRESSFUL ENVIRONMENTS

T hroughout this book, we have described different types of play activities and how they relate to children's development in a variety of cultures and contexts. In particular, Chapters 8 and 9 have explored how play can be encouraged and fostered in familiar settings such as children's homes and schools, settings that are part of children's daily lives. This chapter goes further. Here, play is described in situations that potentially generate high levels of stress for children and are therefore deemed atypical or abnormal. In such contexts, encouraging and protecting children's play is often not a priority for adults. Or if it is, it is usually in the context of therapy. Why is that?

Tamba is a playful 5-year-old Sierra Leonean boy. Yet, Tamba has already experienced quite a lot of stressful events in his short life. In April 1998, he and his family had to escape from Sierra Leone because of the terrible civil war that devastated the country at the beginning of the 1990s. Tamba left his house, his village in the region of Kono, and many relatives behind. . . . Despite his young age, he had to walk in the bush for 3 weeks in extremely difficult conditions, eating roots and trying to avoid the rebels along the way. Tamba was lucky enough to arrive safely in Guinea-Conakry, a neighboring country, where he and his family found refuge. Along with about 20,000 other refugees, he lived in the camp of Massakoundou. The living conditions where precarious, but at least he and his family were safe, though not for very long.

In September 2000, the Sierra Leonean rebels entered Guinea, and the war spread. Most of the refugee camps along the boarder were attacked, and more adults and children were killed or captured as prisoners and child soldiers. Tamba and his family had no choice but to flee again, further away from Sierra Leone, to a place where they hoped to be safe for a little longer.

As soon as Tamba arrived in the new refugee camp of Kountaya, in October 2000, his dad started constructing a new house for the family, making bricks with mud and using branches and leaves as a roof. This would do, he thought, at least until the beginning of the rainy season. While his father worked, Tamba went to the activity and play center newly established in the camp.[1] And what did Tamba do? After having lost his house twice in a few months, he played at reconstructing a house with sticks, sand, and leaves! . . . In play, Tamba was able to process the situation and reconnect.

Does Tamba need therapy? Or is play—along with any potential protective factor at his disposal—enough in this particular case? It is difficult to tell.

To answer these questions and to properly explain the complex yet seldom addressed interaction between stress and children's play, we discuss two types of stressful environments where play is often absent: hospitals and refugee camps. We first analyze the concept of childhood stress and explain why play tends to disappear in stressful contexts.

We also explain that across cultures and contexts, most children react in developmentally appropriate ways when confronted with abnormal environments. In this respect, therefore, we explain that most children do not need therapy. In fact, we also show that play—*just* play—can help children thrive. Why? Because play has restorative powers. In this chapter, we explain how.

Finally, we cannot deny that we face a paradox here: Play tends to disappear in stressful environments, and yet play can help children cope. . . . How can we resolve this paradox? In this chapter, we provide practical suggestions for how restorative play can be encouraged and fostered in abnormal environments, so that children can smile and once again be children.

• STRESS AND ITS EXPECTED CONSEQUENCES IN CHILDHOOD

Stress in childhood is part of the normal process of growing up. Indeed, although theorists differ in how they explain the influence of stress, all agree that stress is part of normal childhood. For instance, Freud (1920) explained how age-appropriate frustrations and challenges help children better balance the id's and the superego's often opposing demands. Slightly departing from Freud's psychosexual theory, Erikson (1963) listed eight successive stressful crises that individuals go through in the process of developing and maturing. The first five (i.e., basic trust vs. mistrust; autonomy vs. shame and doubt; initiative vs. guilt; industry vs. inferiority; and identity vs. role confusion) take place during childhood and the adolescent years. In Piaget's cognitive developmental approach (1951), children constantly use their own stressful confusion to find new ways to adapt. Other theorists have developed different analyses of the stresses associated with the process of growing up. However, no matter how different these theoretical approaches and interpretations may be, all agree that these processes should be seen as a normal component of childhood. As such, they usually lead to a healthy and balanced growth (Elkind, 1981). In fact, the absence of developmental crises and associated stress is now seen as undermining development (Fergusson, Lynskey, & Horwood, 1996).

However, there is no denial that problems can and do occur when children face powerful stressors that go beyond what is deemed normal (Henniger, 1995). Stress in childhood relates to our subject, children's play, because there is an intimate relationship between stress and play. To better establish this relationship and to explain how it operates, we first need to have a clearer understanding of abnormal stress in childhood.

Conceptualizing Stress

Over the past few decades, evidence has accumulated that negative events and experiences can produce levels of stress leading to psychopathology in childhood (Rutter, 1990). Significant risks can be associated with bereavement, divorce and remarriage, chronic physical disorders, man-made and natural disasters, and a broad range of other events that appear to carry long-term psychological threats. Yet, children do not all react in the same ways when facing similar situations, and individual differences need to be taken into consideration. Indeed, variables such as age, personal characteristics, and level of social support operate to reduce or exacerbate levels of stress (Compas & Grant, 2003).

In addition, most researchers now embrace a transactional approach to address the dynamic and reciprocal relations between environmental stressors and individual characteristics. In general, therefore, stress should be seen as a characteristic intrinsic neither to certain environments nor to certain children, but rather as the result of a complex, dynamic, and evolving interaction between environment and child (Bronfenbrenner, 1999). Yet, certain types of environments do contain such high levels of stressors for children that children's reactions to the environment need to be assessed in a somewhat different way. As we shall see later in this chapter, play appears all the more important in such abnormal environments.

Two Examples of Stressful Environments: Hospitals and Refugee Camps

Several examples of environments potentially leading to high levels of stress in childhood could be listed (e.g., homeless shelters, courtrooms, etc.). Unfortunately, the list of such environments can be quite long. In this chapter, we choose to focus on two specific environments: hospitals and refugee camps. By focusing on these two specific examples, we do not intend to provide an exhaustive review of the stressful situations and environments that children can be exposed to, but we do intend to suggest a frame of analysis for assessing how children may react in abnormal and stressful environments in general. Even more important, we intend to suggest how play can help children better cope in many such circumstances.

Can we compare such radically different types of environments and draw analogies between them with regard to how play can help children cope? Our answer is yes. Indeed, though they differ in important respects, hospital settings and refugee camps have in common the potential for creating harmful stress. In both environments, children face the combined effects of an acute event (e.g., illness, war, natural disaster) and being in a new and unfamiliar environment. These effects can lead to high levels of stress. In fact, adults usually expect most children to be distressed while in these environments. In this respect, they recognize and acknowledge that children in these environments may need additional support. Here, we go beyond an intuitive understanding by explaining how and why children tend to react in certain ways when experiencing abnormal environments. In doing so, we lay the base for subsequent sections of this chapter, in which we explain how play can significantly contribute to the additional support most children need in such environments. But first, let us take a closer look at how these environments often lead to high levels of stress in children.

Children in Hospitals

Being hospitalized as the result of an illness can be highly stressful for a child. Indeed, this experience usually departs quite drastically from what the child has encountered before in her life, and can therefore produce anxiety and stress. It is often difficult to disentangle the respective effects of being in a hospital and away from home from the effects of the illness itself and its treatment (Wolff, 1981). In fact, several variables need to be taken into consideration, such as the seriousness of the illness, the length of the hospitalization, and the level of unfamiliarity in the hospital setting. As previously explained, individual differences in terms of personal characteristics—sometimes referred to as "prehospital personality" (Thompson & Stanford, 1981, p. 21)—and the level of family and social support are key variables affecting how a given child might react to the hospital environment.

Another crucial variable is age. Indeed, a developmental approach is useful to better understand how children perceive their global situation and react to it. Children of different ages conceptualize the causes of illness in different ways (O'Jessee, Wilson, & Morgan, 2000), and certain conceptualizations can cause stress, as the following example of Jennifer indicates.

Jennifer is a 5-year-old little girl who has had a benign heart abnormality since birth. Last year, as she does every year, Jennifer went to the hospital with her mom for a routine examination. But, when the doctor pulled out the stethoscope to listen to her heart, Jennifer suddenly became very nervous, and several questions popped out of her mouth: What if the doctor did not hear anything? Would that mean that her heart had stopped beating? Would she be dead then? Instead of taking such a risk, Jennifer simply refused to be examined.

Research has suggested that children's notions of illness causality, prevention, and treatment follow the same developmental sequence as Piaget's major stages of development (Bibace & Walsh, 1980; Moss-Moris & Paterson, 1995). For younger children, misconception of their own illness and pain often leads to confusion, panic, and guilt. Between ages 2 and 6, children think in a prelogical manner. This stage is mainly characterized by the predominance of magical thinking and a difficulty to decenter from one's own experiences. As a result, children tend to explain things in terms of the immediate spatial and temporal cues that dominate the situation, and may even think that they get sick because of a naughty action or a bad thought.

This intellectual stage coincides with the stage of emotional development at which children appear to be most preoccupied with bodily integrity, especially between 3 and 6 years of age (Wolff, 1981). Take the following example to see what this means.

At the Tufts Educational Day Care Center, Band-Aids are used on a daily basis. It is not so much that the children hurt themselves here more than anywhere else. In fact, most of the injuries are minor and hardly noticeable. But the teachers there understand something essential: Young children have a very blurry conception of their body envelope and limits. Therefore, any little hole in their skin can cause great anxieties: What if the cut never stops bleeding? What if all the "inside stuff" goes away? . . . At the day care center, a simple Band-Aid can alleviate a lot of stress, especially if it is colorful and funny looking.

In addition, especially for children between 7 months and about 4 years of age, the emotional effects of separation from a primary caregiver are believed to be at their maximum (Freud, 1946). Young children appear, therefore, to be particularly vulnerable when hospitalized. Somewhat coincidentally, as we already explained in Chapters 2 and 3, it is also during this age period that pretend play usually emerges and develops, at least if the context allows for play. As we shall see in the next section of this chapter, pretense can reduce the young child's sense of being vulnerable.

When children become older and reach the concrete operational cognitive level, they begin to consider the cause of illness as located inside the body but originating from an external source. School-age children seem to have several advantages over younger children in dealing with illness and hospitalization (Thompson & Stanford, 1981). Most of them have a better capacity to understand what's happening, to deal with the separation from home that accompanies the experience, and to develop relationships with other hospitalized children. However, being hospitalized is seldom a stress-free experience for school-age children. Indeed, issues associated with fear of isolation, loss of control, fear of injury, mutilation, and/or death, and abrupt separation from peers and family can quite often lead to feelings of abandonment, insecurity, distrust, and stress (Manheimer, 2000).

Finally, as children reach adolescence, their thinking becomes increasingly sophisticated in terms of understanding their internal bodily functioning and how illness affects different body systems (O'Jessee et al., 2000). However, hospitalization often complicates the developmental tasks that preadolescents and adolescents face. Indeed, while they are struggling for independence from adult authority, hospitalized adolescents have no choice but to become dependent on adults once again (Manheimer, 2000). In addition, separation from their peer group and fears that their medical condition may affect their appearance and their developing sexuality can create high levels of stress.

It is clear now that each age has specific anxieties about hospitalization—anxieties that cause unusual stress. Play, therefore, has different potentials depending on the child's age.

Children in Refugee Camps

The amount of literature devoted to how children in refugee camps perceive and react to their environment is scarce. This is not surprising given the instability of this type of environment and the difficulty of following the same refugee children across extended periods of time. As a result, the few studies that do investigate children in refugee camps tend to focus on case studies (Williams-Gray, 1999; Weine, Becker, McGlashan, & Vojvoda, 1995). However, many relief organizations have been actively involved in a global

effort to understand and address the specific needs of refugee children. Anthropologists, psychologists, social workers, pediatricians, and nurses have contributed to the global effort. In the past 20 years, an increasing awareness has progressively emerged that children in refugee camps have other important needs beyond the obvious material ones of food, shelter, and medicine.

Children come to refugee camps via different pathways. Understanding the variety of pathways helps us to better understand the variety of children's reactions to being in refugee camps and the variety in their ability to cope through using play. Some of the most crucial variables include the reason for migrating (e.g., civil war, natural disaster, famine); the conditions and length of the migration (e.g., by foot, across unsafe areas, alone or with family members, etc.); the length of time spent in camps, before returning to the original land or resettling in a new location; the level of support received from the host population, the civil authorities, and the international community; the degree of freedom experienced on a daily basis (e.g., open or closed camp, presence of land mines, etc.); and the level of access to basic services (e.g., schools, health care units). All these variables make the experience more or less stressful for refugee children and also affect their capacity to play.

Given the wide range of situations experienced, therefore, and the associated impact on the psychological well-being of the children, it is difficult to make generalizations as to precisely how the experience of being in a refugee camp affects children. However, most adults agree that living in a refugee camp is a highly stressful experience for most children. Indeed, even when provided with adequate food, medicine, and shelter (which is far from being the norm), most refugee children display signs of distress. In most cases, refugee children play less or in quite different ways.

When the Problem Is in the Environment, Not in the Child

These two situations—children in hospitals and children in refugee camps—illustrate how most children react with developmentally appropriate and expected behaviors when facing high levels of stress. Their anxieties and confusion are normal. In most cases, therefore, the problem is not in the child; the problem is in the environment.

This is not to say that all children fall in this range. Some children cope extremely well. They play by themselves and with others, make new friends, and grow from their experience. In fact, some of them might even find opportunities in these circumstances that they never had before. For instance, children who come from rural communities where education is not an option sometimes get a chance to go to school in refugee camps. In some cases, children go as far as coping almost too well, in ways that might seem adaptive in the short term but that may lead to further complications later on. At the other extreme, some children display such intense negative reactions that they need appropriate and culturally sensitive therapeutic intervention such as play therapy or traditional ways of healing.

At this stage, we would like to emphasize that the type of play described in this chapter is not play therapy. Indeed, play therapy has specific goals and entails particular settings and dynamics. By using play, the most elaborate means of communication available to young children, play therapy aims at diminishing emotional problems and disturbances through the establishment of a relationship between the child and the therapist and through making useful interpretations (Hellendoorn, van der Kooij, & Sutton-Smith, 1994b). The theories and implications associated with play therapy will be fully developed in the next chapter.

Here, we address the needs of the majority of the children, those who react normally to abnormal, stressful environments. For these children, instead of speaking of the clinical value of play, we speak of the restorative value of play. In doing so, we emphasize that play holds a key function in restoring some level of normality in children's lives—a preventive function rather than a clinical one. Indeed, play can provide children with the ego support they need to remain on the positive side of the imaginary and subtle line that separates adaptive or "normal" from maladaptive or pathological. In other words, play is viewed as a powerful protective factor. In the next section, we explain why.

PLAY AS A MEANS TO ASSESS AND RELIEVE STRESS ●

Carefulness and humility are essential when conducting assessments or intervening in cultures where the place and role of children in society and the meaning of play might be radically different from traditional European or North American cultures. However, play seems to hold a special role in stressful environments regardless of culture. When children are scared, when they do not understand what is happening to them, when they are unhappy and withdrawn, play can hold restorative powers. Therefore, it is essential that play be preserved, protected, and supported, especially in stressful environments.

Lack of Play as a Means to Assess Stress

As previous chapters document, play is both vital to and reflective of a child's development (Linder, 1990). The purpose here is not to list and detail all the assessment techniques that are increasingly used to assess the level and quality of a child's play. The interested reader will find samples of these instruments in other publications. The purpose here is to look at what happens under stressful conditions when a child does not play.

Beyond individual differences, many children reach a breaking point where they are unable to cope when the environment becomes too stressful (Henniger, 1995). For young children especially, this breaking point can be observed in the play experience or, more often, in the lack of play. Lack of play, or what is called "play disruption," may be a signal of a child's inability to express thoughts and feelings related to her situation (Schaefer, 1994). Erikson (1963) was the first to describe "play disruption" and its effects. He defined it as "the sudden and complete or diffused and slowly spreading inability to play" (p. 223). Going further, Erikson describes how play disruption can be seen as the "counterpart, in waking life, of the anxiety dream: it can keep children from trying to play just as the fear of night terror can keep them [and many adults] from going to sleep" (p. 221).

However, one should not always assume that a child's not playing constitutes "play disruption." Indeed, children might not play for a variety of alternative reasons, one being the lack of opportunities to play. In hospital settings and refugee camps, there are clearly times when children do not get a chance to play—as when they are hooked to IVs in hospitals and when they are enlisted for work in refugee camps. As Thompson and Stanford (1981) have noted, hospitalization seriously threatens the extent and quality of play.

Furthermore, sometimes play has not been part of a child's life prior to the experience, especially for children in refugee camps. As mentioned in other chapters, children in many cultures are expected to contribute to their family and community's activities by engaging in tasks such as gathering wood for the fire, fetching water from the well, caring for their younger siblings, or even holding a full-time apprentice position in a craftsman's workshop. Yet, children usually start learning about these tasks in playful ways, first by imitating their parents or siblings, then by performing the task at a mini-level best suited to their capacities, and then eventually by fully performing it. When writing about the Chiga of Uganda, for instance, Leacock (1976) describes how children start playing with small gourds at a young age and, in the process, progressively learn how to balance the gourds on their heads. The adults in the community encourage such playful activities. Indeed, the children who go to a water source and manage to bring back a little bit of water in their gourds are usually praised and even applauded. Step after step, then, playful activities turn into meaningful contributions to the household and larger community.

In refugee situations, children may carry on doing the tasks that they were used to doing prior to the refugee situation, but they usually do so in a much less playful manner. The presence of land mines, the lack of security in general, the lack of time to wander around, the absence of available siblings or other children to engage in collaborative play, and the lack of access to play materials or toys are among the many reasons why children in such circumstances might not engage in play.

Before the war in Bosnia-Herzegovina, Nermina was living in an affluent household. Both her parents were highly qualified and had well-paying jobs, and Nermina had lots of toys: all kinds of dolls and stuffed animals, a new bike that she had just got for her birthday, and video games.

In July of 1995, Nermina's life changed dramatically: Her hometown, Srebrenica (in the former Yugoslavia, now Bosnia-Herzegovina), was attacked, and her father was one of the several thousands of men who "disappeared." In Srebrenica, only the children, the women, and the elderly were allowed to escape to the town of Tuzla.

Nermina was only 8 at the time, so she had to mature fast. In Tuzla, she and her mom lived in a collective center, where several refugee families shared a limited space. Her mom could not find a job, so, to survive, Nermina started selling candy and cigarettes in the streets. For Nermina, play was not an option. Like so many other children in her situation, she appeared chronically too serious for her age.

In sum, when there is no protected time and space, when adequate materials are scarce or not available, when there is no appropriate adult involvement, and when traditional family and community supports are weak or totally absent, the environment becomes stressful for children, and play hardly takes place.

Play as a Means to Relieve Stress

Why should we be so concerned when a child does not play? What is it that makes play so important in a child's life, especially when the environment becomes stressful? One might wonder, indeed. After all, play is commonly referred to as *just* play, a seemingly naïve and futile activity that children engage in when they have nothing better to do. Thompson and Stanford (1981) describe how, for instance, one director of nursing remarked when considering the option of establishing a child life program: "I don't think the administrator would ever allow us to hire a full-time person just to play with the kids" (p. 63). As this example indicates, play is often seen as a nice leisure activity and a potential diversion for children, but not as something to be taken seriously. In many respects, this once commonly shared view has somewhat evolved. In hospital settings, more and more pediatric health professionals accept the importance of play for hospitalized children and recognize that play is essential to the child's ability to cope with the hospital experience (Wishon & Brown, 1991; Henniger, 1995). Yet, in many hospitals, "play remains an 'extra' activity in the child's day—something to be squeezed in between doctor's visits and treatments" (Wishon & Brown, 1991, p. 45).

In humanitarian crises and emergency situations such as those faced by refugee populations, the general attitude toward play is not very different. Adult refugees (when they are consulted on this matter) tend to show diverse feelings toward play, and these feelings are often influenced by how they viewed children's play prior to the crisis. As far as the relief organizations are concerned, a trend similar to the one observed in hospital settings has recently been operating. Once completely ignored as part of children's needs in times of turmoil, the importance of play has become increasingly emphasized over the past few years. Professionals in the field of humanitarian assistance, from the grassroots level of the social workers in the field to the members of the most prestigious international organizations (e.g., United Nations High Commission for Refugees [UNHCR] and United Nations Children's Fund [UNICEF]), now recommend that play programs be implemented for refugee children when feasible and culturally relevant.

However, despite this trend, play programs in refugee camps remain scarce. When the financial possibilities are strangled, when strategic choices need to be made, these play programs are often the first ones to be considered "extra" and are therefore removed from the overall assistance plan. In both stressful environments, therefore, play is increasingly viewed as a useful and important way to help children cope with the situation, but it is certainly not yet seen as a priority. In the meantime, and somewhat paradoxically, play has consistently been described in the literature as one of the most powerful and effective means of reducing children's stress (O'Jessee et al., 2000).

What Does the Literature Say?

Psychoanalytic theorists provide a good deal of insight into the stress-reducing potential of children's play. They developed the cathartic theory of play, according to which play is a means for children to act out unpleasant experiences and minimize resulting negative psychological impact (Freud, 1920). *Catharsis* means purification in Greek, and the term was first used in Aristotle's time to describe how tragedies and music were believed to purge audiences of their emotions (Henniger, 1995). When applied to play, this notion of catharsis suggests that play can be a means for children to release emotional tensions in a safe, progressive, and nondamaging way. This, in turn, leads to play satiation. Play satiation, in Erikson's view, is the opposite of play disruption; it is "play from which the child emerges as a sleeper from dreams which 'worked'" (1963, p. 229).

To fully understand how play satiation occurs, we need to take a closer look at the notion of "abreactive" play. The concept of abreaction is drawn from the phenomenon of the "repetition compulsion" (Erikson, 1963). It is based on the strong inner drive, in all human beings, to re-create their experiences in order to assimilate them (Schaefer, 1994). For example, adults often keep telling over and over again the very minute details of a stressful or painful event they have recently experienced. By doing so, they unconsciously try to progressively gain mastery over an event that was beyond their capacity to react to or understand at the time. Freud (1920) was the first to apply this concept of abreaction to childhood, suggesting that a similar process may be operating in play. Indeed, when children play, and when they dramatize a traumatic experience, they progressively gain ownership of the experience that was too intense for them to master at the time. In imaginary play, children actively reenact the event that they have passively experienced in real life. They become the master of a game that follows their own rules instead of being the mere victims of a stressful situation. By doing so, they progressively regain control and are better able to cope.

The famous example of a toddler playing with a string, developed by Freud and described in the introduction to this book, shows clearly the implications of childhood play. You may remember in this example, Freud describes how the little boy used a string to symbolize his mother's comings and goings (Erikson, 1963). By throwing the string away and making it come back at his own pleasure, he played at recreating a situation that provoked anxiety when happening in real life. Over time, he learned to accept his mother's absence and to master his fears that she might not return. According to this approach, to play it out is the most natural, self-therapeutic—or restorative—process childhood offers (Erikson, 1963).

However, catharsis does not always occur in play. According to Watson (1994), individual characteristics and interpretation of meaning may lead different children or the same child in different circumstances to engage in other types of play behavior. For instance, he explains how some children entirely avoid the stressful situation and use less threatening themes in their play. Doing so, they progressively retrieve the level of confidence that they need to eventually face the stressful situation.

Other theorists, such as Piaget, also emphasize that play has restorative powers. However, they put more emphasis on the assimilation process than on the accommodative one. According to Piaget (1951), play is the medium that young children use to assimilate new experiences into their existing schemes. In play, children work through past stresses and prepare for future ones, which allows them to assimilate and gain control. Within this frame of analysis and previously discussed in Chapter 3, Piaget identified two distinct but complementary types of play that serve restorative functions: compensatory combinations and liquidating combinations. Compensatory combinations are purely assimilation processes: They are play behaviors that modify real-life events to fit the child's wish and turn a negative or stressful experience into a more pleasant and satisfying one. For example, a child might become the aggressor in reenacting a situation where he or she was the one being aggressed. Liquidating combinations are play behaviors that help children neutralize the strong emotions that were aroused by a specific

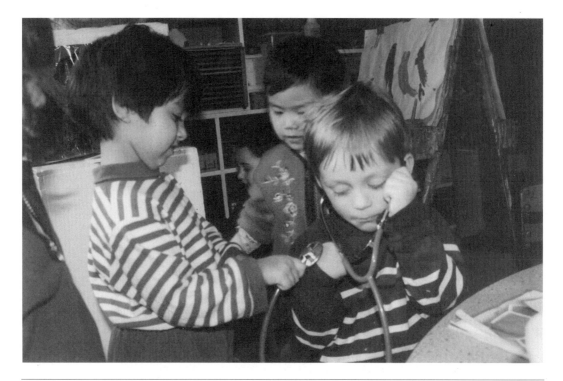

Photo 10.1   Play is the medium that young children use to assimilate new experiences into their existing schemes. Allowing this boy to play with a stethoscope may help him adjust to having the stethoscope placed on his own chest.

event and derive pleasure in the process. For example, a child might engage in spanking a baby doll to release feelings of anger and frustration (Schaefer, 1994).

Vygotsky (1978), on the other hand, while agreeing that play is essential to children's development, insisted that play can lead development instead of simply being an expression of it. In his view, play is central to the development of a child's ability to use symbols. In fact, play creates a zone of proximal development: "In play, a child always behaves beyond his average age, above his daily behavior; in play it is as though he was a head taller than himself" (1978, p. 102). Both Vygotsky and Piaget agree, however, that play is a means for children to emancipate from situational constraints and eventually gain control over them. In general, these theorists and many after them have come to the conclusion that play can have a powerful restorative impact. Play is therefore the activity of choice for children to deal with the normal stressors expected in the process of growing up and also to overcome the abnormal and intense additional stressors that sometimes came their way.

What Do Children Tell Us?

Beyond these theories, there are actually numerous concrete examples of stressful situations where children use play to cope. These examples often speak for themselves. In hospital settings, for instance, play has been associated with more rapid recovery and reduced length of stay (Wishon & Brown, 1991). Research has shown that hospitalized children acquire an increased sense of well-being through play, and that physiological measures such as heart rate, temperature, and blood pressure indicate faster overall healing when play opportunities are available. In addition to helping children cope with their fears, pretend play, especially with medical themes, allows children to gain the sense of control that they often lose while hospitalized. For instance, they can reverse the roles in playing with dolls, and can become the powerful doctor instead of the helpless patient (Hughes, 1991).

Most recently, the introduction of computers in dialysis rooms has proven to be particularly effective in helping children regain some sense of mastery in their lives. By creating virtual realities through Internet connections with one another while being physically bedridden and isolated, children and adolescents recover faster, both at physical and psychological levels (Bers, Gonzales-Heydrich, & de Maso, 2001). Through the illusion of power in imaginary play, therefore, children can change from being passive victims to being active manipulators. This helps them progressively gain control over the fears and negative emotions that they experience in real life. In that respect, play is part of children's survival kit (Harvey, 1984).

Isaiah is a 6-year-old boy who has had quite a few encounters with hospital settings. Although he is now doing much better, he went to the hospital 30 times in the first 3 years of his life! Most of those times, Isaiah did not really have access to play materials during his stays at the hospital. However, Isaiah has an attentive mother, Angela, who soon realized that her son could not remain inactive while in the hospital. She decided to invest in a complete doctor kit for Isaiah to play with. This toy kit soon became the most essential component of the suitcase that Angela always had ready for Isaiah, just in case he would have to go to the hospital. As she puts it, she "could not have made a better investment."

Indeed, Isaiah stopped being withdrawn at the hospital and started actively engaging in play. He would give pretend shots to his stuffed animals and dolls, put Band-Aids on them, comfort them, and so forth.

(Continued)

(Continued)

One of his favorite companions, a replica of the cartoon character Arthur, became the ideal patient: Any procedure that Isaiah had to undergo, Arthur would undergo as well several times before and after the actual procedure took place. Obviously, Arthur was not the only one being fixed in the process.

In refugee camps, play holds similar value and appears to have similar effects, though more research is needed to be sure. As mentioned earlier, research is scarce in such contexts, partly due to the instability and precariousness of the environment, as well as to the many obstacles that make the assessment of children's recovering processes difficult and hazardous. Longitudinal studies or even short-term experiments are usually not an option in those settings. In addition, refugee populations across the world come from highly diverse cultures. This, by itself, adds even more complexity to the whole situation and should not be overlooked. As a result, even the most well-intentioned and properly designed efforts to understand what is really happening in these children's lives appear to be limited. However, much can be said about refugee children and how they cope with their situation through play. In fact, many case stories have shown that play does hold a key function when available to the children. Do you remember Tamba?

These individual trajectories, often reported by social workers, anthropologists, and psychologists, suggest that the abreactive mechanisms described earlier in theory and in hospital settings are also operating in refugee situations. Over time, refugee children who engage in play seem to be less vulnerable to sickness, attend school on a more regular basis (when there is a school nearby and when they are old enough to attend), and engage more in constructive relationships with their peers. Generally speaking, they are simply happier. This really should come as no surprise. We have explained how stressful refugee camps can be for children, and we have detailed how play can be a means to restore childhood in stressful environments in general. It seems logical to hypothesize that play does have restorative powers for most refugee children, provided that play is given a chance to occur—not so easy to do given the often deplorable conditions and desperate circumstances in refugee camps.

Several dimensions need to be given attention, namely, a protected time and space, age-appropriate and culturally adequate play materials, a carefully balanced adult involvement, and involvement of peers, family, and the community at large. In the next and last section of this chapter, we explain why and how.

FOUR DIMENSIONS FOR A ●
GOOD-QUALITY PLAY PROGRAM

Play is not always positive for children, especially when children are exposed to highly stressful situations. For instance, play that takes away initiative from the child and gives him or her a passive role or play that is only a diversion and a denial of what is happening in reality may not provide the support children need to master current experiences (Harvey, 1984). In fact, the critical issue for adults is to ensure that children are given every opportunity to engage in creative and restorative play (Henniger, 1995). Therefore, the theoretical question of whether or not a play program should be implemented becomes a rather empirical one: What kind of play program will best address the children's needs? In other words, what are the dimensions to keep in mind when designing, implementing, and developing good-quality play programs?

In the remaining discussion of this chapter, we have chosen to focus on four main dimensions. They are the same dimensions usually missing in environments such as hospitals and refugee camps and in the absence of which an environment becomes abnormal. We will show how their careful reintroduction can foster play behaviors that are restorative for children. These four dimensions are as follows: (a) a protected time and space; (b) age-appropriate and culturally sensitive play materials; (c) a carefully balanced adult presence and involvement; and (d) the presence and involvement of peers, family, and the community at large. Each dimension encompasses a number of important variables.

The indications that follow reflect current thinking about best practices. However, they are by no means static. Indeed, any planned intervention must approach children as individuals and adapt to children's specific needs. Each situation is unique, and not all dimensions are equally important—or necessary—in all contexts. For instance, one situation might call for a high level of adult involvement and little emphasis on the space, whereas another may benefit from the exact opposite combination. In addition, each situation is subject to a different set of constraints in terms of financial means, human resources, space, or materials and toys available. In speaking of dimensions instead of conditions, then, we acknowledge this diversity.

A Protected Time and Space

First of all, to create a setting in which good play can occur, a child-welcoming and safe climate must be created (Wishon & Brown, 1991). In hospital and refugee camp settings, children often feel unsafe, and for obvious reasons. In hospitals, they usually experience painful or unpleasant situations several times a day: They might undergo surgery, receive shots, and take bad-tasting medicine. In refugee camps, children usually live in temporary shelters, and the fears associated with the reasons and conditions of their exile are usually still vivid. In some cases, the situation may remain unstable even within the host country or region. As a result, the children and their families might live in a permanent state of fear.

For play to occur in such instances, for the children to relax and engage in play, they need to be warmly reassured that nothing harmful or negative will happen to them during play. In hospital settings, children need to know that while in the playroom, they will not be interrupted for a medical procedure (Hellendoorn et al., 1994). Only then will children lower their defenses and become trustful enough to play.

In refugee situations, the level of general security in the camp is unfortunately beyond the control of the adults implementing play programs. However, much can be done to convince children that play areas and times allocated for play are both special and protected. Children usually do not have the fixed schedules that they used to have at home and that they need to regain control of their lives. The time devoted to play can, therefore, begin to hold this regulating function in their lives. For example, when children know that they can go to the play area from 2:00 to 4:00 p.m. every day, and when they begin to trust that caring adults will ensure their safety, then—and maybe only then—can they start to play.

The most resilient children might not need this level of regularity to confidently and spontaneously engage in play. In fact, they might initiate play by themselves, grasping any opportunity they have and making use of what play material they have, compensating with their creativity and imagination for what is missing in their environments. Some children in hospitals use whatever is available, be it ashtrays, IV poles, or light switches to start playing (Thompson & Stanford, 1981). In refugee camps, some children collect whatever they can recycle (e.g., metallic cans, banana leaves, bottle caps, shoe soles, etc.) and transform these "treasures" into the most creative toys. These children are usually those who first catch an observer's attention, because they remain active and playful in even the most stressful times. However, not all children are so creative, resourceful, and resilient. The quieter and sometimes withdrawn children often need encouragement to engage in quality play, the kind of play that leads to play satiation and leaves the child refreshed (Erikson, 1963). In fact, even those children who do play spontaneously can still greatly benefit from a more structured time and space (Thompson & Stanford, 1981).

Once a safe and predictable play area is established, the area itself needs to be given special care. A playroom accessible to all children is recommended (Landreth & Sweeney, 1999), one that allows for privacy, and one that is large enough to allow for different kinds of play. A too-small room restricts children's expression and may lead to frustration and aggressiveness. A too-large room may impair the quantity and quality of contacts among children and with a play facilitator (Landreth & Sweeney, 1999). Obviously, the conditions of the settings and the amount of resources available determine the kind of play setting that will be implemented. Whatever the case, however, it is important that all children, of all ages and conditions, feel welcome and encouraged to come and play. The space is the first key element that triggers children's curiosity and wish to participate.

Age-Appropriate and Culturally Sensitive Play Materials

As summarized by Erikson, "children . . . choose for their dramatizations play materials which [are] available in their culture and manageable at their age" (1963, p. 218). A welcoming and operational playroom, therefore, includes a variety of age-appropriate and culturally sensitive play materials, materials that are familiar to the children or that hold special meanings for them.

Specific toys can be provided in specific circumstances. In hospitals, for instance, children usually undergo painful or intimidating procedures. In the process, they are often exposed to many strange-looking and anxiety-provoking medical instruments such as needles and syringes (Adams, 1976). To help hospitalized children better cope with those specific and temporary anxieties, the play facilitators can provide various medically orientated play materials that replicate in a smaller and less threatening way those very instruments that the children are afraid of or unfamiliar with (e.g., plastic needles and syringes, bandages, a play examination table, small blood-pressure kits, nurse and doctor replicas and/or costumes). An assortment of diverse and more random dolls and puppets can also be assigned various roles in the dramatization of the procedures (Wishon & Brown, 1991).

Because the child controls the pace and contents of those pretend play sessions, personally important or interesting information can be dealt with in a manageable and active way, while those concepts that are too threatening can be put aside and avoided in play until the child is ready to confront them (Oremland, 1988). Through play with adequate materials, therefore, children in hospitals progressively regain mastery of the situation and are better able to cope with it.

The same can hold true in refugee camps, although the specific toys and materials used may be quite different. Children who have experienced war situations may find it helpful to play and replay war scenes, where they become the hero characters instead of being the passive and helpless young victims that they often were in real life. Toys that encourage such play, however controversial they may be when the whole population is eager for peace and forgetting, might nonetheless prove very pertinent and useful. In fact, even when particular toys are not provided in that respect, children appear to engage in war play anyhow, with whatever object they can turn into a gun, soldier, or enemy outfit. By providing the children with what they need to fully engage in war play, and by reassuring them that this type of play is accepted as long as it remains play, children can process the events in a more supportive environment. For example, small replicas to be played with on the floor promote more contained, less impulse-ridden war play, and may therefore be better than materials promoting sociodramatic war play.

However, children affected by war do not only play at war themes. Like any other children, they play at representing what is happening in their daily lives. In refugee camps, they might pretend-play a variety of scenes such as family interactions, going to school, cooking food, and so forth. In addition to knowing what these children have gone through, and what their life is like in the present, play facilitators should also be particularly sensitive to the cultural context surrounding the children. When children are healthy and happy, they might be willing to explore and discover new toys that don't really belong to their culture but that they are curious to integrate into their play. When they are sick, however, or when the environment becomes highly stressful, this capacity might be seriously impaired, and the play activity itself might be compromised if children cannot relate to more familiar objects. A plastic medieval castle or toy "hook and ladder," for instance, does not make much sense in African cultures, as the previous two sketches imply.

Ro, 4 years old, was born in a refugee camp in Thailand. His parents had managed to escape from Cambodia during the Khmer Rouge geno-cide (1975–1978), when one third of the population was killed. In 1998, Ro came back to his family's region of origin, Samlot (northwest of Cambodia, near the border with Thailand). At 4 years of age, he was what people call a "returnee." The land was full of mines, which made playing and wandering around extremely hazardous for children.

Ro did not really engage in play during the first few times he spent at the activity and play center located near his newly reconstructed house. The play materials that the educators had for him were very scarce and not really adequate: a couple of plastic blond dolls "made in Taiwan," a few kappla sticks, a ball, and many "educational games" that the educators made to support the children's learning process at school.

Realizing that the lack of appropriate material might be the reason why Ro did not engage in play, one of the educators, Savuth (himself a returnee), had a brilliant idea: He decided to give his traditional scarf—or *krama*—to Ro so that he could use it as a hammock for the doll. Babies sleep in hammocks in Cambodia, just as many adults do. Sure enough, Ro engaged in play right away: He put the blond doll in the pretend hammock, his face covered with a wide grin, and pretended that he was the father of the baby for a while. With culturally sensitive material, Ro was finally able to play.

A Carefully Balanced Adult Presence and Involvement

When the time and space for play are set, when adequate toys and play materials are provided, children have more opportunities to play. Yet, this is often not enough, and children who face abnormal environments such as hospitals and refugee camps often need more support in addition to those physical and material incentives. In that respect, the presence and guidance of a supportive, consistent, and trustworthy adult who does not threaten or reject is essential (Wishon & Brown, 1991). In fact, in the absence of such a person, many children might simply not play (Henniger, 1995).

Hospitalized and refugee children often hold a distorted view of adults because of the negative experiences that they have had with some of them. In hospitals, children are exposed to many painful procedures, and they often consider the adults who inflict these treatments on them directly responsible for their suffering. Even the most caring nurses and doctors, in such circumstances, can appear quite threatening. Refugee children, for other reasons, might display similar reactions toward adults in general. Those who have seen adults engage in acts of violence, for instance, might remain mistrustful and even distressed when in the presence of a stranger.

For all these reasons, adults who hold the function of play facilitators with these children need to be particularly engaging, warm, and supportive. With refugee children especially, it is best if the play facilitators are from the same cultural origin as the children. Because they have gone through the same events and currently live in the same refugee conditions, they can relate much better to the children's fears and need for comfort. And because they are from the same culture, they are also better able to communicate with the children, both verbally and through play.

Researchers and practitioners traditionally agree that some adult presence is needed in the playroom. The type and level of involvement that play facilitators should display, on the other hand, appears to be much more debated. O'Jessee, Wilson, and Morgan have described, for instance, how directed play and nondirected play are often opposed (2000). In nondirected play, children are the initiators of the activity, and play facilitators hold the role of participant-observer. In directed play, on the contrary, play facilitators predetermine the themes and content of the play experience and assume a much more active role.

In practice, though, the theoretical debate needs to be transcended. Facilitating a child's play involves continuously adjusting the mode of interaction with the child on the basis of each particular child's needs, in a specific context, and at a certain time (Linder, 1990). When dealing with a group of children, play facilitators who remain aware of individual differences and diverse needs can help children find their own comfortable space within the group and engage in play at their pace and level.

Sometimes, children might engage in play that appears inappropriate or disturbing for adult observers. Adams (1976), for example, relates a case in which two young hospitalized boys started stabbing at their puppets with syringes, giving them "shots" in the eyes and genitals. In such circumstances, there is a risk that play may in fact foster more anxieties than relief, both for the children who engage in the dramatization and for the other ones around.

The role of play facilitators, in such circumstances, is clearly to help children step back a little and realize that there is a difference between their play and what might or might not happen in reality. In the example provided by Adams, the play facilitators allowed the boys to continue their play, but reassured them that although it was fine to play like this, such "shots" would never be given to any child in real life.

In other cases, some children regress and feel a need to play with toys that are usually meant for younger children. Such behaviors, given the circumstances and the abnormality of the environment, can be quite common among children who experience high levels of stress. When such behaviors are temporary, they can in fact prove quite adaptive: These children simply need to go back to the safer grounds that they have already mastered before they can move on and cope with the new challenges they face in the present. As the following example illustrates, sensitive play facilitators can provide the additional support children need in such cases.

Sar was 9 years old at the time he returned to his home region in Cambodia. He was born in a refugee camp in Thailand, and his family had been struggling to survive for years. Sar's father, unemployed, soon became an alcoholic after he lost one of his legs as a result of a land-mine injury. Although absent for long periods of time, he was violent when at home and he used to beat Sar and his mother on a regular basis.

When Sar first came to the play and activity center, he appeared quite immature: His speech was that of a 4-year-old, and he spontaneously played in the toddlers' corner, nurturing dolls for extensive periods of time and interacting only with children much younger than himself. The play facilitators, well aware of Sar's family situation, decided to let him play like this for a while. Yet they paid particular attention to Sar's younger playmates. Indeed, although Sar had regressed in many ways, he still had the strength of a 9-year-old and could involuntarily hurt younger children in play.

In the meantime, the play facilitators slowly introduced Sar to more adequate play materials and older playmates. Although Sar remained in the toddlers' corner most of the time, he progressively opened up and started interacting with older children. Thanks to the children's patience and to the play facilitators' insight, Sar was finally able to evolve and progress at his own pace through play.

The Presence and Involvement
of Peers, Family, and the Community at Large

Finally, play facilitators work with each child both in an individual and in a social context. While adopting a child-centered approach and being sensitive to the special needs and wishes of each child, they also need to take into consideration the whole social and cultural context surrounding the child. Peers, family, and the community at large are traditional sources of support in times of turmoil. Sometimes, those supports are weakened due to the circumstances and to the level of stress and fear experienced by these individuals.

In hospitals, a child's traditional peer network is absent, and although visits can take place, there is clearly a separation between the daily life of the hospitalized child and other children's lives, especially if the length of hospitalization is extended. As for parents and relatives, the very fact that they themselves deal with many anxieties linked to the child's sickness often prevents them from being truly supportive (Thompson & Stanford, 1981). In refugee situations, the whole community is usually severely affected by the events. Although peers, parents, and relatives might still be able to provide the child with a caring and supportive environment, they are not always physically and psychologically available to be fully sensitive to the child's specific concerns and fears.

In such instances, play can also help children reconnect with the meaningful persons in their environment. At the peer level, several authors note that group play can help children maintain socialization and experience opportunities for multilateral relationships (Ginott, 1961; Adams, 1976; Landreth & Sweeney, 1999). These authors further explain how group play can provide more opportunity for catharsis than does individual play. For instance, children who are quiet and sometimes fearful of their own feelings can benefit greatly from another child's expression through play in the group. In hospitals, because of the increased isolation of children in one-bed or two-bed rooms, such opportunities for socialization appear all the more important.

For some children, however, solitary play remains "an indispensable harbor for the overhauling of shattered emotions after periods of rough going in the social seas" (Erikson, 1963, p. 221). Play facilitators should remain aware of such needs, and playrooms should always provide safe and quiet areas where these children can engage in play by themselves before they feel secure enough to join the group. In such cases, as in any other, it is the play facilitator's role to sense what is best for a child at a given time and how to best support this particular child in his or her struggles.

Alma's dad "disappeared" during the Srebrenica attack in Bosnia-Herzegovina. In August of 1996, she started going to the play and activity center newly created in Tuzla. One of the play facilitators working there, Jasmina, a displaced person herself, soon noticed that Alma was not playing with the other children. Instead, Alma would sit by herself in a corner of the room and play alone with a plastic telephone. Through careful observation and listening, although not interfering with Alma's play, Jasmina soon realized that the child was talking to her dad through the plastic telephone toy. Each time Alma came to the activity and play center (two to three times a week), she kept repeating the same patterns of play with very few changes.

Not knowing what to do to help Alma and fighting with her own personal issues at the same time, Jasmina followed her intuition and respected Alma's desire to be alone. She decided to let her behave like this as long as she wanted or needed to.

Approximately 1 year later, Alma left her solitary corner, abandoned the plastic telephone toy, and joined the other children playing nearby. Through solitary play, she was finally able to reconnect and engage in group activities with other children.

At the family and community level, much can also be done through play to help children reconnect with their environment and culture. Acknowledging the parents' needs to understand and accept what is happening in their child's life is a first step in that direction. Even when they are distressed by their own situation and sometimes not fully available to answer their children's emotional needs, most parents in stressful and abnormal environments are concerned with their children's well-being.

Finally, as we have conveyed throughout this chapter, sensitivity to the child's cultural context is crucial. In times of crises and turmoil, children often feel lost and unsafe. The traditional and cultural values that they might have taken for granted beforehand often become more salient and sometimes even questionable during and after the events. Children in abnormal environments such as hospitals and refugee camps face such issues as sickness, death, suffering, violence, and helplessness. They might find it difficult to find comfort in the means that they traditionally used before (e.g., religion, spirituality, communal practices, etc.), and they might start doubting the effectiveness of such traditions or beliefs. In times of war, especially civil wars, the very fact that the community and culture as a whole allowed such violence to take place often goes beyond the understanding capacity of children—and of adults as well.

In the Sierra Leonean animist tradition, Kongolee is a spirit that can be quite mischievous. He is represented by a big scary wooden mask and takes part in many traditional feasts and ceremonies. Before the war, the children would pursue Kongolee (whoever was wearing the mask), teasing him and exciting him. However, when Kongolee would turn around and start chasing them, they would be scared and run away.

In the refugee camps, many traditional ceremonies, such as the ritual initiation of boys and girls into adulthood, were delayed. Indeed, those ceremonies were supposed to be practiced in secret and to take place in small villages or in the sacred forest nearby, not in refugee camps. However, some other ceremonies remained, despite the need for adaptation. The Kongolee tradition is one of them. Once in a while, whenever a special occasion had to be celebrated, a man would wear the Kongolee mask, and children would start playing with him in this ambivalent and pleasurable combination of excitement and fear. Through the use of such cultural symbols, they were able to process the present and adapt to it.

When children play with culturally appropriate toys and materials, when they do so in the presence of sensitive adults who belong to their culture, and when the whole community is involved, they can reengage and reconnect with at least certain aspects of their culture. Most important of all, they can reengage and reconnect with themselves within their context and culture.

● SUMMARY

In abnormal environments such as hospitals and refugee camps, most children experience a degree of stress that calls for specific support. Play, in such instances, holds restorative powers by helping children draw from their inner resources and regain some sense of mastery. In a protected time and space, with age-appropriate and culturally sensitive play materials, a carefully balanced adult presence and involvement, and the presence and involvement of peers, family, and the community at large, most children can be children again, cope with the adversity of their situation, and develop to become healthy members of their community.

In this chapter, we have established that restorative play is different from play therapy, both in its theoretical framework and in its practical applications.

We have focused on the majority of the children, those who react normally to an abnormal environment. Yet, some situations and specific individual trajectories call for further intervention. Play, because it is the expression of childhood, still holds a key function in such instances. However, when play is used as a tool within a therapeutic relationship, a different type of dynamic takes place. In the following chapter, we review how theorists and practitioners have conceptualized the clinical uses of play and how they have implemented play therapy.

KEY WORDS, NAMES, AND IDEAS ●

Abnormal environment

Abreactive play

Acute event

Adult involvement

Catharsis

Child life programs

Community

Culturally sensitive

Developmental crises

Developmentally appropriate behaviors

Hospitals

Illness causality

Play disruption

Play satiation

Preventive function vs. therapeutic function

Psychological well-being

Refugee camps

Regularity

Security

Stress

Transactional approach

Unfamiliar environment

● NOTE

1. In this particular story, as in others taking place in refugee camps, the activity and play program mentioned was established by the nongovernmental organization Enfants Réfugiés du Monde (Refugee Children of the World).

CHAPTER 11

PLAY THERAPY

Play Therapy: The Psychoanalytic Tradition
Play Therapy: The Humanistic Tradition
Play Therapy: Cognitive-Developmental Approaches
Play Therapy: Behavioral and Cognitive-Behavioral Approaches
Art Therapy
Training
Concluding Remarks: Does Play Therapy Work?

> During their free-play time at preschool, Jack and Sarah carefully built two towers out of wooden blocks and then placed Lego people on top of each tower. Jack held a plane in his hand and flew it around the buildings while Sarah took the Lego people and dropped them, one by one, to the ground. Jack then slammed the plane into the towers, knocking them down while making noises that sounded like explosions. Sarah stomped on the blocks and Lego people, screaming, "Now they're all dead!" For a few moments Jack looked at Sarah quietly, and then began rebuilding the towers.

The scene of Jack and Sarah reenacting the World Trade Center attacks in their play represents what was commonly observed by parents, teachers, and therapists during the days, weeks, and months following the terrorist attacks of September 11, 2001. Jack and Sarah's play illustrates the fact that children commonly and frequently recreate emotionally difficult and confusing experiences—presumably to master feelings and reduce confusion.

During the aftermath of the September 11th tragedy, adults tried to cope by articulating their thoughts and emotions, by seeking or avoiding information as they saw fit, by engaging in activities that distracted them from their grief, and by making profound changes in their lives that reflected new, altered priorities. Adults had, therefore, several different ways to cope, ways not available to children.

That adults have more ways to cope is made clear by a moment's reflection. First, most adults have the power to make choices—consciously or unconsciously—about how they will deal with difficult circumstances. Second, most adults can articulate their thoughts and emotions and share them with others through discussion or writing. Third, most adults can draw on their experience of adversity, trauma, and tragedy. In short, most adults know how to cope with difficult situations.

However, children—especially young children—do not have an extensive repertoire of coping skills or a history of having coped with difficult situations. They often are not able to articulate their thoughts and emotions, and even if they can, their understanding of what has happened and how it affects them is limited. Furthermore, children's understanding of difficult situations is more likely to be based on inaccurate attributions of cause and effect, which sometimes causes additional worry. For example, following a divorce in the family, some children feel they must have done something wrong for one parent to leave and for the other to be so unhappy.

For all these limitations, children often need help to cope. Play offers help if children can use play naturally, on their own, as a form of self-help. But some cannot—either because their emotional problems have blocked their ability to play or because their play skills are undeveloped. As the clinician and developmental researcher Jan Drucker (1994) put it,

> the children who come to us for treatment are almost always there because the ordinary ways of handling events and emotions, centrally including play, have been insufficient, and symptomatic or other maladaptive means of coping have developed. An inability to play is indeed often one of the reasons for referral to treatment. (p. 64)

When, for whatever reason, children cannot play, their problems may increase. They may withdraw, become depressed, become overly anxious, become contentious, or become all of the above. For any of these problems, they may need help from caring professionals who know how to help children use play to help themselves.

In helping children use play to help themselves, therapists are, therefore, harnessing what is normal and natural in typical childhoods. Play therapy is a homeopathic treatment akin to the physician helping a patient strengthen his or her immune system.

However, play therapy is not one thing. Rather, it is many different things. Different therapists use play in different ways or in similar ways for different reasons. Some focus on the play itself because of play's presumed therapeutic functions. Others use play more as a context for implementing interventions not having directly to do with play.

As we discuss these and other differences, it should become clear that therapists using different theoretical perspectives have different definitions of what are the problems. Some define problems as having mainly to do with children's feelings and others as having mainly to do with children's thinking or behaving. Whatever way a child's problems are defined, in play therapy, play becomes a means to solve and cure. In this chapter, we will discuss different types of play therapy.

● PLAY THERAPY: THE PSYCHOANALYTIC TRADITION

Today, play is a common feature in therapies for children. However, the history of play therapy shows that this was not always the case. In fact, until the late 1800s play was not even recognized as significant for children's development. It was originally viewed as something that simply occupies children's time or that serves as an outlet for excess energy. But after the turn of the twentieth century, Sigmund Freud's psychoanalytic theory brought attention to early childhood development and children's play. He wrote, "We see that children repeat in their play everything that has made a great impression on them in actual life" (Freud, 1961). In developing his idea that children, in play, master their emotions, Freud provided the rationale for play therapy.

However, it was not Sigmund Freud but his daughter Anna, along with Melanie Klein and other child analysts, who developed the theory and practice of play therapy. These pioneers from the psychoanalytic tradition saw in play a means to get at children's troublesome feelings—much like the analyst uses patients' dreams and free associations to get at adults' troublesome feelings. Interpreting children's play became analogous to interpreting adults' dreams and free associations.

The analogy between children's play and adults' dreams and free associations is based on the presumed shared functions of play, dreams, and free associations, the main function being that of expressing the inner (unconscious) life and its feelings surrounding repressed intrapsychic conflicts. However, the actual process of therapy differs greatly for children and adults. In analysis, adult patients need to relax their grip on outer reality to focus on inner reality. This would not work for children, because children are not adept at distinguishing inner and outer reality and because their grip on outer reality is already what might be called "relaxed." However, children can and do use play to express their inner lives and what is troubling them—especially if helped by a professional who knows how to support play so that *clinical themes* get played out.

Play also helps solidify the relationship between child and therapist. For the analyst, no real change can occur until the patient has feelings for the analyst and cares about the relationship, that is, until there is what the analysts call a *therapeutic alliance.* From the analytic point of view, play therapy has the double advantage of helping children form a therapeutic alliance and express their inner lives so that a therapist can, through interpreting, help them understand and master their feelings. To see how this works, consider the following well-known example of the British child analyst Donald Winnicott using play to help his young patient deal with troublesome feelings (Winnicott, 1977).

Winnicott was treating a 2½-year-old girl nicknamed "the Piggle." The Piggle came to therapy following the birth of her younger sister. After the birth, she became easily bored, depressed, and distant from her father. Furthermore, she developed nightmares about a "black mummy" who lived in her tummy and a "babacar" who sometimes came to put her into the toilet.

Through playing with the Piggle, Winnicott very quickly fostered a therapeutic alliance, so that in just the first session he was able to introduce what we are here calling *the clinical theme.* In the Piggle's case, the clinical theme was that of her wanting everything the way it was *before* her sister's arrival— when she had her parents' love and attention all for herself. Here is a description from Winnicott's notes of that first session:

> She went . . . and brought the teddy over for me to show him the toys. She then started playing with them herself, mostly taking parts of trains out of the muddle. . . . Then began something which was repeated over and over again: "Here's another one . . . and here's another one." This had to do mostly with trucks and engines, but it did not seem to matter much what it was that she made this comment about. I took this therefore as a communication and said: "Another baby. The Sush Baby (The Piggle's name for her little sister)." This was evidently the correct thing to say, because now she started giving me an account of the time the Sush Baby came, as she remembered it. (p.10)

During the second session, while in the middle of asking Winnicott about various toys, she asked, "Do you know about the babacar?" Winnicott responded by interpreting,

> "It's the mother's inside where the baby is born from." She added, "Yes, the black inside." The Piggle then began to overfill a bucket with toys while Winnicott interpreted that she was making a Winnicott baby sick.

But then Winnicott initiated a new play sequence—one that clearly expressed the clinical theme and one that offered the Piggle a way out of her dilemma. Here is the brief and charming dialogue Winnicott recorded between himself and the Piggle:

W. Winnicott is the Piggle's baby; it's very greedy because it loves the Piggle, its mother, so much, and it's eaten so much that it's sick.

P. The Piggle's baby has eaten so much.

W. The new thing you want is about the Winnicott baby and the Piggle mother, about Winnicott loving the Piggle (mother), eating the Piggle, and being sick.

P. Yes, you do.

After some playing together, the Piggle left the room to join her father. Winnicott remained on the floor next to the toys. When the Piggle returned, she asked:

P. Can I have a toy?

W. Winnicott very greedy baby; want all the toys.

This round of dramatic play was repeated several times until she left the room to tell her father, "Baby want all the toys." She brought her father back into the therapy room, showed him the Winnicott baby, and then began her own game of "being born." This consisted of her sliding down from her father's lap, head first, and onto the floor while saying, "I'm a baby too." Winnicott responded:

W. I want to be the only baby. I want all the toys.

P. You've got all the toys.

W. Yes, but I want to be the only baby; I don't want there to be any more babies.

P. I'm a baby too.

W. I want to be the *only* baby! (and in a different voice) Shall I be cross?

P. Yes. (p. 25)

Winnicott then made a big noise, knocked over the toys, hit his knees and said, "I want to be the only baby." This pleased the Piggle.

It's obvious what Winnicott accomplished by becoming a greedy baby. In this role, Winnicott offered the Piggle a way of confronting and accepting her own feelings about the Sush baby and her desire to have everything for herself.

Using play to form a therapeutic alliance and interpret feelings remains to this day a cornerstone of psychoanalytically oriented play therapy. Furthermore, this use of play shows up in play therapy from different theoretical traditions, though what is meant by a therapeutic alliance and by interpreting feelings often changes when going from one tradition to another. We see this clearly in the next discussion, of *humanistic* play therapy.

● PLAY THERAPY: THE HUMANISTIC TRADITION

There are lots of distinctions between types of play therapy focusing on children's feelings. However, one distinction in particular stands out. That one is between traditional psychoanalytic play therapy, in which the therapist interprets unconscious, repressed feelings symbolized in a child's play, and humanistic play therapy, in which the therapist *mirrors* a child's surface feelings to convey understanding and *unconditional positive regard.*

Humanistic clinical psychology is most closely associated with the name of Carl Rogers, who developed his theory and approach to therapy based on one big assumption. That assumption was that his clients (he called them clients, not patients) had within themselves the strength to solve their problems, if only they could accept themselves, believe in themselves, and have the needed self esteem and positive sense of self for taking on the goals of growing and healing. From this perspective, what brings so many into therapy is not so much deep and hidden conflicts as it is extensive life experience with others who provide mainly negative or conditional regard. Humanistic therapy focuses, therefore, on providing a "corrective emotional experience," one that has the therapist constantly working to provide *unconditional positive regard.* It sounds easy, doesn't it—providing unconditional positive regard? In fact, it is not easy—as we will soon discover.

Carl Rogers initiated the humanistic, client-centered approach, but like Sigmund Freud before him, he left it to others to develop the approach for children. Of all those who developed Rogerian therapy for children, no one has been more influential than Virginia Axline, so it is her work that we will feature.

Axline's humanistic play therapy with children clearly illustrates the basic humanistic assumptions about problems and what is needed to bring about change. It also illustrates the skill needed to implement this approach effectively. To demonstrate this, consider the following example from Axline's widely read book, *Play Therapy* (1980). The example is of a 6-year-old boy, "Oscar," described by Axline as being "aggressive, belligerent, negative, insecure, defiant, dependent" (p. 80). (While reading this passage, pause after Oscar announces he is going to bust up the toys in the playroom. Ask yourself, "What would I say to Oscar?" Answer honestly. Ask too what you would say if your goal was to convey unconditional positive regard by mirroring Oscar's feelings? After answering these two questions, read on and note how your responses differ from Axline's.)

(Therapist and Oscar go into the playroom. Therapist starts to close the door.)

Oscar
(screaming):   Don't shet the door! Don't shet the door! (Tears roll down his cheeks.)

Therapist: You don't want me to shut the door. You're afraid to stay here with me if we shut the door. (Oscar looks up amazed, and then nods his head. The therapist continues.) Very well. We'll leave the door open and you close the door when you feel like it.

Oscar (as he
thaws out):   I'll bust up everything in here!

Therapist: You're feeling tough now.

Oscar (glaring
at therapist): I'll bust you up too.

Therapist: You're still feeling tough.

Oscar: I'll—(suddenly laughs) I'll—(He wanders around the play-room and picks up the toy telephone.) What's this? (p. 81)

Axline responded to Oscar's threat by saying he was feeling tough. Was this how you would have responded? When faced with a child threatening to be destructive, most adults respond quite differently. Most provide some counter-threat (such as, "If you do that, you won't be able to play with the toys") or mildly negative argument (such as, "Other children want to play with the toys"). Even when remaining true to the guiding principles of humanistic therapy, most adults would not likely say what Axline said. They might instead say something such as, "You feel like busting everything up" or "You're feeling angry."

If your responses fall roughly into what most are likely to say in response to Oscar's threat, you are in an excellent position to appreciate the skill and expertise of Axline. Axline's response was perfect. Not only did it mirror Oscar's feelings, it conveyed something wonderfully positive. Few 6-year-old boys fail to appreciate being called "tough" (directly or by implication)—and Oscar obviously is not among the few. Clearly Oscar was pleased with Axline's choice of words. As a result, he became pleased with himself.

Note that Axline's choosing just the right words to mirror Oscar's feelings did the opposite of encouraging him to bust up everything. Feeling both understood and accepted by Axline and feeling good about himself, Oscar did not need to demonstrate his toughness through being destructive. He could focus on what he most wanted to do, which was to explore and play with the toys in the therapy room.

Humanistic play therapy, therefore, frees children from having to act on their negative feelings. It shares with psychoanalysis a focus on children's feelings, but the feelings focused on are those at the surface and not those hidden in repressed conflicts.

In the next discussion, the focus shifts from feelings to thinking, though thinking and feelings are never disconnected.

PLAY THERAPY: COGNITIVE-DEVELOPMENTAL APPROACHES ●

Half-way through his monumental treatise, *Play, Dreams, and Imitation* (*in Childhood,* 1962), Piaget discusses why it is that children often do not know the deeper meaning of their play—a fact that psychoanalysts attribute to repression and humanists treat as largely irrelevant. He wrote,

> the field of unconscious symbolism is wider than that of repression, and consequently of what can be censored. The question that then arises is whether its unconscious character, i.e., the subject's ignorance of its meaning, does not merely result from the fact that he is incapable of direct and complete consciousness of it. For Freud, censorship is a product of consciousness, and symbolism a product of unconscious associations which elude censorship. In our opinion, it is worth considering whether these two terms might not be reversed, censorship being merely the expression of the unconscious, uncomprehended character of the symbol, and the symbol itself being the result of a beginning of conscious assimilation, i.e., an attempt at comprehension. (p. 191)

What this difficult-to-decipher though insightful comment suggests is that we treat children's play, at least their make-believe play, as their way of attempting to comprehend and become more conscious, not as attempts to conceal and remain unconscious. From Piaget's perspective, children start out unconscious and, with development, become increasingly conscious through adopting and constructing new tools for thinking—the symbolizing found in narrative make-believe play being a prime example.

To show how relevant this point is to understanding the cognitive-developmental perspective on play therapy, consider the previous example of Winnicott playing at being a greedy baby. For Winnicott, his play was a substitute for interpreting—a way to draw out the wishes and feelings that the Piggle had repressed. But for Piaget and cognitive-developmentalists, Winnicott's play supported the Piggle's developing a new tool for thinking, a tool she could use in the future to manage her feelings (Scarlett, 1994). In sum, developing children's thinking and their tools for thinking is the focus in cognitive-developmental play therapy.

One of the most significant areas of thinking to develop is thinking about what others are thinking—what today's cognitive-developmentalists are likely to call "theory of mind" (Perner, 1991). For clinicians within a cognitive-developmental tradition, children with serious emotional and relationship problems often need help because they have bad or undeveloped theories about what others are thinking.

Nowhere is this last assumption better shown than in the cognitive-developmental therapist's concern for helping children overcome their egocentricity. By *egocentricity* they mean, of course, not selfishness, but relative inability to take the point of view of another. *Pair therapy* offers a nice example of using play to help children overcome their egocentricity.

Pair therapy was developed by Robert Selman and his associates at the Judge Baker Guidance Clinic in Boston (Selman & Hickey Schultz, 1990). In pair therapy, joint play between two children paired with one another provides the therapist opportunities for helping them learn new, less egocentric ways to relate well to one another. Here is an example:

> Two boys, Mitchell and Arnie, had been in pair therapy for several months when, during one play session, both boys began to quarrel, and Arnie said something hurtful. Mitchell turned to the therapist and said, "Tell him to shut up." The therapist responded by suggesting a more mature alternative: "Can you tell Arnie his insults hurt your feelings?" (p. 257)

Here the therapist helps both boys by encouraging Mitchell to make explicit to Arnie how Arnie's words hurt his feelings. Arnie's egocentricity had prevented him before he spoke from understanding that his words might hurt, and Mitchell's egocentricity prevented him from seeing the need to make his feelings explicit if Arnie was to understand.

The kind of help given by therapists adopting a cognitive-developmental approach is common in early childhood classrooms. This observation coupled with the fact that in these days of managed health care, the only therapy that is likely to be given to many troubled children is school-based therapy (Drewes, 2001) is why the next example is of a teacher rather than a clinician. In this example, the teacher uses co-play to help a child understand and become responsive to the feelings and thinking of her play partners (Scarlett, 1998).

Susie, age 5, had become so bossy that her classmates were beginning to avoid her. To help Susie become less bossy, her teacher began co-playing with her, at first by following Susie's lead (to establish rapport) but then by playing as an equal and by occasionally insisting that Susie follow her (the teacher's) lead.

When they first played together, Susie started off by being bossy. "Let me pick a person (doll) for you, and here is one for me. Okay, okay, now you make yours sick." Her teacher responded, "I'll make my person cough." "No, no," said Susie, "Make her throw up, like this." (She demonstrates.) "Okay, now I'll drive her to the hospital. Okay, lie yours here. (The teacher puts her toy figure down.) The doctor says you ate too much. That's why you're sick."

The teacher had been passive throughout, not being allowed by Susie to be active. Finally, the teacher had her toy figure say, "I'm feeling better now.

I'm ready to go home." Susie was not pleased by this initiation and said, "Not so soon, young lady. You ate too much junk. Just lie down. I have a shot for you." The play sequence continued with Susie remaining the boss and firmly in control.

In a subsequent co-playing session, the teacher began the session quite differently, by leading, not following: "Susie, let's play with these cars and the garage." Susie responded, "I want to play with you but with the Legos." "Well, I'm playing with the garage now," said the teacher. "We can use the Legos another time." Susie folded her arms and said sternly, "No, I'm wanting the Legos now." The teacher proceeded to set up things around the garage. Slowly, Susie inched her way over. The teacher began to play. "I'm pushing a police car with a woman in it." Susie whined. "I want the police car with the lady in it." She grabbed for it, but the teacher intervened. "No, I'm using this now; you'll have to choose another one." "I want YOU to pick another one," said Susie, to which the teacher replied, "I had this one first, and I want to keep using it. When I'm done, I'll give you a chance." Susie started to look around. She found another figure. "I'm using her. She's even better."

After several of these argument-filled co-playing sessions, the co-playing began to have fewer arguments and become more like normal play. Susie seemed to be slowly giving up trying to control so much. Here is an example:

> Susie and her teacher were playing with matchbox cars. Pointing to the cars, Susie suggested, "Let's pretend they are police." Her teacher responded, "That's a good idea." Then taking another car, the teacher said, "Let's pretend this guy was speeding, and we go to catch him." "No, no," said Susie, "Let's make them go after that person because they got into a terrible accident." The teacher then suggested, "How about if we use both ideas? Let's pretend he was speeding and then got into an accident." "Okay," Susie agreed, "If I get to save him." She then pro-ceeded to make the car speed and flip over. Her teacher said, "I like using both our ideas." Susie said that she liked using just her own ideas better. Then the teacher explained to Susie that she had more fun play-ing with her when they could use both of their ideas. To this Susie responded, "At least you don't get mad and leave." (Scarlett, 1998, p. 73)

In subsequent co-playing sessions, Susie's teacher reminded her of this last remark, an obvious insight and milestone. From then on, Susie began to see the connection between giving in a little and making friends.

In the examples given so far, we see play being used to express and inter-pret feelings, as well as to guide children into thinking differently. In the fol-lowing examples, the focus narrows to individual behaviors, as we see how play is used in behavioral and cognitive-behavioral play therapies.

● PLAY THERAPY: BEHAVIORAL AND COGNITIVE-BEHAVIORAL APPROACHES

In behavioral therapies, individual behaviors, or in the case of cognitive-behavioral therapy, individual thoughts (Beck, 1976), are targeted for change either because they are "inappropriate" or "harmful" (tantrumming, hitting, thinking all mistakes are evidence for being dumb, etc.) or because they are "appropriate" or valued (cooperating, playing constructively, discriminating between when mistakes are matters of intelligence and matters of effort or inexperience). One might say, therefore, that the job description of the behavioral therapist is someone who decreases inappropriate and harmful behaviors and increases appropriate and valued behaviors—or teaches others to do so.

Furthermore, although there are many types of behavioral therapies, the most common have to do with operant conditioning (Skinner, 1953) or controlling which behaviors serve as stimuli for target behaviors and which serve as reinforcers. Following this approach, all we have to do is eliminate the stimuli or reinforcers setting off or rewarding unwanted behaviors and implement the stimuli or reinforcers setting off or rewarding desired behaviors. Sounds easy, doesn't it? But, just as we found in the case of Axline's providing unconditional positive regard, in the case of the behavioral therapist managing stimuli and reinforcers, it rarely is easy. Consider just the first step in the process of designing a behavioral treatment program.

Once a target behavior has been chosen, the behaviorist must identify what stimuli and reinforcers are setting up and maintaining the target behavior. But when observing a child in some natural setting such as the child's home or school, one rarely sees immediately what are the stimuli and reinforcers. In fact, what might appear to be a reinforcer (e.g., praising a child) could turn out to be a punisher, as happens sometimes when praising a child will put an end to that child's appropriate behavior. (If you have not experienced this phenomenon, believe us, it happens.) Furthermore, what might appear to be irrelevant behavior to an observing adult might be the stimulus setting off the unwanted, target behavior, as happens sometimes when it is the seemingly reasonable behavior of an adult that sets off tantrumming in a child. The behaviorist, therefore, must observe and measure carefully to find the true stimulus-target behavior-reinforcement patterns and not simply the ones that might be expected.

But what, you might ask, has all this to do with play therapy? For most of the history of behavioral child therapy, the answer has been "not much," because the focus on decreasing and increasing target behaviors has not been on play. However, there have been a few notable exceptions, one that we will discuss here both because it is well-known and because it shows the potential for using play within behavioral therapies.

The exception is Forehand and his associates' training for parents of children with "conduct problems" (Forehand & McMahn, 1981). In this training, parents are taught to punish and avoid reinforcing maladaptive behaviors and to reinforce and avoid punishing prosocial behaviors. The training comes in phases, and each phase uses play as the context and medium for training.

In Phase 1, while their child is playing, parents are taught how to use praise and give attention selectively to reward desired behavior and to extinguish or punish undesired behavior. In other words, Phase 1 play sessions focus on teaching parents how to be behaviorists, especially with regard to controlling the consequences of their child's behavior.

In Phase 2, the focus shifts from consequences to antecedents as parents are taught how to give commands and instructions. In particular, they are taught to give concise, specific demands (e.g., "Put on the smock before you start to paint") rather than vague or question commands (e.g., "Would you like to put on the smock before you start to paint?").

Phase 3 is an extension of the standard training supplied in the first two phases. It consists of letting a child lead his or her parent(s) in some play activity. However, rather than this being the kind of co-play described in the example of Susie and her teacher, Phase 3 serves more as a time when parents are to practice and consolidate the operant skills learned in Phase 1, using every opportunity presented by a child to give praise and attention selectively.

In one sense, the use of play in behavioral therapies does not make it play therapy, because it is not the play itself that is seen as being therapeutic. The same could be said of cognitive-developmental therapies such as pair therapy. However, in another sense, play figures so centrally in some behavioral therapies, such as Forehand's, that we believe it is acceptable to group them under the label of play therapy.

Also, the behaviorist perspective allows us to reinterpret the meaning of what other types of play therapies say they are doing, just as we could reinterpret Winnicott's greedy baby play from a cognitive-developmental perspective. We can, in fact, do the same using a behaviorist perspective. That is, we can reinterpret to show that Winnicott's play can fit into a behaviorist's design for treatment. While Winnicott saw his greedy baby play as a kind of action interpretation helping the Piggle to become conscious of her feelings, cognitive-behavioral therapists might see it as modeling an adaptive thought such as the thought that "naughty" feelings can be played with. This is the kind of explanation given by today's cognitive-behavioral play therapists (Knell, 1998).

Photo 11.1   Being creative can have healing powers. This girl is holding up the artwork she has created.

● ART THERAPY

We could not leave this subject of play therapy without mentioning the related field of art therapy. As we have seen in previous chapters, art (drawing, sculpting, etc.) and play overlap—at least in childhood. This overlap suggests the rationale for linking discussions of art and play therapy.

Art therapy differs from the play therapies discussed in this chapter in at least two important ways. First, art therapy is less theory driven, though its roots lie within the psychoanalytic tradition (Kris, 1952) and art therapy is incorporated into all the major theoretical traditions (Malchiodi, 2003). Second, in art therapy, it is the creative process itself that becomes the major focus, because being creative seems to have healing powers (Waller, 1992).

Certainly it appears to make good sense to give children, including troubled children, plenty of opportunities to be creative, if for no other reason than the fact that being creative is an index of thriving. Therefore, it may be irrelevant whether or not art therapy successfully incorporates the theories and methods of psychoanalytic, humanistic, or any other clinical psychological tradition.

This last point may need clarifying. Among those who study or work with children with clinical problems, there is an ongoing debate as to whether to view these children through a medical lens that emphasizes their defects and deficiencies or through a more developmental and contextual lens that emphasizes their strengths and their being children. For example, Cambone points out that the troubled children in many residential treatment programs can just as well be described as resourceful, resilient, clever, creative, and tenacious as they can be described as maladaptive, deficient, and deviant (Cambone, 1994). Art therapy may, therefore, be an important way for certain children to at least momentarily experience themselves in positive ways—in particular, as being creative.

TRAINING ●

We have described the main approaches to play therapy, highlighting their backgrounds and particular advantages, but how does one become a play therapist? What is appropriate training?

Play therapists, regardless of their backgrounds, commonly have an education in psychology or child development and have received further training in the specific approaches that they utilize. Although there are no global standards of training or credentials, there are organizations that provide play therapy instruction and certification. Play Therapy International (PTI) is an international organization of play therapists and child psychotherapists that provides training and promotes discussion and advancement in the field. The International Board of Examiners of Certified Play Therapists (IBECPT) is a professional body of play therapists that governs accreditation and certification on an international level. In addition, the American Psychological Association (APA) approves organizations that provide continuing education in play therapy for psychologists (Play Therapy International, 2004; Society for Play and Creative Arts Therapies, 2003). There are, then, many training opportunities.

CONCLUDING REMARKS: DOES PLAY THERAPY WORK? ●

Perhaps asking the question "Does play therapy work?" is unfair, because play therapy is not, as we have seen, one thing. A better question might be, "Do any play therapies work?" But even this broader question might be unfair because of the nature of clinical work with children. In working with children and their families, it is often near impossible to measure the most important results quantitatively, though, of course, we must always try.

In the end, we have to admit that there is little empirical evidence to support continuing play therapy of any type. As Hellendoorn, van der Kooij, and Sutton-Smith (1994a) concluded, "Because the different therapy theories and 'schools' remain the most important source of thinking about play therapy, work in this field is largely deductive" (p. 218).

However, the fact that play therapy cannot be justified on the basis of quantitative, scientific studies makes the situation regarding play therapy no different from a great deal of clinical work, both medical and psychological (Paauw, 1999). Furthermore, swearing by play therapy makes good sense if skilled people with lots of clinical experience provide satisfactory qualitative accounts of their work with children, which seems to be the case with play therapy.

Whatever the case, play therapies seem to be here to stay and for one simple reason: Play is the child's natural way of being and interacting. If we are to relate to children, help them with their problems, and support their development, there is no way of doing so without considering and enlisting the help of play.

● KEY WORDS, NAMES, AND IDEAS

Art therapy

Clinical themes

Cognitive-behavioral

Cognitive-developmental

Egocentricity

Humanistic

Pair therapy

Psychoanalytic

Reinforcers

Stimuli

Therapeutic alliance

Unconditional positive regard

WEB RESOURCES

A word of caution: These Web sites vary in the quality of the information they provide. In addition, their content is likely to evolve over time. Therefore, as with any Web site, we encourage the reader to exert caution in the analysis and use of their content.

I. ACROSS CHAPTERS ●

Tufts University Child and Family Webguide
   http://www.cfw.tufts.edu

II. FOR SPECIFIC CHAPTERS ●

Chapter 2: The Emergence of Play in Infancy and the Toddler Years

Toys' safety
   www.cpsc.gov/cpscpub/pubs/281.html
   www.toy-tia.org
   www.safekids.org/tier2_rl.cfm?folder_id=179

Chapter 4: Play in Late Childhood: Rule-Governed Play

Games with rules
   www.everyrule.com
Guidelines for distinguishing aggression from play fighting
   www.cfchildren.org/parent_aggression.shtml
Relational aggression
   www.opheliaproject.org/issues/issues_RA.shtml

Chapter 6: Electronic Play: Computer, Console, and Video Games

Game Spot—information and resources regarding games
   http://www.gamespot.com
Penny-Arcade—information and resources regarding games and the game industry
   http://www.penny-arcade.com
Entertainment Software Association[1]
   http://www.theesa.com
Entertainment Software Rating Board
   http://www.esrb.com
National Institute on Media and the Family
   http://www.mediafamily.org

Chapter 7: Organized Youth Sports

Sport in Society
   http://www.sportinsociety.org
Center for Sports Parenting
   http://www.sportsparenting.org/csp/
National Alliance for Youth Sports
   http://www.nays.org
National Youth Sports Safety Foundation
   http://www.nyssf.org
University of Michigan: Institute for the Study of Youth Sport
   http://www.ed-web3.educ.msu.edu/ysi
Youth Sports on the Web
   http://www.infosports.net
North American Youth Sports Institute
   http://www.naysi.com
Youth Sports Trust
   http://www.youthsporttrust.org
Special Olympics Web site
   http://www.specialolympics.org

Chapter 8: Home and Outdoor Play

London Play
   http://www.londonplay.org.uk/playground.htm

Chapter 9: Schooling and Play

Lego curriculum @ Netlab
http://www.netlab.co.uk/robotics/index.htm
Robot Education @ NASA
http://www.netlab.co.uk/robotics/index.htm
Lego Related Links
http://www.asccxe.wpafb.af.mil/Robotics/Related%20Links.htm
Seymour Papert
http://www.papert.org/
Microworlds
http://www.microworlds.com
National Association for the Education of Young Children
http://www.naeyc.org
George Forman
http://www.videatives.com

Chapter 10: Restorative Play in Stressful Environments

Child Life Council
http://www.childlife.org
UN Convention on the Rights of the Child
http://www.unicef.org/crc/crc.htm

Chapter 11: Play Therapy

Play Therapy International
http://www.playtherapy.org
Play Therapy Training Institute
http://www.ptti.org

NOTE ●

1. Formerly known as the Interactive Digital Software Association (IDSA).

REFERENCES

Adams, M. A. (1976). A hospital play program: Helping children with serious illness. *American Journal of Orthopsychiatry, 46*(3), 416–424.

Ainsworth, M. (1979). Attachment as related to mother-infant interactions. In J. S. Rosenblatt, C. Beer, & M. Busnel (Eds.), *Advances in the study of behavior* (Vol. 9). Orlando, FL: Academic Press.

Allen, L. (1968). *Planning for play.* Cambridge, MA: MIT Press.

Anderson, C. A., & Bushman, B. J. (2001). Effects of violent video games on aggressive behavior, aggressive cognition, aggressive affect, physiological arousal, and pro-social behavior: A meta-analytic review of the scientific literature. *Psychological Science, 12*(5), 353–359.

Anderson, D. R., & Evans, M. K. (2001). Peril and potential of media for infants and toddlers. *Zero-to-Three, 22*(2), 10–16.

Ariel, S. (2002). *Children's imaginative play.* Westport, CT: Praeger Publishers.

Armchair Empire. (2002). *PC reviews: Grand Theft Auto III.* Retrieved August 14, 2002, from http://www.armchairempire.com/Reviews/PC%20Games/grand-theft-auto-iii.htm

Bainum, C. K., Lounsbury, K. R., & Pollio, H. R. (1984). The development of laughing and smiling in nursery school children. *Child Development, 55,* 1946–1957.

Baker, E., Herman, J., & Yeh, J. (1981, Spring). Fun and games: Their contribution to basic skills instruction in elementary school. *American Educational Research Journal, 18*(1), 83–92.

Bariaud, F. (1989). Age differences in children's humor. In P. E. McGhee (Ed.), *Humor and children's development: A guide to practical applications* (pp. 15–45). New York: Haworth Press.

Beatty, B. (1995). *Preschool education in America.* New Haven, CT: Yale University Press.

Beck, A. (1976). *Cognitive therapy and the emotional disorders.* New York: International Universities Press.

Beentjes, J. W. J., Koolstra, C. M., Cees, M., Marseille, N., & van der Voort, T. H. A. (2001). Children's use of different media: For how long and why? In S. Livingstone & M. Bovill (Eds.), *Children and their changing media environment: A European comparative study* (pp. 85–111). Mahwah, NJ: Lawrence Erlbaum Associates.

Belsky, J., Lerner, R., & Spanier, G. (1984). *The child in the family.* Reading, MA: Addison-Wesley.

Belsky, J., & Most, R. (1981). From exploration to play: A cross-sectional study of infant free play behavior. *Developmental Psychology, 17*(5), 630–639.

Berger, M. (1999). *101 Spooky Halloween jokes.* New York: Scholastic.

Berlyne, D. E. (1972). Humor and its kin. In J. Goldstein & P. McGhee (Eds.), *The psychology of humor: Theoretical perspectives and empirical issues.* New York: McGraw Hill.

Berryman, J. (1996). The rise of boys' sports in the United States, 1900 to 1970. In F. Smoll & R. Smith (Eds.), *Children and youth in sport: A biopsychological perspective.* New York: McGraw-Hill.

Bers, M., Gonzales-Heydrich, G., & de Maso, D. (2001). Identity construction environments: Supporting a virtual therapeutic community of pediatric patients undergoing dialysis. In *Proceedings of the symposium on computer-human interaction 2001* (pp. 380–387). Seattle, WA: ACM.

Bers, M., Ponte, I., Juelich, K., Viera, A., & Schenker, J. (2002). Teachers as designers: Integrating robotics in early childhood education. *Information Technology in Childhood Education,* 123–145.

Bibace, R., & Walsh, M. E. (1980). Development of children's concepts of illness. *Pediatrics, 66*(6), 912–917.

Bigelow, T., Moroney, T., & Hall, L. (2001). *Just let the kids play: How to stop other adults from ruining your child's fun and success in youth sports.* Deerfield Beach, FL: Health Communications.

Biklen, D. (1989). Redefining schools. In D. Biklen, D. Ferguson, & A. Ford (Eds.), *Schooling and disability.* Chicago: University of Chicago Press.

Bjorklund, D. F. (2000). *Children's thinking: Developmental functions and individual differences* (3rd ed.). Pacific Grove, CA: Brooks/Cole.

Blatchford, P. (1998). *Social life in school.* London: Falmer.

Blatchford, P., & Sumpner, C. (1998). What we know about break time: Results from a national survey of break time and lunch time in primary school in primary and secondary schools. *British Educational Research Journal, 24,* 79–94.

Bloch, M., & Pellegrini, A. (1989). Young boys' and girls' play at home and in the community: A cultural-ecological framework. In M. Bloch & A. Pellegrini (Eds.), *The ecological context of children's play.* Norwood, NJ: Ablex.

Block, J., & King, N. (1987). *School play: A source book.* New York: Teachers College Press.

Boulton, M. J. (1996a). A comparison of 8- and 11-year-old girls' and boys' participation in specific types of rough and tumble play and aggressive fighting: Implications for functional hypotheses. *Aggression & Behavior, 22,* 271–287.

Boulton, M. J. (1996b). Lunchtime supervisors' attitude towards playful fighting and ability to differentiate between playful and aggressive fighting: An intervention study. *British Journal of Educational Psychology, 66,* 367–381.

Bowlby, J. (1969). *Attachment and loss: Vol. 1: Attachment.* New York: Basic Books/Cole.

Brazelton, T. B., Koslowski, B., & Main, M. (1974). The origins of reciprocity: The early mother-infant interaction. In M. Lewis & L. Rosenblum (Eds.), *The effect of the infant on its caregiver* (Vol. 1, pp. 49–76). New York: John Wiley & Sons.

Brett, A., Moore, R., & Provenzo, E. (1993). *The complete playground book.* New York: Syracuse University Press.

Bronfenbrenner, U. (1999). Environments in developmental perspective: Theoretical and operational models. In S. L. Friedman, & T. Wachs (Eds.), *Measuring environment across the life span: Emerging methods and concepts* (pp. 3–30). Washington, DC: American Psychological Association.

Bronson, B. C. (1981). Toddlers behaviors with agemates: Issues of interaction, cognition, and affect. In M. Rosenzweig & L. Porter (Eds.), *Monographs on infancy* (Vol. 1). Norwood, NJ: Ablex Publishing Corporation.

Bruner, J. (1972). The nature and uses of immaturity. *American Psychologist, 27,* 687–708.

Bruner, J. (1982). The organization of action and the nature of adult-infant transaction. In M. von Cranach & R. Harré (Eds.), *The analysis of action* (pp. 313–327). New York: Cambridge University Press.

Bruner, J. (1986). *Actual minds, possible worlds.* Cambridge, MA: Harvard University Press.

Bruner, J. (1995). From joint attention to the meeting of minds: An introduction. In C. Moore & P. J. Dunham (Eds.), *Joint attention: Its origins and role in development* (pp. 1–14). Hillsdale, NJ: Erlbaum.

Bruner, J., Jolly, A., & Sylva, K. (Eds.). (1976). *Play: Its role in development and evolution.* New York: Basic Books.

Bruner, J., Jolly, A., & Sylva, K. (1986). *Actual minds, possible worlds.* Cambridge, MA: Harvard University Press.

Bruner, J., & Sherwood, V. (1976). Peekaboo and the learning of rule structures. In J. Bruner, A. Jolly, & K. Silva (Eds.), *Play: Its role in evolution and development* (pp. 277–285). Harmondsworth, UK: Penguin.

Cambone, J. (1994). *Teaching troubled children.* New York: Teachers College Press.

Carlsson-Paige, N., & Levin, D. (1987). *The war play dilemma: Balancing needs and values in the early childhood classroom.* New York: Teachers College Press.

Carson, D. K., Skarpness, L. R., Schultz, N. W., & McGhee, P. E. (1986). Temperamental and communicative competence as predictors of young children's humor. *Merrill-Palmer Quarterly, 32,* 415–426.

Cassell, J., & Jenkins, H. (1998). *From Barbie to Mortal Kombat: Gender and computer games.* Cambridge, MA: The MIT Press.

Chen, K. (2000). Heuristic search and computer game playing. *Information Sciences, 122*(1), 1–2.

Cicchetti, D., Beeghly, M., & Weiss-Perry, B. (1994). Symbolic development in children with Down's syndrome and in children with autism: An organizational, developmental psychopathology perspective. In A. Slade & D. Wolf (Eds.), *Children at play: Clinical and developmental approaches to meaning and representation.* New York: Oxford University Press.

City of Helsinki. (2002). *Helsinki—The city of the future.* Retrieved September 1, 2002, from http://www.hel.fi/english/info/Yleis_eng.pdf

Coakley, J. (1998). *Sport in society: Issues and controversies* (6th ed.). New York: McGraw-Hill.

Cohen, U., McGinty, T., & Moore, G. (1979). *Recommendations for child play areas.* Milwaukee: University of Wisconsin School of Architecture and Urban Planning.

Collis, G. M. (1979). Describing the structure of social interaction in infancy. In M. Bullowa (Ed.), *Before speech: The beginning of interpersonal communication* (pp. 111–130). Cambridge, UK: Cambridge University Press.

Compas, B. E., & Grant, K. E. (2003). Processes of risk and resilience during adolescence: Stress, coping and stress reactivity. In R. M. Lerner, & D. Wertlieb (Eds.), *Handbook of applied developmental science: Promoting positive child, adolescent, and family development through research, policies, and programs.* Thousand Oaks, CA: Sage Publications.

Crawford, M., & Gressley, D. (1991). Creativity, caring, and context: Women's and men's accounts of humor preferences and practices. *Psychology of Women Quarterly, 15,* 217–231.

Crick, N. R., Wellman, N. E., Casas, J. F., O'Brien, K. M., Nelson, D. A., Grotpeter, J. K., et al. (1999). Childhood aggression and gender: A new look at an old problem. In D. Bernstein (Ed.), *Nebraska symposium on motivation* (p. 45). Lincoln: University of Nebraska Press.

Csikszentmihalyi, M. (1979). The concept of flow. In B. Sutton-Smith (Ed.), *Play and learning* (pp. 257–274). New York: Gardner.

Dattner, R. (1969). *Design for play.* New York: Van Nostrand Reinhold Company.

Devereux, E. C. (1978). Backyard versus Little League baseball: The impoverishment of children's games. In R. Martins (Ed.), *Joy and sadness in children's sports* (pp. 115–129). Champaign, IL: Human Kinetics.

DeVries, R., & Kohlberg, L. (1990). *Constructivist early education: Overview and comparison with other programs.* Washington, DC: National Association for the Education of Young Children.

Dill, K. E., & Dill, J. C. (1998). Video game violence: A review of the empirical literature. *Aggression & Violent Behavior, 3*(4), 407–428.

DiPietro, J. A. (1981). Rough and tumble play: A function of gender. *Developmental Psychology, 17,* 50–58.

Drewes, A. A. (2001). Play objects and play spaces. In A. A. Drewes, L. J. Carey, & C. E. Schaefer (Eds.), *School-based play therapy* (pp. 62–80). New York: John Wiley & Sons.

Drewes, A., Carey, L., & Schaefer, C. (Eds.). (2001). *School-based play therapy.* New York: John Wiley & Sons.

Drucker, J. (1994). Constructing metaphor: The role of play in the treatment of children. In A. Slade & D. Wolf (Eds.), *Children at play: Clinical and developmental approaches to meaning and representation.* New York: Oxford University Press.

Eckerman, C. O., Davis, C. C., & Didow, S. M. (1989). Toddlers emerging ways of achieving social coordination with a peer. *Child Development, 60,* 440–453.

Edelson, D. C. (2001). Learning-for-use: A framework for the design of technology-supported inquiry activities. *Journal of Research in Science Teaching, 38*(3), 355–385.

Electronic Arts. (2001). *The Sims—Tips and tricks.* Retrieved September 1, 2002, from http://thesims.ea.com/us/about/tipsandtricks/index.html

Elkind, D. (1981). *The hurried child.* Reading, MA: Addison-Wesley.

Elkind, D. (1988). *Miseducation: Preschoolers at risk.* New York: Alfred A. Knopf.

Elkind, D. (1994). *Ties that stress: The new family imbalance.* Cambridge, MA: Harvard University Press.

Elkind, D. (2003). *The commercialization of play.* Paper presented at the Play and Time, Lego Conference. Copenhagen, Denmark.

Entertainment Software Rating Board. (2003). *ESRB game ratings: Game rating and descriptor guide.* Retrieved September 14, 2003, from http://www.esrb.com/esrbratings_guide.asp

Erikson, E. (1950). *Childhood and society.* New York: Norton.

Erikson, E. H. (1963). *Childhood and society* (2nd ed.). New York: Norton.

Esman, A. H. (1983). Psychoanalytic play therapy. In C. E. Schaefer & K. J. O'Conner (Eds.), *Handbook of play therapy* (pp. 11–20). New York: John Wiley & Sons.

Ewing, M., & Seefeldt, V. (1996). Patterns of participation and attrition in American agency-sponsored youth sports. In F. Smoll & R. Smith (Eds.), *Children and youth in sport: A biopsychosocial perspective.* New York: McGraw-Hill.

Fein, G. (1981). Pretend play in childhood: An integrative review. *Child Development, 52,* 1095–1118.

Fein, G., & Kinney, P. (1994). He's a nice alligator: Observations on the affective organization of pretense. In A. Slade & D. Wolf (Eds.), *Children at play: Clinical and developmental approaches to meaning and representation.* New York: Oxford University Press.

Feinburg, S. (1976). Combat in child art. In J. Bruner, A. Jolly, & K. Sylva (Eds.), *Play: Its role in development and evolution.* New York: Basic Books.

Feinman, S. (1992). *Social referencing and the social construction of reality in infancy.* New York: Plenum.

Fergusson, D. M., Lynskey, M. T., & Horwood, L. J. (1996). Factors associated with continuity and changes in disruptive behavior patterns between childhood and adolescence. *Journal of Abnormal Child Psychology, 24,* 533–553.

Fine, G. (1987). *With the boys.* Chicago: University of Chicago Press.

Fjertoft, I. (2001). The natural environments as a playground for children: The impact of outdoor activities in pre-primary school children. *Childhood Education, 29,* 111–117.

Fleming, M. J., & Rickwood, D. J. (2001). Effects of violent versus nonviolent video games on children's arousal, aggressive mood, and positive mood. *Journal of Applied Social Psychology, 31*(10), 2047–2071.

Foote, H. C., & Chapman, A. J. (1976). The social responsiveness of young children in humorous situations. In A. J. Chapman & H. C. Foote (Eds.), *Humor and laughter: Theory, research, and applications.* New Brunswick, NJ: Transaction Publishers.

Forehand, R., & McMahon, R. (1981). *Helping the noncompliant child: A clinician's guide to parent training.* New York: Guilford.

Forman, G. (1998). Constructive play. In D. Fromberg & D. Bergen (Eds.), *Play from birth to twelve and beyond.* New York: Garland Publishing.

Forman, G., & Hill, F. (1980). *Constructive play: Applying Piaget in the preschool.* Monterey, CA: Brooks/Cole.

Forman, G., & Hill, F. (1984). Constructive play: Applying Piaget in the preschool. Menlo Park, CA: Addison-Wesley.

Freitag, P. (1998). Games, achievement, and the mastery of social skills. In D. Fromberg & D. Bergen (Eds.), *Play from birth to twelve and beyond.* New York: Garland.

Freud, A. (1946). *Normality and pathology in childhood: Assessment of development.* New York: International Universities Press.

Freud, S. (1920). Beyond the pleasure principle. In J. Strachey (Ed.), *The standard edition of the complete psychological work of Sigmund Freud (SE).* London: Hogarth Press.

Freud, S. (1953). Three essays on the theory of sexuality. In *The standard edition of the complete psychological work of Sigmund Freud* (pp. 123–245). London: Hogarth. (Original work published 1905)

Freud, S. (1961). *Beyond the pleasure principle.* New York: Norton.

Frost, J. (1992). *Play and playscapes.* Albany, NY: Delmar.

Frost, J., & Klein, B. (1979). *Children's play and playgrounds.* Boston: Allyn and Bacon.

Frost, J., Shinn, D., & Jacobs, P. (1998). Play environments and children's play. In O. Saracho & B. Spodek (Eds.), *Multiple perspectives on play in early childhood education.* New York: State University Press.

Funk, J. B., & Buchman, D. D. (1996). Playing violent video and computer games and adolescent self-concept. *Journal of Communication, 46*(2), 19–29.

Funk, J. B., Buchman, D. D., & Germann, J. N. (2000). Preference for violent electronic games, self-concept and gender differences in young children. *American Journal of Orthopsychiatry, 70*(2), 233–241.

Funk, J. B., Flores, G., Buchman, D. D., & Germann, J. N. (1999). Rating electronic games: Violence is in the eye of the beholder. *Youth & Society, 30*(3), 283–312.

Funk, J. B., Hagan, J., Schimming, J., Bullock, W. A., Buchman, D. D., & Myers, M. (2002). Aggression and psychopathology in adolescents with a preference for violent electronic games. *Aggressive Behavior, 28,* 134–144.

Garbarino, J. (1989). An ecological perspective on the role of play in child development. In M. Bloch & A. Pellegrini (Eds.), *The ecological context of children's play.* Norwood, NJ: Ablex.

Gardner, H. (1983). *Frames of mind: The theory of multiple intelligences.* New York: Basic Books.

Garvey, C. (1977). *Play.* Cambridge, MA: Harvard University Press.

Gaskins, S. (2003). *The cultural construction of play.* Paper presented at the 33rd Annual Meeting of the Jean Piaget Society: Play and Development, Chicago, IL.

Giddings, M., & Halverson, C. (1981). Young children's use of toys in the home environments. *Family Relations, 30,* 69–74.

Ginott, H. G. (1961). *Group psychotherapy with children.* New York: McGraw-Hill.

Glassman, M. (2001). Dewey and Vygotsky: Society, experience, and inquiry in educational practice. *Educational Researcher, 30*(4), 3–14.

Goldstein, J. (1994a). Sex differences in toy play and use of video games. In J. Goldstein (Ed.), *Toys, play, and child development* (pp. 110–129). Cambridge: Cambridge University Press.

Goldstein, J. (1994b). *Toys, play and child development.* New York: Cambridge University Press.

Goldstein, J. (1995). Aggressive toy play. In A. D. Pelligrini (Ed.), *The future of play theory: Multidisiplinary inquiry into the contributions of Brian Sutton-Smith* (pp. 127–159). New York: State University Press.

Goldstein, J. H., & McGhee, P. E. (1972). An annotated bibliography of published papers on humor in the research literature and an analysis of trends: 1900–1971. In J. Goldstein & P. McGhee (Eds.), *The psychology of humor: Theoretical perspectives and empirical issues.* New York: McGraw Hill.

Goodwin, M. H. (1990). *He-said-she-said: Talk as social organization among black children.* Bloomington: Indiana University Press.

Goodwin, M. H. (2002). Exclusion in girls' peer groups: Ethnographic analysis of language practices on the playground. *Human Development, 45,* 392–415.

Gould, R. (1972). *Child studies through fantasy.* New York: Quadrangle Books.

Green, R. (1977). Atypical sexual identity: The "feminine" boy and the "masculine" girl. In E. K. Oremland & J. D. Oremland (Eds.), *The sexual and gender development of young children: The role of the educator.* Cambridge, MA: Ballinger Publishing.

Greenfield, P. (1984). *Mind and media: The effects of television, video games, and computers.* Cambridge, MA: Harvard University Press.

Greer, R. (1977). Atypical sex identity: The "feminine" boy and the "masculine" girl. In E. K. Oremland & J. D. Oremland (Eds.), *The sexual and gender development of young children: The role of the educator.* Cambridge, MA: Ballinger Publishing Company.

Guerney, L. F. (1983). Child-centered (nondirective) play therapy. In C. E. Schaefer & K. J. O'Connor (Eds.), *Handbook of play therapy* (pp. 21–64). New York: John Wiley & Sons.

Haight, W., & Miller, P. (1993). *Pretending at home.* Albany, NY: State University of New York Press.

Harris, M. J., & Began, J. K. (1993). Make-believe: A descriptive study of fantasies in middle-childhood. *Imagination, Cognition, and Personality, 13,* 125–145.

Harris, P. (2000). *The work of the imagination.* Malden, MA: Blackwell Publishers.

Harris, P. (2003). *Hard work for the imagination.* Paper presented at the 33rd Annual Meeting of the Jean Piaget Society: Play and Development, Chicago, IL.

Harris, P. E. (1928). *Changing conceptions of school discipline.* New York: Macmillan.

Hart, C. (1993). *Children on playgrounds.* Albany, NY: State University of New York Press.

Hartup, W. (1983). Peer relations. In E. M. Hetherington (Ed.), *Handbook of child psychology* (Vol. 4, pp. 103–196).

Harvey, S. (1984). Training the hospital play specialist. *Early Child Development and Care, 17,* 277–290.

Hawker, D. S., & Boulton, M. J. (2003). Twenty years' research on peer victimization and psychosocial maladjustment: A meta-analytic review of cross-sectional studies. *Annual progress in child psychiatry and child development 2000–2001, Part IV,* 505–534.

Hayward, G., Rothenberg, M., & Beasley, R. (1974). Children's play and urban playground environments. *Environment and Behavior, 6,* 131–168.

Healy, J. M. (1998). *Failure to connect: How computers affect our children's minds—For better and worse.* New York: Simon and Schuster.

Hellendoorn, J., van der Kooij, R., & Sutton-Smith, B. (1994a). Epilogue. In J. Hellendoorn, R. van der Kooij, & B. Sutton-Smith (Eds.), *Play and intervention* (pp. 215–224). Albany, NY: State University of New York Press.

Hellendoorn, J., van der Kooij, R., & Sutton-Smith, B. (Eds.). (1994b). *Play and intervention.* Albany, NY: State University of New York Press.

Henniger, M. L. (1995). Play: Antidote for childhood stress. *Child Development and Care, 105,* 7–12.

Hodapp, R. M., Goldfield, E. C., & Boyatzis, C. J. (1984). The use and effectiveness of maternal scaffolding in mother-infant games. *Child Development, 55,* 772–781.

Holland, N. N. (1982). *Laughing: A psychology of humor.* Ithaca, NY: Cornell University Press.

Hollis, L. Y., & Felder, B. D. (1982). Recreational mathematics for young children. *School Science and Mathematics, 82*(1), 71–75.

Hong, J. C., & Liu, M. C. (2003). A study on thinking strategy between experts and novices of computer games. *Computers in Human Behavior, 19*(2), 245–258.

Howe, F. C. (1993). The child in elementary school. *Child Study Journal, 23*(4), 227–372.

Howes, C. (1988). Peer interaction of young children. *Mongraphs of the Society for Research in Child Development, 53*(1, serial No. 217).

Howes, C., Unger, O., & Matheson, C. (1992). *The collaborative construction of pretend.* Albany, NY: State University of New York Press.

Hughes, F. (1991). *Children's play and development.* Needham Heights, MA: Allyn and Bacon.

Humphrey, A. P., & Smith, P. K. (1987). Rough and tumble, friendship, and dominance in school children: Evidence for continuity and change with age. *Child Development, 58,* 201–212.

Hutt, C. (1970). Specific and diverse exploration. In H. W. Reese & L. P. Lipsitt (Eds.), *Advances in child development* (Vol. 5, pp. 119–180). New York: Academic Press.

Hutt, S., Tyler, S., Hutt, C., & Christopherson, H. (1989). *Play, exploration, and learning: A natural history of the pre-school.* London: Routledge.

Interactive Digital Software Association. (2001). *Video games and youth violence: Examining the facts.* Washington, DC: IDSA.

Johnson, L. (1987). The developmental implications of home environments. In C. Weinstein & T. David (Eds.), *Spaces for children.* New York: Plenum Press.

Jones, R., & Tanner, L. (1981). Classroom discipline: The unclaimed legacy. *Phi Delta Kappan, 494–497.*

Jordan, A. B., & Woodard, E. H. (2001). Electronic childhood: The availability and use of household media by 2- to 3-year-olds. *Zero-to-Three, 22*(2), 4–9.

Kafai, Y. B. (1996). Gender differences in children's constructions of video games. In P. M. Greenfield & R. R. Cocking (Eds.), *Interacting with video: Advances in applied developmental psychology* (Vol. 11, pp. 39–66). Norwood, NJ: Ablex.

Katz, L. (1998). Mothering and teaching: Some significant distinctions. In L. Katz (Ed.), *Current topics in early childhood.* Norwood, NJ: Ablex.

Kaye, K. (1982). *The mental and social life of babies: How parents create persons.* Chicago: The University of Chicago Press.

Kaye, K., & Fogel, A. (1980). The temporal structure of face-to-face communication between mothers and infants. *Developmental Psychology, 16*(5), 454–464.

Keegan, P. (1999). *Culture quake.* Retrieved June 1, 2002, from http://www.motherjones.com/mother_jones/ND99/quake.html

Kellert, S., & Wilson, E. (1995). *The biophilia hypothesis.* Washington, DC: Shearwater Books.

Kline, S. (1995). The promotion and marketing of toys: Time to rethink the paradox? In A. Pellegrini (Ed.), *The future of play theory.* Albany, NY: State University of New York Press.

Knell, S. (1998). Cognitive-behavioral play therapy. *Journal of Clinical Child Psychology, 27,* 28–33.

Kohn, M. (1966). The child as a determinant of his peers' approaches to him. *Journal of Genetic Psychology, 109,* 91–100.

Konner, M. (1976). Relations among infants and juveniles in comparative perspective. In M. Lewis & L. Rosenblum (Eds.), *Friendship and peer relations.* New York: Wiley.

Kris, E. (1952). *Psychoanalytic explorations in art.* New York: International Universities Press.

Lampert, M. (1996). Studying gender differences in the conversational humor of adults and children. In D. Slobin & J. Gerhard (Eds.), *Social interaction, social context, and language: Essays in honor of Susan Earvin-Tripp.* Mahwah, NJ: Lawrence Erlbaum.

Landreth, G. L., & Sweeney, D. S. (1999). The freedom to be: Child-centered group play therapy. In D. S. Sweeney & L. Homeyer (Eds.), *The handbook of group play therapy: How to do it, how it works, whom it is best for* (pp. 39–64). San Francisco: Jossey-Bass.

Lascarides, V., & Hinitz, B. (2000). *History of early childhood education.* New York: Falmer Press.

Leacock, E. (1976). At play in African villages. In In J. S. Bruner, A. Jolly, & K. Sylva (Eds.), *Play: Its role in development and evolution* (pp. 466–473). New York: Basic Books.

Lerner, C., Singer, D. G., & Wartella, E. (2001). Computers, TV, and very young children: What impact on development? *Zero-to-Three, 22*(2), 30–33.

Leslie, A. M. (1987). Pretense and representation: The origins of "theory of mind." *Psychological Review, 94,* 412–422.

Lillard, A. (2003). *Why children don't get confused by others' pretense.* Paper presented at the 33rd Annual Meeting of the Jean Piaget Society: Play and Development, Chicago, IL.

Linder, T. W. (1990). *Transdisciplinary play-based assessment: A functional approach to working with young children.* Baltimore: Brookes.

Lord, R., & Kozar, B. (1996). Overuse injuries in young athletes. In F. Smoll & R. Smith (Eds.), *Children and youth in sport: A biopsychological perspective.* Boston: McGraw Hill.

Lubeck, S. (2001). Early childhood education and care in England. *Phi Delta Kappan, 83,* 216–226.

Lynch, K. (1997). *Hard-to-manage children and how to play: A study of the play of children with behavior problems.* Unpublished master's thesis, Tufts University, Medford, MA.

Maccoby, E. (1998). *The two sexes: Growing up apart, coming together.* Cambridge, MA: Belknap.

Magill, R., & Anderson, D. (1996). In F. Smoll & R. Smith (Eds.), *Children and youth in sport: A biopsychological perspective.* New York: McGraw-Hill.

Mahler, M. S., Pine, F., & Bergman, A. (1975). *The psychological birth of the infant.* New York: Basic Books.

Malchiodi, C. A. (2003). *Handbook of art therapy.* New York: The Guilford Press.

Manheimer, L. (2000). Summer and the school-age child in the hospital. In E. Oremland (Ed.), *Protecting the emotional development of the ill child: The essence of the child life profession* (pp. 157–170). Madison, CT: Psychosocial Press.

Markward, M. J., Cline, S. S., & Markward, N. J. (2001). Group socialization, the Internet and school shootings. *International Journal of Adolescents and Youth, 10*(1–2), 135–146.

Martin, P., & Caro, T. (1985). On the functions of play and its role in behavioral development. In J. Rosenblatt, C. Beer, M. Busnel, & P. Slater (Eds.), *Advances in the study of behavior* (Vol. 15). New York: Academic Press.

Masten, A. M. (1986). Humor and competence in school-aged children. *Child Development, 57,* 461–473.

McCune, L. (1993). The development of play as the development of consciousness. In M. Bornstein & A. O'Reilly (Eds.), *The role of play in the development of thought* (pp. 67–79). San Francisco: Jossey-Bass.

McCune-Nicolich, L. (1981). Toward symbolic functioning: Structure of early pretend games and potential parallels. *Child Development, 52,* 785–797.

McGhee, P. E. (1980). Development and the sense of humor in childhood: A longitudinal study. In P. E. McGhee & A. J. Chapman (Eds.), *Children's humor.* Chichester, UK: Wiley.

McGhee, P. E. (2002). *Understanding and promoting the development of children's humor.* Dubuque, IA: Kendall/Hunt.

McGhee, P. E., & Lloyd, S. A. (1982). Behavioural characteristics associated with the development of humor in young children. *Journal of Genetic Psychology, 141,* 253–259.

McHale, S., Crouter, A. C., & Tucker, C. J. (2001). Free-time activities in middle-childhood: Links with adjustment in early adolescence. *Child Development, 72*(6), 1764–1778.

Meany, M., Stewart, J., & Beatty, W. (1985). Sex differences in social play: The socialization of sex roles. In J. Rosenblatt, C. Beer, M. Busnel, & P. Slater (Eds.), *Advances in the study of behavior* (Vol. 15). New York: Academic Press.

Medrich, E. A., Roizen, J. A., Rubin, V., & Buckley, S. (1982). *The serious business of growing up: A study of children's lives outside school.* Berkeley: University of California Press.

Meltzoff, A. (1995). Understanding the intentions of others: Re-enactment of intended acts by 18-month-old children. *Developmental Psychology, 31,* 838–850.

Miedzian, M. (1991). *Boys will be boys: Breaking the link between masculinity and violence.* New York: Doubleday.

Moller, L. C., Hymel, S., & Rubin, K. H. (1992). Sex typing in play and popularity in middle childhood. *Sex Roles, 26*(7/8), 331–353.

Moore, G. (1987). The physical environment and cognitive development in child-care centers. In C. Weinstein & T. Davis (Eds.), *Spaces for children: The built environment and child development* (pp. 41–72). New York: Plenum.

Moss-Moris, R., & Paterson, J. (1995). Understanding children's concepts of health and illness: Implications for developmental therapists. *Physical and Occupation Therapy in Pediatrics, 14,* 95–108.

Mueller, E., & Lucas, T. (1975). A developmental analysis of peer interaction among toddlers. In M. Lewis & L. A. Rosenblum (Eds.), *Friendship and peer relations* (pp. 223–258). New York: John Wiley & Sons.

New, R. S. (1994). Child's play—una cosa naturale: An Italian perspective. In J. Ropnarine, J. E. Johnson, & F. H. Hooper (Eds.), *Children's play in diverse cultures* (pp. 123–145). Albany, NY: State University of New York Press.

New, R. (2003). *Documentation as storytelling.* Chicago: National Association for the Education of Young Children.

Newman, H. (2003, July 3). Monitoring video-game violence is getting easier. *Detroit Free Press.*

Nicolich, L. M. (1977). Beyond sensorimotor intelligence: Assessment of symbolic maturity through analysis of pretend play. *Merrill-Palmer Quarterly, 23*(2), 89–99.

Niec, L. N., & Russ, S. (2002). Children's internal representations, empathy, and fantasy play: A validity study of the SCORS-Q. *Psychological Assessment, 14*(3), 331–338.

Nokia. (2002). *Nokia on the Web.* Retrieved September 1, 2002, from www.nokia.com

O'Jessee, P., Wilson, H., & Morgan, D. (2000, Summer). Medical play for young children. *Childhood Education,* 215–218.

Opie, I., & Opie, P. (1969). *Children's games in street and playground.* Oxford, UK: Clarendon Press.

Oremland, E. (1988). Mastering developmental and critical experiences through play and other expressive behaviors in childhood. *Children's Health Care, 16*(3), 150–156.

Paauw, D. (1999). Did we learn evidence-based medicine in medical school? Some common medical mythology. *Journal of the American Board of Family Practice, 12*(2), 143–149.

Papert, S. (1980). *Mindstorms: Children, computers, and powerful ideas.* New York: Basic Books.

Papert, S. (1996). *The children's machine: Rethinking schools in the age of the Internet.* New York: Basic Books.

Papousek, H., & Papousek, M. (1982). Vocal imitation in mother-infant dialogues. *Infant Behavior, 5,* 176.

Parten, M. (1932). Social participation among preschool children. *Journal of Abnormal and Social Psychology, 27,* 243–369.

Passer, M. (1996). At what age are children ready to compete? Some psychological considerations. In F. Smoll & R. Smith (Eds.), *Children and youth in sport: A biopsychological perspective.* New York: McGraw-Hill.

Peel, K. (1997). *The family manager's guide for working moms.* New York: Ballantine Books.

Pellegrini, A. D. (1988). Elementary-school children's rough and tumble play and social competence. *Developmental Psychology, 24*(6), 802–806.

Pellegrini, A. D. (1995). *School recess and playground behavior.* Albany, NY: State University of New York Press.

Pellegrini, A. D., Blatchford, P., Kato, K., & Baines, E. (in press). A short-term longitudinal study of children's playground games in primary school: Implications for adjustment to school and social adjustment in the USA and the UK. *Social Development.*

Pellegrini, A., & Davis, P. (1993). Relations between children's playground and classroom behavior. *British Journal of Educational Psychology, 63,* 88–95.

Pellegrini, A., Huberty, P., & Jones, I. (1995). The effects of recess timing on children's playground and classroom behaviors. *American Educational Research Journal, 32,* 845–864.

Pellegrini, A., Kato, K., & Banies, E. (2002). A short-term longitudinal study of children's playground games across the first year of school: Implications for social competence and adjustment to school. *American Research Journal, 39,* 991–1015.

Pellegrini, A., & Perlmutter, J. (1989). Classroom contextual effects on children's play. *Developmental Psychology, 25,* 289–296.

Pellegrini, A., & Smith, P. (1993). School recess: Implications for education and development. *Review of Educational Research, 63,* 51–67.

Perner, J. (1991). *Understanding the representational mind.* Cambridge, MA: MIT Press.

Phillips, C., Rolls, S., Rouse, A., & Griffiths, D. (1995). Home video game playing in schoolchildren: A study of incidence and patterns of play. *Journal of Adolescence, 18*(6), 687–691.

Piaget, J. (1951). *Play, dreams, and imitation in childhood.* London: Routledge.

Piaget, J. (1952). *The origins of intelligence in children.* New York: International Universities Press.

Piaget, J. (1962). *Play, dreams, and imitation in childhood.* New York: Norton.

Piaget, J. (1965). *The moral judgment of the child.* New York: The Free Press.

Pien, D., & Rothbart, M. K. (1980). Incongruity humor, play, and self-regulation of arousal in young children. In P. E. McGhee & A. J. Chapman (Eds.), *Children's humour.* Chichester, UK: Wiley.

Pitcher, E., & Hickey-Schultz, L. (1983). *Boys and girls at play.* New York: Praeger.

Play Therapy International. (2004). *Play therapy international.* Retrieved February 1, 2004, from http://www.playtherapy.org

Politsky, R. H. (1995). Toward a typology of research in the creative arts therapies. *The Arts in Psychotherapy, 22*(4), 307–314.

Pollowy, A.-M. (1977). *The urban nest.* Stroudsburg, PA: Dowden, Hutchinson, and Ross.

Posner, J. K., & Vandell, D. L. (1999). After school activities and the development of low-income children: A longitudinal study. *Developmental Psychology, 35,* 868–879.

Power, J. J., & Radcliffe, J. (2000). Assessing the cognitive ability of infants and toddlers through play: The symbolic play test. In K. Gitlin-Weiner, A. Sandgrund, & C. Schaefer (Eds.), *Play diagnosis and assessment* (pp. 58–79). New York: John Wiley & Sons.

Power, T. G. (2000). *Play and exploration in children and animals.* Mahwah, NJ: Lawrence Erlbaum Associates.

Ratner, N., & Bruner, J. S. (1978). Games, social exchanges, and the acquisition of language. *Journal of Child Language, 5,* 1–15.

Reckers, G. (1981). Psychosexual and gender problems. In E. J. Mash & L. G. Terdal (Eds.), *Behavioral assessment of childhood disorders* (pp. 483–526). New York: Guilford Press.

Reiss, S. (1989). *City games: The evolution of American urban society and the rise of sports.* Chicago: University of Chicago Press.

Resnick, M., Berg, R., & Eisenberg, M. (2000). Beyond black boxes: Bringing transparency and aesthetics back to scientific investigation. *Journal of the Learning Sciences, 9*(1), 7–30.

Risinger, M., & Yates, P. (1996). *The biggest joke book in the world.* New York: Sterling.

Rivkin, M. (1995). *The great outdoors: Restoring children's right to play outside.* Washington, DC: National Association for the Education of Young Children.

Rivkin, M. (1998). Children's outdoor play. In D. Fromberg & D. Bergen (Eds.), *Play from birth to twelve and beyond: Contexts, perspectives, and meanings.* New York: Garland Publishing.

Roe, K., & Muijs, D. (1998). Children and computer games: A profile of the heavy user. *European Journal of Communication, 13*(2), 181–200.

Rogoff, B. (1991). *Apprenticeship in thinking: Cognitive development in social context.* New York: Oxford University Press.

Rogoff, B. (2003). *The cultural nature of human development.* New York: Oxford University Press.

Roopnarine, J., Johnson, J., & Hooper, H. (1994). *Children's play in diverse cultures.* New York: State University Press.

Rothbart, M. K. (1973). Laughter in young children. *Psychological Bulletin, 80*(3), 247–256.

Rubin, K., Fein, G., & Vandenberg, B. (1983). Play. In P. Mussen & E. M. Hetherington (Eds.), *Handbook of child psychology* (4th ed., Vol. 4). New York: Wiley.

Russ, S. W., & Kaugars, A. S. (2001). Emotion in children's play and creative problem solving. *Creativity Research Journal, 13*(2), 211–219.

Rutter, M. (1990). Psychosocial resilience and protective mechanisms. In J. Rolf, A. S. Masten, D. Cicchetti, K. H. Nuechterlein, & S. Weintraub (Eds.), *Risk and protective factors in the development of psychopathology* (pp. 181–204). Cambridge, UK: Cambridge University Press.

Salguero, R. A., & Moran, R. M. (2002). Measuring problem video game playing in adolescents. *Addiction, 97*(12), 1601–1606.

Sanford, S., & Eder, D. (1984). Adolescent humor during peer interaction. *Social Psychology Quarterly, 47,* 235–243.

Scarlett, W. G. (1980). Social isolation from agemates among nursery school children. *Journal of Child Psychology and Psychiatry, 21,* 231–240.

Scarlett, W. G. (1994). Play, cure, and development. In A. Slade & D. Wolf (Eds.), *Children at play: Clinical and developmental approaches to meaning and representation.* New York: Oxford University Press.

Scarlett, W. G. (1998). *Trouble in the classroom: Managing the behavior problems of young children.* San Franciso: Jossey-Bass.

Scarlett, W. G., & Myers, K. (1998). Programming, the physical environment, and behavior problems. In W. G. Scarlett (Ed.), *Trouble in the classroom: Managing the behavior problems of young children.* San Francisco: Jossey-Bass.

Scarlett, W. G., & Wolf, D. (1979). When it's only make-believe: The construction of a boundary between fantasy and reality in storytelling. In E. Winner & H. Gardner (Eds.), *Fact, fiction, and fantasy in childhood.* San Francisco: Jossey-Bass.

Schaefer, C. (1994). Play therapy for psychic trauma in children. In K. O'Conner & C. Schaeffer (Eds.), *Handbook of play therapy: Vol. 2. Advances and Innovations* (pp. 297–318). New York: John Wiley & Sons.

Sehaffer, H. R., Collis, G. M., & Parsons, G. (1977). Vocal interchange and visual regard in verbal and preverbal children. In H. R. Schaffer (Ed.), *Studies in mother-infant interaction* (pp. 291–324). London: Academic Press.

Schultz, T. R., & Horibe, F. (1974). Development of the appreciation of verbal jokes. *Developmental Psychology, 10,* 13–20.

Selman, R., & Hickey Schultz, L. (1990). *Making a friend in youth.* Chicago, University of Chicago Press.

Senda, M. (1992). *Design of children's play environments.* New York: McGraw- Hill.

Shaffer, D. R. (2000). *Social and personality development.* Belmont, CA: Wadsworth/ Thompson Learning.

Sherman, L. W. (1988). Humor and social distance in elementary school children. *Humor: International Journal of Humor Research, 1,* 389–404.

Shotton, M. A. (1991). The costs and benefits of "computer addiction." *Behavior & Information Technology, 10*(3), 219–230.

Shultz, T. R. (1976). A cognitive-developmental analysis of humor. In A. J. Chapman & H. C. Foote (Eds.), *Humor and laughter: Theory, research, and applications.* New Brunswick, NJ: Transaction Publishers.

Simon, B. (2002). *The Sims online: 60 Minutes II special recap.* Retrieved December 30, 2002, from http://www.worldsims.org/modules.php?name=News&file=article&sid=280

Singer, D. G., & Singer, J. L. (1990). *The house of make-believe: Play and the developing imagination.* Cambridge, MA: Harvard University Press.

Singer, J. L. (1994). Imaginative play and adaptive development. In J. H. Goldstein (Ed.), *Toys, play, and child development* (pp. 6–26). Cambridge, UK: Cambridge University Press.

Singer, J. L. (1995). Imaginative play in childhood: Precursor of subjunctive thought, daydreaming, and adult pretending games. In A. D. Pellegrini (Ed.), *The future of play theory: A multidisciplinary inquiry into the contributions of Brian Sutton-Smith* (pp. 187–220). Albany, NY: State University of New York Press.

Skinner, B. F. (1953). *Science and human behavior.* New York: Macmillan.

Slade, A., & Wolf, D. (Eds.). (1994). *Children at play: Clinical and developmental approaches to meaning and representation.* New York: Oxford University Press.

Smilansky, S. (1968). *The effects of sociodramtic play on disadvantaged preschool children.* New York: Wiley.

Smith, P., & Vollstedt, R. (1985). On defining play: An empirical study of the relationship between play and various play criteria. *Child Development, 56,* 1042-1050.

Smolucha, L., & Smolucha, F. (1998). The social origins of mind: Post-Piagetian perspectives on pretend play. In O. N. Saracho & B. Spodek (Eds.), *Multiple perspectives on play in early childhood education* (SUNY Series, Early Childhood Education: Inquiries and Insights pp. 34–58). Albany, NY: State University of New York Press.

Socha, T. J. (1994). Children making "fun": Humorous communication, impression management, and moral development. *Child Study Journal, 24*(3), 237–253.

Society for Play and Creative Arts Therapies. (2003). *Training and resources.* Retrieved February 1, 2004, from http://www.playtherapy.org.uk/TrainResources PTIIBECPT.htm

Sroufe, L. A., & Wunsch, J. P. (1972). The development of laughter in the first year of life. *Child Development, 43*(4), 1326–1344.

Stafford, B. M., & Terpak, F. (2001). *Devices of wonder: From the world in a box to images on a screen.* Los Angeles: Getty Research Institute.

Steele, W. (2003). Using drawing in short-term trauma resolution. In C. A. Malchiodi (Ed.), *Handbook of art therapy* (pp. 139–151). New York: The Guilford Press.

Steinsieck, S., & Myers, K. (1998). Curriculum and behavior problems. In W. G. Scarlett (Ed.), *Trouble in the classroom: Managing the behavior problems of young children.* San Francisco: Jossey-Bass.

Stevenson, H., & Stigler, J. (1992). *The learning gap.* New York: Summit Books.

Strommen, E. F., & Revelle, G. L. (1990). Research in interactive technologies at the children's television workshop. *Educational & Training Technology International, 38,* 65–80.

Sutton-Smith, B. (1986). *Toys as culture.* New York: Gardner Press.

Sutton-Smith, B. (1994). Does play prepare the Future? In J. H. Goldstein (Ed.) *Toys, Play, and Child Development.* Cambridge: Cambridge University Press.

Sutton-Smith, B. (1995). Does play prepare the future? In J. Goldstein (Ed.), *Toys, play, and child development.* New York: Cambridge University Press.

Sutton-Smith, B., Gertsmyer, J., & Meckley, A. (1988). Play-fighting as folk play amongst preschool children. *Western Folklore, 47,* 161–176.

Sutton-Smith, B., & Kelly-Byrne, D. (1984). The idealization of play. In P. K. Smith (Ed.). *Play In Animals and Humans.* Oxford: Basil Blackwell.

Swanson, J. (2001). *What's the difference?* Retrieved September 1, 2002, from http://www.girltech.com/Mentors/MN_research.html

Tamis-LeMonda, C. S., & Bornstein, M. H. (1991). Individual variation, correspondence, stability, and change in mother and toddler play. *Infant Behavior and Development, 14,* 143–162.

Taylor, M. (1999). *Imaginary companions and the children who create them.* New York: Oxford University Press.

Taylor, M., & Carlson, S. (2000). The influence of religious beliefs on parental attitudes about children's fantasy behavior. In K. Rosengren, C. Johnson, & P. Harris (Eds.), *Imagining the impossible: Magical, scientific and religious thinking in children.* New York: Cambridge University Press.

Tejeiro, R. (2001). Video games addiction: A review [Spanish]. *Adicciones, 13*(4), 407–413.

Thomas, A., & Chess, S. (1986). The New York longitudinal study: From infancy to early adult life. In R. Plomin & J. Dunn (Eds.), *The study of temperament: Changes, continuities, and challenges.* Hillsade, NJ: Erlbaum.

Thompson, R. H., & Stanford, G. (1981). *Child life in hospitals: Theory and practice.* Springfield, IL: Charles C Thomas.

Tobin, J. (1989). *Preschool in three cultures.* New Haven, CT: Yale University Press.

Tomasello, M., & Mannie, S. (1985). Pragmatics of sibling speech to one-year-olds. *Child Development, 56,* 911–917.

Tronick, E. (1982). *Social interchange in infancy: Affect, cognition, and communication.* Baltimore: University Park Press.

U.S. Consumer Product Safety Commission. (1991). *Handbook for public playground safety.* Washington D.C. 20207, Publication # 325, web document: http://www.cpsc.gov/cpscpub/pubs/325.pdf

Vandell, D. L., & Wilson, K. S. (1987). Infants' interactions with mother, sibling, and peer: Contrasts and relations between interaction systems. *Child Development, 58,* 176–186.

Varga, D. (2000). Hyperbole and humor in children's language play. *Journal of Research in Childhood Education, 14*(2), 142–151.

Veatch, T. C. (1988). A theory of humor. *Humor, 11*(2), 161–215.

Vygotsky, L. (1976a). *Mind in society.* Cambridge, MA: Harvard University Press.

Vygotsky, L. (1976b). Play and its role in the mental development of the child. In J. Bruner, A. Jolly, & K. Sylva (Eds.), *Play: Its role in development and evolution.* New York: Basic Books.

Vygotsky, L. S. (1978). *Mind in society: The development of higher psychological processes.* Cambridge, MA: Harvard University Press.

Waller, D. E. (1992). Different things to different people: Art therapy in Britain—A brief survey of its history and current development. *The Arts in Psychotherapy, 19,* 87–92.

Walsh, D., Gentile, D., Van Overbeke, M., & Chasco, E. (2002). *Mediawise video game report card.* Retrieved February 16, 2003, from http://www.mediafamily.org/research/report_vgrc_2002-2.shtml

Watson, M. W. (1994). The relation between anxiety and pretend play. In A. Slade & D. P. Wolf (Eds.), *Children at play: Clinical and developmental approaches to meaning and representation* (pp. 33–47). New York: Oxford University Press.

Wegener-Spohring, G. (1994). War toys and aggressive play scenes. In J. Goldstein (Ed.), *Toys, play, and child development.* New York: Cambridge University Press.

Weine, S., Becker, D., McGlashan, T. H., & Vojvoda, D. (1995). Adolescent survivors of "ethnic cleansing": Observations on the first year in America. *Journal of the American Academy of Child and Adolescent Psychiatry, 34*(9), 1153–1159.

Weinstein, C., & David, T. (1987). *Spaces for children.* New York: Plenum Press.

Weisler, A., & McCall, R. B. (1976). Exploration and play: Resume and redirection. *American Psychologist, 31,* 492–508.

Weisz, J., Chaiyasit, W., Weiss, B., Eastman, K., & Jackson, E. (1995). A mulitmethod study of problem behavior among Thai and American children in school: Teacher reports versus direct observations. *Child Development, 66,* 402–415.

Weisz, J., Suwanlert, S., Chaiyasit, W., Weiss B., & Jackson, E. (1991). Adult attitudes toward over-controlled and undercontrolled child problems: Urban and rural parents and teachers from Thailand and the United States. *Journal of Child Psychology and Psychiatry, 32,* 645–654.

Weisz, J., Weiss, B., & Mosk, J. (1993). Parent reports of behavioral and emotional problems among children in Kenya, Thailand, and the United States. *Child Development, 64,* 98–109.

Weitzman, I., Blank, E., & Green, R. (2000). *Jokelopedia: The biggest, best, silliest, dumbest joke book ever.* New York: Workman.

Wellhousen, K., & Kieff, J. (2001). *A constructivist approach to block play in early childhood.* Albany, NY: Delmar.

Whiting, B. (1988). *Children of different worlds.* Cambridge, MA: Harvard University Press.

Wiegman, O., & van Schie, E. G. M. (1998). Video game playing and its relations with aggressive and prosocial behaviour. *British Journal of Psychology, 37*(3), 367–378.

Wiggins, D. (1996). A history of highly competitive sport for American children. In F. Smoll & R. Smith (Eds.), *Children and youth in sport: A biopsychosocial perspective.* New York: McGraw-Hill.

Williams-Gray, B. (1999). International consultation and intervention on behalf of children affected by war. In N. B. Webb (Ed.), *Play therapy with children in crisis: Individual, group, and family treatment* (2nd ed., pp. 448–467). New York: The Guilford Press.

Winner, E., & Gardner, H. (Eds.). (1979). *Fact, fiction, and fantasy in childhood.* San Francisco: Jossey-Bass.

Winnicott, D. W. (1977). *The Piggle: An account of the psychoanalytic treatment of a little girl.* New York: International Universities Press.

Wishon, P. M., & Brown, M. H. (1991). Play and the young hospitalized patient. *Early Child Development and Care, 72,* 39–46.

Wolff, S. (1981). *Children under stress* (2nd ed.). New York: Pelican Books.

NAME INDEX

Adams, M. A., 222, 224, 225, 226
Ainsworth, M., 47
Allen, L., 167, 168
American Psychological
    Association (APA), 245
Anderson, D. R., 122, 128, 129
Ariel, S., 33, 65
Armchair Empire, 129
Axline, V., 237, 238

Baines, E., 75, 78, 79, 194
Bainum, C. K., 101
Baker, E., 190
Banazewski, T., 179
Beasley, R., 170
Beatty, W., 14, 178
Beck, A., 242
Becker, D., 208
Beeghly, M., 16
Beentjes, J. W. J., 116
Began, J. K., 87
Belsky, J., 35, 164
Berg, R., 193
Bergman, A., 46
Berlyn, D. E., 107
Berryman, J., 140
Bers, M., 217
Bibace, R., 207
Bigelow, T., 144, 145, 148, 150, 151
Biklen, D., 16
Bjorklund, D. F., 32
Blatchford, P., 75, 78, 79
Bloch, M., 162
Block, J., 183, 185, 189
Bornstein, M. H., 35, 36, 39
Boulton, M. J., 80, 81, 82
Bowlby, J., 47
Boyatzis, C. J., 30
Brazelton, T. B., 40
Brett, A., 170
Bronfenbrenner, U., 205
Bronson, B. C., 41

Brown, M. H., 213, 217, 219, 222, 224
Bruner, J., 10, 13, 30, 38, 57
Buchman, D. D., 127, 128, 129, 131
Buckley, S., 77
Bullock, W. A., 128

Cambone, J., 245
Carlson, S., 68
Carlsson-Paige, N., 69
Caro, T., 5
Casas, J. F., 82
Cassell, J., 116
Cees, M., 116
Chaiyasit, W., 195
Chapman, A. J., 102
Chasco, E., 131
Chess, S., 47
Christopherson, H., 26
Cicchetti, D., 16
City of Helsinki, 118
Cline, S. S., 131
Coakley, J., 138, 143, 146, 148, 153, 154
Cohen, U., 167
Collis, G. M., 29, 41
Compas, B. E., 204
Crick, N. R., 82
Crouter, A. C., 76, 77
Csikszentmihalyi, M., 193

David, T., 167
Davis, C. C., 44, 45, 46
Davis, P., 194
De Maso, D., 217
Devereux, E. C., 90, 138, 157, 168
DeVries, R., 180
Dewey, J., 179
Didow, S. M., 44, 45, 46
DiPietro, J. A., 75
Drucker, J., 233

Eastman, K., 195
Eckerman, C. O., 44, 45, 46

SUBJECT INDEX

ABOUT THE AUTHORS

W. George Scarlett is Professor in the Eliot-Pearson Department of Child Development at Tufts University. He is a graduate of Yale and Clark universities, has authored numerous articles on children's play, and has coauthored books on parenting, managing behavior problems, and religious-spiritual development. His past research includes research on play and its development in diverse media during early childhood, play assessment techniques for work with atypical children, and play of children with serious problem behavior. For over two decades he has taught undergraduate and graduate courses on children's play.

Sophie Naudeau currently writes and conducts research on positive youth development and play among war-affected children and children of incarcerated parents. She is a graduate of the Sorbonne and a former Fulbright fellow. She has done extensive fieldwork with refugee children in diverse cultures (Bosnia, Guinea-Conakry, Sierra Leone, Thailand, and Cambodia).

Dorothy Salonius-Pasternak is Senior Researcher at the Harvard Medical School Center for Mental Health and Media and also conducts research on resilience and chronic illness through the Judge Baker Children's Center, Joslin Diabetes Center, and Tufts University. She is a graduate of Wesleyan and Tufts universities and was formerly affiliated with the National Research Institute in Finland and the Yale New Haven Hospital.

Iris Ponte has worked for Sesame Street Research at the Children's Television Workshop in New York and has been an early childhood educator for the Department of Child Development's laboratory school at Tufts University. She is a graduate of Holy Cross College and a former Watson Scholar. She has conducted research on preschools in the United Kingdom, Taiwan, China, Japan, and Newfoundland.